The Happy Traveler

THE HAPPY TRAVELER

UNPACKING THE SECRETS OF BETTER VACATIONS

JAIME KURTZ

OXFORD
UNIVERSITY PRESS

OXFORD
UNIVERSITY PRESS

Oxford University Press is a department of the University of Oxford. It furthers
the University's objective of excellence in research, scholarship, and education
by publishing worldwide. Oxford is a registered trade mark of Oxford University
Press in the UK and certain other countries.

Published in the United States of America by Oxford University Press
198 Madison Avenue, New York, NY 10016, United States of America.

Library of Congress Cataloging-in-Publication Data
Names: Kurtz, Jaime, author.
Title: The happy traveler : unpacking the secrets of better vacations / Jaime Kurtz.
Description: New York, NY : Oxford University Press, [2017]
Identifiers: LCCN 2016038064 | ISBN 9780190638986 (paperback : alk. paper)
Subjects: LCSH: Vacations—Planning.
Classification: LCC GV186 .K + | DDC 306.4/8125—dc23
LC record available at https://lccn.loc.gov/2016038064

1 3 5 7 9 8 6 4 2

Printed by LSC Communications, United States of America

To my parents, who always let me go.

CONTENTS

I Had One Job

I write this from the comfort of a quiet hotel room in the heart of Santa Fe, New Mexico. I was invited here to give two talks on happiness slated for the end of the week. Since it's my spring break, I figured I'd make a little vacation out of it, arriving Sunday, arranging inexpensive lodging until my healthy per diem kicks in, and devoting a couple of days to the sheer pleasure of being someplace entirely different.

For months, I've been fantasizing about this trip. As much as I love my home in Virginia, I spent part of my twenties out West and sometimes long to lose myself in its vast, dramatic landscapes. And I visited Santa Fe once before, years ago, but it was a quick visit tacked onto the end of a work conference, just long enough to leave me wanting more. Santa Fe is the perfect backdrop for travel wish-fulfillment. It has renowned spas and restaurants, cultural and historic appeal, and an air of artsy sophistication. I came here hoping for moments of clarity, wonder, gratitude, renewal . . . all of those things you expect from a vacation.

Today was my first full day. With the surge of motivation that often accompanies the start of a journey, I was eager to hit the road. The plan was to drive north to Taos, a small town an hour or so away, which has been on my to-see list for quite a while. I was up insanely early due to the two-hour time change, the weather was clear, and I left my hotel excitedly, ready to reacquaint myself with mountain roads, ear-popping changes in elevation, open spaces, and that feeling of unbridled freedom that only a road trip out West can evoke.

While central Virginia's rolling topography seems to exist on a human scale, northern New Mexico is vast beyond comprehension. As I left the city for the highway, I had to take a moment to adjust to and make sense of the enormity of it all, feeling both dizzied and diminished in the process. I was awed. The stage was set for a great day.

But as the miles ticked by, rather than a sense of continuous, unqualified wonder, I began to feel unwelcomed pressures arise in me. First, there was my music selection. Was it the right brand of inspiring, pensive, sing-along chill? And which scenic views were worth stopping to photograph? They seemed to get consistently more breathtaking, but my moments of appreciation were interrupted by assessments of their worth. *Is this one the best?* I wondered. *Should I pull over and take a picture here?* As I entered the small town of Dixon, a midpoint enthusiastically highlighted in my guidebook, did I want to stop and eat in the small café praised for having some of the best green chile in the state, even though it was only 10 a.m. and I was still digesting breakfast? Would I be sorry if I didn't? Good sense prevailed and I pressed on, but a small sense of regret nagged at me.

I got to Taos, parked, and began to wander around. It was lovely. Truly. Adobe buildings with historical markers explaining their fascinating origins. Little shops with one-of-a-kind jewelry, paintings, and pottery. Cute cafés and restaurants. But the real star was the landscape. Acres of ranchland dotted with horses. Snow-capped peaks. The ancient dwellings and ceremonial buildings of the Taos Pueblo. After a couple of hours wandering, snapping pictures, shopping, and having a drawn-out lunch, I drove back to Santa Fe on what was termed the "high road" and it was truly breathtaking: pristine wilderness beyond my wildest dreams of what a scenic drive in New Mexico could be.

But at the risk of sounding utterly ungrateful, I arrived back in Santa Fe more relieved than happy. I had crossed a place off my list. I'd seen Taos. *Check!* The pressure was off. I caught myself thinking things like, "Okay, now I can do what I want," and "Now I can enjoy myself." *What?* These thoughts crept back when I consulted the weather app on my phone. There was an unmistakable twinge of relief upon seeing that tomorrow is supposed to be rainy. Great! I can focus on work and pleasure reading without guilt or fear of missing out.

Because, you know what? I'm tired. Trying to craft this amazing day for myself—one that maximized my time and took full advantage of my location—was exhausting! My goals weren't just to look at the pretty scenery, window shop, and eat decent enchiladas. I could do that at home. I wanted so much *more* from my day in Taos. I wanted joy. Wonder. Freedom. Transcendence, even. I wanted to be Thelma and Louise, Jack Kerouac, and Elizabeth Gilbert all rolled into one, minus the crime spree, drugs, and depression. I was unknowingly projecting all of my travel wishes onto this one day.

The result? My thoughts were less about the otherworldly landscapes of New Mexico and more about whether I was making the best possible choices and having the best time I could. These expectations exerted a tremendous weight. *This restaurant is good, but could I have found something even better? This scenic drive is pretty, but that other one sounded amazing as well.* How could that possibly be any fun? I had one job, to relax and enjoy, and I had somehow blown it. I had made it into *work*. Poor Taos never had a chance.

Let's back up. This wasn't the first trip of mine that didn't quite live up to expectations. Three years ago, reveling in the good fortune of having both some free time and a bit of money to spend, I had decided to treat myself to a vacation. I settled on a solo tour of Eastern Europe and felt nothing but excitement as I mapped out my itinerary. Two weeks into it, after another morning spent wandering the gorgeous cobblestoned streets of Hvar, a seaside town in Croatia, I realized that I was over it. I was over touring ancient cathedrals and world-class museums. Over dodging crowds from the cruise ships. Over living out of a suitcase, and *definitely* over carrying one. I was even over dinners of delicate risotto studded with seafood fresh from the Adriatic.

Dejected and angry with myself (because what kind of ingrate can't enjoy *this!*), I returned to my hotel room and powered up my laptop. Maybe

I just needed a break. A change in perspective. Maybe hearing friends' complaints about their workaday lives would remind me of just how lucky I was to be relaxing on the beautiful Dalmatian coast. But what I found in my inbox was an email from a good friend, detailing the latest juicy gossip. Facebook flaunted ordinary but suddenly enviable moments: friends idling away an afternoon at a winery, others happily crossing the finish line of a 5K race, and still others dancing at an outdoor concert. Two weeks into my month-long trip, it suddenly hit me how lonely I was and how much I missed all that I had once longed to escape.

Let me be clear. I am generally a happy person. Grateful. An optimist. I usually wake up energized and excited for what the day brings. If you're not a morning person, I'd be too much for you. And I deeply, wholeheartedly, passionately love travel. Growing up, my family rarely ventured more than an hour from home, so my first trip abroad in my late teens led to a seismic shift in my worldview and created an unquenchable wanderlust. I now take undergraduates to Europe in the summer, hoping they might experience some of the same. Nothing enlivens me or immediately pulls me out of a funk like planning my next trip. My heart races when I approach the travel section of a bookstore and a world of possible journeys is laid out before me. And when I meet someone else who loves to travel, my natural reticence vanishes and I can't help but lean into these conversations, curious and animated. Yet sometimes, as a trip actually plays out, the pressures of it are just too much for me. Sometimes, it's just *not fun*.

Clearly, I'm doing something wrong.

Perplexed and searching for answers, I started bringing up the challenges of "happy travel"—*travel that is pleasurable, meaningful, and engaging*—to a wide range of friends and colleagues.[1] As I sheepishly shared my mixed experiences and growing ambivalence, something interesting happened: I began hearing stories of travel gone wrong from every direction. Clearly, I wasn't alone here. Nearly everyone I know—from other happiness researchers to the most wanderlust-stricken of my friends—seemed unsure about how to travel happily. And it didn't matter whether they'd spent thousands of dollars on a luxury experience halfway around the world or road-tripped to a bed and breakfast for the weekend. Money was no indicator that a trip would be fulfilling. Neither was distance, or duration, or even location.

Maybe *a lot* of us are doing something wrong.

This is why I'm compelled to write this book. I'm fascinated by the difficulty we have in what seems to be the easiest and most privileged of tasks: crafting a pleasurable experience for ourselves. Really, what in our lives is earmarked for pleasure quite like travel is? And we literally have the entire *world* to work with in pursuit of this pleasure.

But you know what? This is exactly why it's hard. With a world of options before us, with the explicit goals of fun, meaning, challenge, romance, or whatever other special feeling we seek, and armed with the misguided assumption that happy travel is simple and natural, we are setting ourselves up for disappointment.[2] Of course, we all know that sometimes travel disappoints for reasons far beyond our control. Flights are cancelled, luggage is lost. It rains every day of our beach holiday or backpacking adventure. However, we fail to realize just how much our own decisions, habits, and goals can undermine even the best-laid travel plans. It turns out that, in truth, *many of the challenges to happy travel lie within us.*

WHY TRAVEL?

As I set out to unpack the challenges of happy travel, I first had to confront my assumption that travel truly is a worthwhile investment of time and money. We certainly seem to *think* it is. When people sit down to construct a bucket list, travel goals shoot right to the top. A quick browse through the website bucketlist.org reveals a deep longing for far-flung adventures: taking a hot air balloon ride, seeing Niagara Falls, swimming with dolphins, visiting all seven continents, and even throwing a dart at the map and going wherever it lands.

Why? For one, travel is a life-in-miniature, a bookended period of time in which we experience a wealth of highs and lows. As the Danish writer Peter Høeg said, "Traveling tends to magnify all human emotions." From crippling fatigue to exuberance, from a search for solitude to shared belly laughs and deep connections, from cultural bumblings to heightened understanding of the world outside of ourselves: it's all there, and many of us consider that full range of inner experiences to be essential for a well-lived life.

Our reverence for travel is also woven deeply into our cultural ethos. America's short history can be summed up as one of movement and expansion. From the early explorers venturing to the New World to nineteenth-century author Horace Greeley's advice to "go West, young man," from Kerouac's iconic *On the Road* to Bill Bryson's *A Walk in the Woods*, we are captivated by travel and believe in its restorative and transformative powers. Elizabeth Gilbert's 2006 runaway hit *Eat Pray Love*, in which the author spends a year discovering herself in Italy, India, and Indonesia, propelled countless women onto the path to self-awareness, healing, and empowerment. Tourism to the areas Gilbert visited skyrocketed on the heels of her book's success. Ten years after its release it even inspired the essay collection *Eat Pray Love Made Me Do It: Life Journeys Inspired by the Bestselling Memoir*. More recently, Cheryl Strayed's best-seller *Wild: From Lost to Found on the Pacific Crest Trail* chronicled her arduous and transformative three-month hike through rough California and Oregon terrain. Because of the number of women seeking a glimmer of this redemption for themselves, the trail has seen a spike in foot traffic since the book and subsequent Reese Witherspoon film were released. One hiker said, "It makes your own personal struggles and problems seem so small. Starting a new life for her was finding herself on this trail and I kind of was in that same point in my life.

It's such an empowering story for women. It will encourage a lot of people to find themselves on a trail."[3]

Indeed, so many of us are seeking to better ourselves and to come into deeper acquaintanceship with ourselves. We desire that elusive *something* that will serve as a catalyst for clarity, inspiration, personal growth, or a renewed sense of wonder. And with these narratives as evidence, we have come to the collective conclusion that this something lies elsewhere. To find it, we must take a break from our lives of routine and set off in search of something wholly different, a place where we can test out slightly altered versions of ourselves, free from the constraints of daily life. Through this process of exploration we might just be transformed or revived by the trail, the beach, the foreign city, or the open road.

And even if we can't jet off to our dream destination, the spark of travel's life-changing promise can live in us. Frances Mayes's 1996 memoir *Under the Tuscan Sun* chronicled her restoration of a neglected Italian farmhouse and inadvertently ignited an obsession for all things Tuscan, from Subway's Tuscan Chicken Melt to rustic bathroom tiles and hardware to Beneful's Tuscan Style Medley dog food. Lacking the wherewithal to buy and restore a crumbling Italian villa *a la* Mayes, we can still live out a small bit of the fantasy through our food, furniture, and housing fixtures.[4]

My recent travels pale in comparison to these rich narratives. Could these beloved travel memoirs be glamorizing something pretty unexceptional or even unpleasant? Creating an enviable, unattainable fiction?

The question remained: in real life, does travel actually do anything for us?

WHAT THE RESEARCH REVEALS

As a behavioral scientist, I felt that the real answer was to be found not in memoirs, guidebooks, or cultural myths but in carefully crafted experiments and psychometrically sound surveys. And—drum roll, please—the empirical evidence reveals that travel actually *does* have the potential for numerous benefits, and these can be experienced before, during, and after a trip. An upcoming vacation gives us something to eagerly anticipate.[5] It's linked to a reduction in work-related stress and burnout as well as enhanced feelings of joy and interest.[6] And travel can shape our personalities. When traveling for an extended period of time, desirable changes—increased openness to experience, emotional stability, agreeableness, and creativity—emerge. A getaway can also boost relationship satisfaction, feelings of connection, and familial bonds. It can even stretch our perception of time. And if happiness is our goal, spending money on life experiences like travel buys us more than spending on material items. Travel adds richness and depth to our life stories. As aging people look back on their lives, they often express gratitude for their travel experiences, while others express regret for not having traveled more.[7]

So as I suspected, travel is more than just a good idea in theory. It really can enhance our lives in so many important ways. And I'm not ready to throw in the towel.

WE CAN DO TRAVEL BETTER

Funny thing. As I began thinking more deeply about the challenges of travel and how we might do it better, I ran headlong into my own research areas. These include positive psychology, which is the relatively new science of happiness and the good life; social psychology, the study of how people think, feel, and act in the real or imagined presence of others; personality psychology, which focuses on individual differences; and judgment and decision-making, which unpacks exactly how we go about making choices. These fields offer practical, evidence-based advice on how to improve our lives, directly addressing questions such as,

Why do my decisions fail to bring me the happiness I expected?
How should I spend my money, if I want to feel happy?

How do I really pay attention to and savor my experiences?

Why are some people naturally more optimistic, more grateful, or happier than others?

How can I maintain and even enhance my close relationships?

How do I fill my life with happy memories?

I knew this research. I'd studied it. I'd written about it. I'd enthusiastically taught it to hundreds of undergraduates over the past ten years. Some of it I had even carried out myself. But never before had I seen it applied to travel.[8] This is both surprising and unfortunate. Travel is expensive and our opportunities to do it are limited, making mistakes costly and regrettable. But as you will see, psychological science can help all of us craft much happier travel experiences.

YOUR EMOTIONAL GUIDEBOOK

Of course, anyone who's ever channel-surfed, browsed the Internet, or wandered through a bookstore knows that there is a wealth of information on the ins and outs of travel out there. But it is information of a very specific kind: geographic, logistical, financial, *external*. Travel guidebooks, magazines, TV programs, and websites will lay out all of the details of where to go, what to pack, where to stay, and how to prudently navigate one of the world's largest and most seductive industries. Vital information, to be sure, but they make little to no mention of human psychology: all of our mysterious inner workings that can make happy travel a surprising challenge.

Don't get me wrong. I subscribe to several travel magazines. I have my favorite travel blogs bookmarked on my web browser. I lose myself in Pinterest's travel dream boards. I open the Sunday newspaper immediately to the travel section every week. I love money-saving tips, lists of clever hacks, enticing images and descriptions of faraway places, and vivid, first-hand accounts of travel's glories and woes. And even though they add extra weight to an already overstuffed suitcase, I adore guidebooks. I have a whole shelf full of them, dog-eared and scribbled in. For me and many others, their appeal exists for obvious reasons: they give you a briefing on the history, the culture, and the must-sees in a place. They help you maximize your short vacation time. Some go so far as to provide detailed walking tours, plotting out the exact path you should take for maximum efficiency. As you walk, you are instructed on what you should look at, why you should look at it, even where to stop for a coffee break. Nothing is left to chance. Except, of course, the ability to kick back and relax, savor and enjoy, explore and immerse, anticipate and reminisce. The problem is that guidebooks, Pinterest, magazines, and blogs might tell us what to see, but they don't teach us *how* to see. All of that difficult mental and emotional work is up to us. And, as I and many others have learned, we aren't always up to the challenge.

To travel happily we need to learn not only a bit about where we're going; we need to understand some fundamental and surprising truths about ourselves, truths revealed by psychological science. We make decisions irrationally. Our ability to notice and appreciate is limited. Comforts entice us. People annoy us. Adventures scare us. The list goes on and on.

Armed with recent research, I will put the rules of happiness, savoring, anticipation, memory-making, and sound decision-making to work to make your travels more pleasurable, more engaging, and more meaningful, whether you're driving to Taos, sneaking away for a romantic weekend, setting sail on a Caribbean cruise, or venturing halfway around the world.

Let's hit the road.

ONE

FLYING BLIND: WHY YOU DON'T KNOW WHAT WILL MAKE YOU HAPPY SIX MONTHS FROM NOW

It is always wise to look ahead, but difficult to look further than you can see.
—Winston Churchill

Imagine that you're in the early stages of planning a much-needed vacation. You ask yourself, "Six months from now, where would I *most* like to be?" You envision lying on the deck of a cruise ship, basking in the sun while sipping a mai tai, not a care in the world. Sounds like just what you need. But then your mind wanders to something entirely different—people-watching in a Parisian café after a day strolling through the Louvre. Absorbing the culture of a vibrant city appeals to you in a whole other way. You *then* recall a friend's recent trip hiking the mountainous and breathtaking terrain around Machu Picchu and consider challenging yourself to do the same.

As you construct and compare these three vastly different experiences, you can't help but also wonder what your life might be like in six months, and you naturally feel stuck. Sure, you may feel exhausted and ready to relax *now*, but in half a year you might be in a vastly different mental place, stuck in a rut rather than stressed out, wanting to be challenged instead of pampered. So how do you decide between these three entirely wonderful and yet vastly different experiences?

SIMULATING FOREIGN FUTURES

In everyday life, when we're confronted with a choice and are trying to gauge how we might feel about it, trial and error is a reasonable strategy. Want to know if you like Indian food? Drive down the street to the nearest Indian restaurant, order up some chicken tandoori, and give it a go. If you decide it's not your thing, you're out a few dollars and maybe an hour of your life. But want to know if you like India? Here, trial and error—as in, flying there to try it out for yourself—makes little sense. If you decide it's not the right place for you, you're out a big chunk of time and money. That's not to say that we don't learn a lot about our travel ideals by experimentation, by getting out there and trying new things. In fact, that is one of the great joys of travel. But as a primary means of teasing out our likes from our dislikes, trial and error is highly inefficient.

Instead, we do our best to figure out what we like through *mental simulation*, projecting into a distant time and place of our own creation, envisioning what it might be like, and making our best guess about how it would feel to be there.[1] I guarantee that you have done this before—for vacations, yes, but also when choosing colleges, partners, and professions. In fact, if you think about it, pretty much *all* decisions involve a prediction of future feelings.[2]

Not surprisingly, this sort of complicated guesswork leaves us at risk for error. The process of predicting future feelings makes travel-related decisions—where to go, what to do, and for how long—more challenging than we might think. Who knows: maybe you would actually go stir crazy on a cruise ship. Maybe the hustle and bustle of Paris would overwhelm you. Maybe hiking through the cold, thin air of the Andes would be far more challenging than you could possibly foresee. It's so hard to really know. However, by understanding more about how we predict and choose, we can learn to anticipate possible errors and make better travel decisions.

Social psychologists Tim Wilson and Dan Gilbert have spent the last twenty years carefully unpacking the ways we estimate our future feelings.[3] They call this process *affective forecasting*, and it is something we do multiple times a day in many small ways ("Would I enjoy a burger or a salad more?") and throughout our lives, often in major ways ("Should I take the job in Portland or the one in Los Angeles?"). Given all of our practice at affective forecasting, you might think we'd be pretty good at it, but Wilson and Gilbert have found that time and time again, we make mistakes. From the outcomes of elections, promotions, breakups, winning the lottery, losing a football game, and much more, we systematically misjudge the intensity and duration of our emotional reactions to future life events, thinking that our sorrows and joys will impact us for longer than they actually do.[4] In short, we don't always know what will make us happy and for how long. Our emotional crystal ball is far from clear.

Now if these mistakes happen in our mundane, everyday lives, with all of their predictability, imagine how much poorer we are when making decisions about what kind of travel is best for us. These kinds of affective forecasts are difficult for several reasons. First, we're required to cross great psychological distances to predict our feelings across time and place, while also weeding through multiple desirable options. How would you really feel if you went to the Caribbean, or to Paris, or to Machu Picchu? How do you accurately conjure up these vastly different and wholly unknown futures? How do you pit one against the other? These are some serious mental gymnastics. Second, accurate forecasting demands open-minded consideration of what *research* suggests makes people happy, even if it goes against our deeply held personal theories. In this chapter, you will encounter several strategies that might not be terribly intuitive. Third, we exacerbate the problem by thinking that we're better at forecasting than we actually are—overconfidence abounds.[5] The end result? We are probably making less than perfect travel decisions and failing to realize it.

NOT ANOTHER SCENIC OVERLOOK!

Ask yourself, "If I won the lottery next month, how happy would I be? And how long would my happiness last?" If you're like participants in a classic study, you would overestimate how much this event would change your life, forgetting that while you do indeed have newfound riches, real life carries on, with all of its hassles and stressors.[6] Chances are, you actually wouldn't be happy about your winnings for nearly as long as you think you would.

You don't need to hit the jackpot to appreciate this fact. Think back to some of your greatest moments in life: maybe college graduation, your wedding day, or finding out that you landed your dream job. Recall the joy or pride you felt on that day. Then recall how, over the subsequent weeks and months, the event gradually lost its emotional power over you. Sure, it's still pleasant to look back on, but it is certainly not as intense, nor do you think about it as much as you did when it first happened. One reason for this is the process of *hedonic adaptation*, in which our experiences, good and bad, lose their emotional impact over time.[7] You made sense of the amazing event and, in so doing, you got used to it. New events and experiences have taken its place in your emotional and mental world. Hedonic adaptation is a normal, natural, well-documented psychological process. It doesn't make you an ingrate, but it is absolutely a stumbling block on the path to everyday happiness.[8]

The process of adaptation is part of what makes travel so great; in a brand-new place, we are *unadapted* and are presented with the rare opportunity to see with new eyes. Travel writer Bill Bryson observed, "To my mind, the greatest reward and luxury of travel is to be able to experience everyday things as if for the first time, to be in a position in which almost nothing is so familiar it is taken for granted."[9] The white sand beach and the mountain vista possess an inherent beauty, but they are also striking in their novelty, in their ability to fully command our attention. Sadly, but inevitably, if we saw these wonders daily, their wow factor would gradually begin to fade as they become the new nor-mal. As author Alexandra Horowitz notes, when we travel, "two things happen: we actually do see new places and, the second, we bother to look. I suspect that some of our fondness for so-called vacation locales is due to this *simply looking*. Before we know it, we have become entirely accustomed to how that vacation spot looks. We have routines, we know the way—and we stop looking."[10]

When planning a trip, we can fail to consider the all-important role of hedonic adaptation. This is why more time in a location isn't always better.[11] Our first day on the beach or in the mountains would likely be incredible, even awe-inspiring. But our tenth day might feel quite ordinary, an idea that is unfathomable when we're in the planning stages. My recent road trip through the fjords of Norway highlighted this for me in dramatic fashion. There I was, in the presence of some of the most jaw-droppingly gorgeous scenery I had ever seen. It seemed almost criminal how, after a week or so of ever-present beauty, its power to impress me had been so diminished. One mountain lake begot another and snowcapped peaks were ever-present. I can even recall wishing away the scenic country miles that were keeping me from a cup of convenience store coffee. I look back over my photographs and wonder how I could have been anything but awestruck, forgetting that it's just not in my—or maybe in anyone's—nature to be constantly amazed for days. We accommodate what we see to what we already know, make sense of it, put it in the back of our minds, and are on the lookout for the next new thing.[12] Therefore, the novel will almost always win the battle for our limited attention, even when the constant is utterly breathtaking.

The Guidebook Myth of Perpetual Joy

It's no wonder that we don't realize the extent to which we will adapt to new surroundings. Page through a guidebook or browse a travel website. You would be hard-pressed to find images of jet-lagged travelers standing in an endless museum ticket line, idly scrolling through social media, or killing time in their hotel room.[13] Common as these occurrences actually are, they certainly don't encourage tourism. No, what we see are those perfect, fantastical moments, which can fuel our expectations and help us ignore the inevitable neutral or annoying ones.

In essence, the tourism industry perpetuates the *impact bias*, the pervasive belief that an emotional event will affect us for longer than it actually does.[14] Wandering the Louvre won't just be pleasant, it will be awesome. And the awesomeness will extend throughout the entirety of the day there. Fussy children, maddening crowds, and tired feet have no place in this fantasy. And we buy into the hype because, well, it's more fun to think about the upsides of our upcoming adventures. It also helps us rationalize the high price of travel. Would you be so eager to fly to Paris if you were giving proper weight to both the highs and the *lows*? Maybe not. The tourism industry certainly isn't willing to take that risk. But these unrealistic beliefs can easily lead to disappointment because chances are, you *won't* be awestruck during the entirety of your vacation.[15] It's not in our nature to be so consistently joyful.

Keeping It Fresh

Understanding how to keep things fresh and exciting—essentially combatting hedonic adaptation—is a chief goal of happiness researchers, and it should be a consideration for travelers as well. It is so vitally important that I will come back to it with specific strategies multiple times in subsequent chapters. For now, in these early planning stages, know that adaptation is a pernicious and automatic process. Know that it can easily detract from happy travel. And know that no one is immune. You must keep it in mind as you plan. Ask yourself how you will maintain a sense of wonder, even in a place that is wonderful. You might consider varying activities or going several different places. Or you might even think about staying one week instead of two and save some money for your next vacation. It may be hard to fathom from the confines of your office cubicle, but two weeks at the beach might just start to get old. Accept this possibility, and truly think about how you can keep your travels fresh and exciting.

A DETAILED NOW,
AN IDEALIZED FUTURE

Think fast: do you want a free ticket to London for next year at this time?

I'm willing to bet that as images of Big Ben, Covent Garden, and Buckingham Palace spring to mind, your answer is an emphatic "yes!" I would also be willing to bet that as the day of your departure gets increasingly closer, your focus would change from the vague fantasies that led to that spontaneous yes to the less-fun intricacies of travel. You'll start having thoughts like, "I wish I'd known how grey and chilly it was going to be in London this time of year," "I hope I don't fall behind at work while I'm away," or "What if my flight gets cancelled?"

Travel decisions require traversing through time, often projecting many months into the future. Where we might like to go today can be quite different from what we end up being in the mood for half a year later. The obvious explanation is that our needs simply change over time. A sunny island getaway sounds ideal in the cold, dark months of winter, but seems less extraordinary come June. Less obvious is the fact that we think about situations differently based on their relationship to us in time.[16] Things that are temporally distant, say, months or years off, we think about rather abstractly, focusing on the big picture: "What's good for me? What would be challenging, broadening, or healthy?" But as the event draws near, the details come to the fore, and our priorities change from what's good for us to what feels good.

I see this sometimes in my students. Months before the new semester is to start, they may register for an 8 a.m. class, saying that this way, they can "get a jump on the day." But they almost always come to rue the decision when classes begin, early mornings are cold, they annoy their roommates with their alarm clock, and they have to say goodbye to late nights. Or think about something as commonplace as grocery shopping. If you're like many shoppers, the nutritious foods you buy for "someday soon" don't get eaten. In the moment of hunger, the immediate desire for a donut likely overwhelms those well-intentioned high-fiber crackers or carrot sticks.[17] What you want now versus what you think you'll want down the road often just don't align. And the further you are from the event in question, the more confident you are that you'll know just what you will want when the time comes.[18]

This is important to consider when planning travel, as I've learned. I love to visit new cities to run races. When I sign up, usually months in advance of the race date, I am thinking about the big picture: the palpable energy present in a big city race, the fun of seeing a new place in a novel way, and how strong and fit I will feel as I cross the finish line. But as race day approaches, small but important details come to the fore. I realize what a nuisance race-day traffic will be, grumble at the weather report, worry about my aching knee, and note just how much money I'm spending on incidentals like hotels, parking, and the prerace pasta pig-out. These details are far less central well in advance of the event, when my mind wants to create images of abstract perfection.

Other travel-related examples abound. Booking that 6 a.m. flight seemed like a good idea when your trip was months away—you'll get to your destination early and have almost a full day to spend!—but as your departure date arrives, deep dread kicks in as you set your alarm for 3 a.m. and realize that no one loves you nearly enough to take you to the airport at that hour. Similarly, taking a red-eye flight or overnight train to save money on a hotel seems like a great idea in advance, but far less so as you try to sleep sitting upright in a cramped chair next to a screaming child.

Taking an abstract view of a future event is beneficial in some ways. Would we ever buy healthy food if we were shopping only based on our immediate cravings? Would I register for those races if I was so focused on the possibility of a rainstorm or some minor aches and pains? Probably not. There's something motivating about thinking about abstract, big-picture features such as personal betterment or goal attainment. That said, neglecting to appreciate the challenges of psychological time travel can also contribute to regret and discontent when the future comes to be, because small details are actually quite important. Anyone who ever mutters "It seemed like a good idea at the time" may be falling prey to the unintended consequences of grappling with a highly abstract future.

Bridging the Psychological Gap

As you plan, try to project into the future as best you can. One idea is to do a prospective diary, laying out exactly what a day of travel might actually look like—the good, the bad, and the ugly. This technique has helped people pull focus from that one big thing that may exert excessive weight on their overall judgments.[19]

For example, imagine your excitement at the thought of your first trip to Paris. The focus is on that broad concept: *Paris*, which evokes happy but vague images of baguettes, berets, sidewalk cafes, and Impressionist paintings. That broad perspective isn't *wrong*, but it's also not very specific or helpful. Concretely, what would a day there be like? Lay it out, from morning until night. Although there is some guesswork involved because you certainly can't know everything that will happen (and what a downer that would be), there is valuable information to be gained through this mental exercise. For example, by getting more detailed, you might realize that the chunk of a day you expect to spend riding buses to reach the center of the city isn't worth the money you might save by staying in the outskirts. As a result, you book a hotel room in the center of Paris—a decision that may cost a little extra but is likely to enhance your experience greatly. If you're debating the relative merits of a 6 a.m. flight, map out just what the night before and morning of might look like. That can get you out of abstract, big-picture mode ("I can get a jump on the day!") and help you focus on the sorts of nitty-gritty details that might really matter when flight time arrives ("Ugh, I'll be waking up in the middle of the night" or "I'll need to pay for a cab"). The prospective diary can help make the experience seem closer to you in time and, as a result, a little more grounded in reality.

PACKING YOUR ROSE-COLORED GLASSES

It's a well-accepted fact that memory is a reconstruction of past events, subject to numerous biases and errors.[20] What is less known is that certain *kinds* of life events are prone to a unique reconstructive bias known as the *rosy view*.[21] Specifically, experiences that are generally positive, bounded in time (they have a clear beginning and an end), and free from an evaluative outcome (there is no win or lose) are often recalled as better than they were when they were actually happening.

Given these criteria, travel experiences should be especially prone to the rosy view: travel is generally good, there is a clear start and end date to a trip, and there is seldom a win or lose outcome at play. To test the rosy view in a group of travelers, researchers surveyed cyclists on a three-week tour of California. While their daily experiences were characterized by high points such as pedaling along the Pacific coastline or eating lunch in a pretty meadow, they also had a lot of neutral and negative moments to deal with—rain, heat, hills, traffic, and so on. When asked to think back and report on their overall experience of the trip, however, they consistently reported it as being better than the sum of its reported moments. A different study found a similar pattern for families on a Disneyland vacation.[22] In the moment, parents grappled with screaming children, exorbitant prices, endless lines, and sweltering heat. Somehow, their seemingly miserable experiences were twisted and shaped into an overall positive memory later. I guess they don't call it the Magic Kingdom for nothing.

Why does the rosy view happen? There are several likely reasons. First, while we know whether a past experience was generally good or bad, we don't store specific and exact memories of our bodily or physical feelings.[23] Conceptually, you know that gorging yourself on Thanksgiving dinner feels awful, but you can't conjure up and recreate those exact physical feelings. The result? It's hard to learn from your mistakes. As you finally put your fork down you might moan, "I'm never eating like that again!" but the next year you're going back for a second helping of pumpkin pie once more. From hangovers to marathon-running to childbirth, we just can't recall exactly how badly things feel, which can affect our choices to pursue similar things in the future, for better or for worse.[24]

This reminds me of backpacking through Southeast Asia during the oppressively hot, humid summer months. Looking back on it now, I know that the heat was just awful, draining, and inescapable. I even have photographs of myself hauling not one but two large backpacks, one on my front and the other on my back, drenched in sweat and looking nothing short of miserable. But absent the actual physical feelings, this knowledge doesn't keep me from wanting to go back. After all, this trip was also adventurous and eye-opening, with delicious food, welcoming locals, and white sand beaches. And it was gloriously inexpensive. These are concepts that I can easily call to mind, even years later. But if I could truly recreate my deep sense of lethargy, discomfort, and grubbiness, I might feel differently about returning.

Other reasons underlying the rosy view seem to be more motivated. Because travel is an investment of time and money, there is a particular urgency to look back on it positively. We can all think back to a trip that didn't turn out so well, and this realization can often come with a bit of psychological discomfort known as *cognitive dissonance*.[25] Essentially, when we have two conflicting beliefs, such as "I know the value of a dollar!" and "I just blew my entire vacation budget on this dreadful, rainy, hilly cycling tour," we feel uncomfortable and are motivated to resolve this feeling. What we often do is spin the information in a way that preserves our self-esteem. Concluding "Well, I guess I'm a real fool when it comes to planning trips!" is much more unsettling than "The rain was actually refreshing, and, as they say, what doesn't kill you makes you stronger!" Time and time again, we interpret situations in a way that makes us feel good about ourselves, and this may lead us to remember our vacations as being better than they actually were.

Also fueling the rosy view of vacations are the *types* of moments we choose to preserve and share. Any trip is sure to be marked by some boring or annoying moments—waiting in line, arguing over which restaurant to try, fighting jet lag—but those aren't the moments that make it into the photo albums or the stories we tell. No, we naturally choose to preserve the beautiful, noteworthy, unique moments, and as we look at our photographs and relive the trip, those experiences take center stage, making the entire experience seem better than it may have been.[26]

Rosy Realism

The rosy view is not necessarily a problem. One of the joys of travel is the memories and rich stories it adds to our lives, so why not remember a trip as being just a little better than it actually was? The primary consideration—and it's a big one—is that the rosy view can bias future decision-making. Tripadvisor.com offers examples in the form of reviews of hotels, restaurants, and tourist attractions headlined, "I said 'Never Again' yet made the same mistake twice!!!!" or "I made the mistake of eating here a second time!"[27]

One study had college students track their moods during their week-long spring break trip, as well as predicting and recalling their moods before and after the trip.[28] They found that students overestimated how happy they thought they would feel during the trip, compared to how they actually felt. They also remembered the trip as being more positive than it was as it unfolded in the moment, and—this is key—it was those positive memories that predicted whether they would like to take a similar trip in the future. Our memories are powerful. They don't only create warm feelings but drive future decisions. The constant challenge is to strike a balance between accuracy, so that we learn from our mistakes, and positivity, so we can feel good about ourselves and our decisions.

CHECKING YOUR
PSYCHOLOGICAL BAGGAGE

When we travel, we aren't just paying for a change of scene. We don't just want beauty to merely surround us. We expect an *internal* change—serenity, gratitude, or joy—to happen too. However, putting ourselves in that just-right location doesn't guarantee that we'll feel a certain way. In *The Art of Travel*, Alain de Botton recounts a trip to Barbados.[29] He describes the experience of sitting down by the edge of the sea to bask in the very same view that had so captivated him in a travel agent's brochure. But it doesn't exactly go as planned: "I may have noticed a few birds careening through the air in matinal excitement, but my awareness of them was weakened by a number of other, incongruous and unrelated elements, among them a sore throat I had developed during the flight, worry over not having informed a colleague that I would be away, a pressure across both temples and a rising need to visit the bathroom. A momentous but until then overlooked fact was making itself clear: I had inadvertently brought myself with me to the island."

Indeed, a massive stumbling block to happy travel is, regrettably, our own selves. The psychological baggage we all carry can naturally put a damper on our fun and relaxation. After all, we don't leave our anxieties, irritations, and bad habits behind when we leave home. They come along for the ride, and can make immersion and enjoyment a real challenge. You might be in Italy, staring out at a Venetian piazza with a perfect cappuccino in hand. And for a little while, your attention is fully captured by what lies before you. But gradually, your mind can't help but wander to that work project left unfinished, to what your friends back home might be posting on Facebook, or even to whether you packed enough underwear. And as your mind wanders, the scene before you recedes into the background of your mental and emotional experience. You might as well be back at home.

Overestimating the ability to be present-focused is a lapse in self-knowledge that has important implications for enjoyment. We can miss the fact that just putting ourselves in a nice, new setting doesn't guarantee happiness. Happiness is a mindset, not a physical setting.[30] So set the mental stage. Before you leave for your trip, make it as easy as possible to disconnect from work. If possible, don't leave projects unfinished. Put up an email auto-response telling people that you're away. Tell your family and friends back home that you need to check out for awhile and not to worry if they don't hear from you. Consider what things might stress you out on your trip and try to lay these things to rest before you depart. In later chapters, we'll discuss many more strategies for being present and appreciative in the moment.

WHO'S BEEN THERE, DONE THAT?

Let's return to the question I posed at the beginning of the chapter. If you're considering traveling to a new place, how will you know if you'll like it? A very reasonable strategy would be to consult people who've been there before. Even better if they are people like you in age, energy level,

degree of cultural interest, or whatever other similarities you deem important. No one's preferences are exactly alike, of course, but it's also true that
some experiences are almost universally grim or glorious. No traveler likes
waiting in endless lines, being ripped off, or getting food poisoning, while
the vast majority enjoy cool ocean breezes, exquisite meals, and impeccable service. So when wondering what a trip to a certain place might
be like, why not consult an expert, such as a friend who has taken a very
similar trip in the past?

This strategy, known as *surrogation*, makes a lot of sense. Consider any
foreign destination that appeals to you. As many guidebooks as you consult, as many Pinterest board as you create, and as many daydreams as you
may enjoy, there are privileged, unvarnished details available only to those
who have actually been there. But do we realize this?

In one study, a group of college women were given the facts about
someone they were about to meet on a five-minute speed-date.[31] Let's call
him Mike. Each woman learned facts like Mike's hometown, age, height,
and favorite movie, and they also saw his photograph. It wasn't unlike
reading over a dating profile. Armed with this information, she could
imagine what the date might actually be like. Other participants were
instead given a *different* woman's account of how her date with him actually
went. Think about this. If you were deciding how much you might like
to meet a potential love interest, would you value your own opinion of
Mike's profile more, or would you give special weight to the opinion of
an acquaintance who had recently gone out with him?

If you said, "I'd value my own opinion more," you'd be in the majority. After all, you have a lifetime of dating experience under your belt and
know all the quirky things that you find attractive. How could someone else know that your dream guy simply must be a great cook, dog
lover, and ardent *Game of Thrones* fan? But actually, your intuition has failed
you. Even though you claim to know what you want in a mate, only the
other woman in the study knows what this guy was really like (at least,

what could be revealed in the span of five minutes); whether he was basically personable and interesting. And, indeed, the study found that the women's actual impression of Mike, after meeting him, aligned with that of the surrogate—the woman who had spent time with him previously. Importantly, participants failed to realize this, believing that their own impressions would be much more useful. This can give rise to overconfidence when simulating future feelings.[32] In short, we overestimate our ability to accurately imagine and predict our feelings about future events, and undervalue the experiences of people in our social networks.

The advice here is clear. You don't always know best. You might make a more informed travel decision if you give proper weight to neighborly advice. Debating Orlando in July? Talk to a relative who went there recently and get the lowdown on the costs, crowds, and summer heat. Considering taking your family on a Colorado ski trip? Talk to a friend who went on one recently. All told, how expensive was it, really? What were the highs and lows? Would she do it over again, if she could? Heed your inner voice as well, but remember that there are experts all around you. From them, you can get the sort of frank opinions and advice you won't get from a travel agent or a guidebook.

THE BLACK HOLE OF OPTIONS

So far, I've discussed the disconnect between what you think you want now and what you will actually enjoy in the future. If you're not disheartened enough, consider another set of decision-making challenges: wading through a vast sea of options, trying to determine what it is you really and truly want.

Recently, I attended a travel industry conference in Washington, DC. While wandering the gigantic exhibit hall, I mindlessly amassed an armload of pamphlets trying to sell me on timeshares, wine tours, cruises, hot air balloon rides . . . you name it. One booth in particular reeled me in; it was a tour company that's known for reasonably priced, small-group adventures that are socially and environmentally friendly. I grabbed their massive catalog, which resembled the September issue of *Vogue* much more than it did the flimsy fliers I'd picked up elsewhere. A few weeks later, I finally got around to paging through their offerings. Almost immediately, I felt my heart start to race as phrases like "lush cloud forest," "city of eternal spring," and "winding streets of ancient medinas" seemed to jump off the page. I gazed at glossy images of fit, happy people cycling past Vietnamese rice paddies, riding camels in Morocco, taking Thai cooking classes, viewing the Northern Lights, and sailing the Galapagos Islands. Here were all of my travel fantasies, cataloged by region, planned out by experts, and there for the taking. I wanted to do it all.

And, it seemed, I *could* do it all. This company offers upward of three hundred different travel experiences, from Antarctica to the Amazon, from Beijing to Borneo. As I sometimes do, I let my mind wander and indulged in some fantasy trip-planning. Which of these tours would I most like to take, if I could go anywhere? That question quickly proved overwhelming, so I laid out some parameters: two weeks was my max, I couldn't break the bank, and weather concerns (I like to be warm) ruled out a good chunk of the globe. This effectively whittled down the list from three hundred, but I was still left with an unwieldy set of options. Hmmm. Okay, so what did I really want my next big trip to be like? Well, I've never been to South America and I've always wanted to hike through Patagonia and see the Chilean wine region. I checked the index. Hey, there's a trip for that! But taking a small boat through the Galapagos Islands, seeing the abundant wildlife up close and personal? I could do that too! In fact, there are twenty different ways to experience the Galapagos . . . how was I going to narrow this down?

Whether you're planning a daytrip, a weekend getaway, or a multiweek adventure, making travel decisions is seldom easy. Internal and external pressures collide, creating a perfect storm of decision-making challenges. First, as discussed previously, deciding how to use your precious vacation days and dollars requires taking a mental leap into a future with which you have no acquaintance. Then there's the tourism industry, a billion-dollar marketing juggernaut, expertly delivering images of perfection like the ones I was so taken in by. And you have—literally—an entire world of options to choose from. These forces conspire to overwhelm and perplex, making it easy to be swayed toward an experience that might not quite be "you," or to be so mentally taxed by options that you lose sight of what you really want.[33]

To really see how choices pervade daily life, consider a nontravel example. Imagine that you need to buy a new car. When there are very few options out there, the best choice may be obvious and the cost of weighing the alternatives is minimal. The problem is, the modern marketplace is glutted with options. In the case of cars, this can translate into countless hours scouring the Web, reading reviews of various makes and models, and noting details like gas mileage, safety ratings, repair costs, trunk space, warranty options, and scores of other details. A spreadsheet may be involved. You'll ask everyone you know for their opinions, test-drive countless models, and listen to sales pitch after sales pitch. Finally, after weeks of this, you finally choose a Subaru Forester.

Given the labor that went into making this decision, your new Forester should deliver nothing short of unadulterated bliss. After all, you did all of that research and made an extremely careful choice. Surprisingly, though, you might not be as enamored of your new car as you might expect. For one, you may have been so distracted by gobs of information—much of which came from external sources rather than from your own set of priorities—that you downplayed or even ignored your own gut feelings of liking. Somewhere between hour five and hour fifty-five of research, you lost sight of what you truly wanted.[34] Secondly, because of all those other cars that were also under consideration, you have some highly salient comparison points, like that Honda, that Toyota, and that Volvo that you *didn't* buy.[35] You might reasonably wonder if one of those would have been better. Versions of this doubt creep up over and over: "the Honda was zippier on curves," "the Toyota had a bigger trunk," "the Volvo had more cup holders." You might conclude that you should have done more research. You likely won't realize that your discontent exists *because* you did so much research.[36]

A car is a huge purchase and I am not suggesting that it be made in a cavalier, devil-may-care fashion. But the fact is, you can research and test-drive *forever*. In the modern marketplace, there are so many options that getting the absolute best is an impossibility. So it's no wonder that *maximizing*—searching through options trying to find the absolute best— is linked to regret and displeasure.[37]

Consider a different strategy. You do your research and make a list of, say, five models that have the features that are most important to you: reasonable price, solid safety ratings, good gas mileage, and enough space for your two Golden Retrievers. You test-drive them and you decide you like the Subaru the best. It meets your needs and feels right to you. Maybe there's something ever-so-slightly better out there, but that's okay. You know the Subaru is a good car and you like it. Done. This strategy, known as *satisficing*, is far less time-consuming and agonizing, and is more likely to lead to fulfillment. Notice that you didn't just settle for any old car; you had your standards, but you also didn't get bogged down by what could easily become an overwhelming decision-making process. As a result, you won't find yourself endlessly ruminating over your choice and comparing your new Subaru to all the other great options out there.

Back to travel. Ask yourself the simple question, "Will I enjoy a Caribbean cruise?" Barring any nautical disasters, this is a no-brainer. You probably would have a pretty good time. But what would make this your best possible cruise experience? Small ship or large? All-inclusive or a la carte dining? Inside or outside cabin? And which excursions would you like to add on? Explore enough options and you may just throw your hands up in frustration, and decide to stay home and queue up old episodes of *The*

Love Boat instead. Or, you might decide on specifics but have all the other options you *didn't* choose nagging at you. "Was this really the best I could do?" you might ask yourself.

There is a psychological cost to the abundant choices that proliferate in the modern marketplace.[38] This is true for everyday, inexpensive items but also for larger-scale purchases like houses, cars, and, yes, vacations.[39] Spend too much time and effort agonizing over the perfect trip and you may end up creating the exact opposite. In fact, tourism researchers directly advise against juggling too many options.[40] In one study, college students were asked to weigh the relative merits of different numbers of popular spring break destinations, such as Orlando, Hawaii, and Acapulco. Some students were asked to rate a single option, while others rated three, ten, twenty, or thirty. Students could deal with a small number of options, indicating clear preferences and attitudes toward each. But once they got to twenty options, they seemed to lose sight of what they wanted.[41] For those students who did manage to tease out a preference, they still expressed regret with their decision when they were grappling with a large number of choices. It's just too much.

Only the Best

The burden of choice weighs most heavily on a certain kind of person dubbed a *maximizer*.[42] Consider the following thirteen questions and the extent to which you agree or disagree with each of them.[43] Use a scale from 1 (completely disagree) to 7 (completely agree).

1. No matter how satisfied I am with my job, it's only right for me to be on the lookout for better opportunities.
2. When I am in the car listening to the radio, I often check other stations to see if something better is playing, even if I am relatively satisfied with what I'm listening to.

3. When I watch TV, I channel surf, often scanning through the available options even while attempting to watch one program.
4. I treat relationships like clothing: I expect to try a lot on before finding the perfect fit.
5. I often find it difficult to shop for a gift for a friend.
6. Renting videos is really difficult. I'm always struggling to pick the best one.
7. I'm a big fan of lists that attempt to rank things (the best movies, the best singers, the best athletes, the best novels, etc.).
8. When shopping, I have a hard time finding clothing that I really love.
9. I find that writing is very difficult, even if it's just writing a letter to a friend, because it's so hard to word things just right. I often do several drafts of even simple things.
10. I never settle for second best.
11. Whenever I'm faced with a choice, I try to imagine what all the other possibilities are, even ones that aren't present at the moment.
12. I often fantasize about living in ways that are quite different from my actual life.
13. No matter what I do, I have the highest standards for myself.

If you responded with mostly low numbers, you're likely a satisficer, the sort of person who tends to manage choices successfully. But a lot of high numbers indicate a general maximizing tendency, where only the best will do.[44]

Maximizing on the Road

If you're a maximizer, someone who finds everyday decision-making tough, imagine the *extra* pressure you might feel when making travel decisions. The stakes are enormous as the calendar dictates that you only have so many meals to enjoy, so many hikes you can take, or so many cathedrals or museums you can visit. You want to experience *the best*, and you don't have a lot of time in which to do it. Mistakes are costly and can be the source of much regret.[45] Plus, there's the very real chance that you might not get to eat at the best restaurant, see the perfect sunset, or stand before the most significant and moving piece of art. Clearly, the maximizing tendency can put a real damper on travel, creating anxiety, negative emotion, distraction, mental fatigue, and a feeling of missed opportunity.

When I travel, especially on my own, my maximizing tendencies emerge with full force as I feel the urgency of time and the consequences of my choices acutely. Every experience chosen carries the weight of loss because there is, necessarily, some other experience that I'm sacrificing in order to do what I'm currently doing. And that thing I'm not choosing *might just be better*. Being a travel maximizer often leads me to disappointment when I fear I've spent my time suboptimally. And when I conclude that I *have* chosen well, I often feel more relieved than happy. Travel FOMO—fear of missing out—takes hold firmly.

I've let the research guide me to some solutions, which my fellow traveler maximizers may also find useful. First, in the planning phase, when you're deciding where to go, consider limiting your options. *Filter, filter, filter.* Yes, this flies in the face of logic. After all, the more choices there are, the more likely you are to find that perfect thing. However, when you're literally considering a world of options, many of which are utterly foreign to you, the decision of where to travel can easily become paralyzing. Consider your needs, budget, and priorities, and force yourself to shorten your list of options.

Because you're somewhat blindly jumping into an unknown place, consider surrendering control and *outsourcing some of the decision-making to the experts*. People report finding this to be a relief.[46] Use the surrogation strategy I mentioned earlier.[47] Consult a well-regarded travel agent and defer to his or her expertise. Also, travel guidebooks suggest hotels, restaurants, and activities that have been vetted and are known to be good. Go there. Websites like TripAdvisor and Yelp provide detailed user reviews, with ratings in order from best to worst. Apply some filters (price, location, etc.), pick the best one that matches what you're looking for, and take comfort in knowing you've made a good, informed decision. Sure, there's a real value in exploring and discovering things on your own, but extreme maximizers might just find this unpleasant.

Traveling with others naturally limits your options. Your companions might have strong preferences of what they want to see and do, which might remove some of the burden you would otherwise experience. This has a clear upside for those who feel overwhelmed by making decisions. You will naturally shift your priorities from finding "the best" to finding something that your partner or kids might really like. Indeed, one of the unsung benefits of social ties is that they limit our options from the seemingly infinite to what is manageable.[48] I felt overwhelmed with all of the trips offered in my aforementioned Catalog of Travel Dreams, but seeing my boyfriend's face fall as I pitched a fourteen-day Patagonian hiking and camping adventure was enough to remove that particular trip from my list. And, you know what? It was a relief.

Finally, an unorthodox suggestion for the extreme maximizer: let your maximizing tendencies dictate where you travel. *Go somewhere that offers few choices.* Recognize that a large city with a multitude of options may overwhelm you, and your quest for the best will be futile and exhausting. For example, I found four days in the food mecca of Barcelona to be just too much pressure. Each meal chosen carried an opportunity cost: a different meal that I *wasn't* choosing. I was sure I could be doing better. And given the fact that Barcelona has over seven thousand restaurants, I was probably right. It's the land of food FOMO. This is why I'm much happier in smaller places that have a few top-notch selections. After Barcelona, I traveled to the tiny, enchanting town of Fornalutx, in the mountains of Majorca. Eleven eateries altogether: a few nice linen-napkin places, a couple casual cafes, and a bakery. There, I wasn't comparing my meal to anything else. There really *wasn't* anything else. The experience was wonderful in its own right, no doubt. I recall one meal of local seafood fresh from the Balearic Sea and homemade pie made from lemons picked from nearby groves, stunning views of the countryside from the hillside terrace, and not a word of English to be heard. But it was made more wonderful because the burden of choice was removed.

Realize that fewer choices means less opportunity for regret. Consider traveling to a small town, a mountain lodge, a secluded resort, or taking a cruise. You don't want zero options. We all like *some* freedom. But too much freedom, too many options, can be surprisingly crippling to many of us. If there are fewer decisions to be made, you may be better able to relax and be satisfied with what lies before you. Which, after all, is often the goal of travel.

Lock It In

Say you're torn between two similarly priced resorts. One features a really nice in-room Jacuzzi and the other boasts a renowned golf course. Both of these amenities appeal to you greatly. The Jacuzzi would be incredibly relaxing, while the easy access to golf would give you good reason to dust off your clubs. You feel paralyzed by indecision. Now what?

Here's your solution: stop agonizing. Do enough research to be informed on the two and then *just pick one*. Flip a coin if you must. I promise that once you commit to the Jacuzzi room, golf will suddenly seem like a relatively unimportant thing to have cared about. You might quickly tell yourself, "A nice golf course is just a short drive away." Or, "If the weather isn't ideal, the golf-resort would have been a terrible choice." Or any number of other justifications.

Why? First, as mentioned, we are excellent at rationalizing our decisions. But also, after you make your choice, the focus of your attention shifts. When you're in the process of weighing options, you're actively comparing similar things to one another in what is known as *joint-evaluation mode*. This naturally highlights and magnifies their differences. Once you decide on something, you're in *single-evaluation mode*. The differences between options become irrelevant and the thing you chose comes to stand on its own merits.[49] A very straightforward example is shopping for a new television set. In the store, the difference between the 42-inch and the 45-inch set seems meaningful. But once you pick one, that comparison ceases to exist and you start focusing on the uniquenesses of your new purchase: the complexity of the remote control, the sharpness of the picture, how the set fits in with your living room decor, and so on. In the case of the competing resorts, once you decide on one you will start to focus on its unique features, such as the room service options, balcony access, and on-site spa, and you'll probably come to feel surprisingly good about your choice.

This will be especially true if you can't change your mind later. We are excellent rationalizers, easily coming to love what we own, but the freedom to change our minds can interfere with this natural process.[50] Thus, *make your decision irreversible*. Lock yourself into a hotel room, a dinner reservation, or a particular guided tour. Even though we often prefer the freedom of an escape clause, we actually focus on the positive sides of our choices if we can't back out of them.[51]

HAPPY TRAVEL TIPS FOR SOUND DECISION-MAKING

Think back to your three hypothetical vacation options: a Caribbean cruise, Paris, or Machu Picchu. As you try to determine which one might be the best choice, consider each one and ask yourself:

- What might a typical day look like, from morning until night? What will I find pleasant, unpleasant, or neutral?
- Is there anything about this trip that might be especially prone to adaptation? What might get old?
- What bad habits, anxieties, and stressors might I be bringing with me? Will they interfere with my enjoyment? How can I leave those things behind?

- Do I know anyone who has been to this place before? Talk to this person about the realities of going there.
- Will I be paralyzed by options and decisions? How can I manage or eliminate some of these?

While all three trips sound great, maybe, just maybe, one of them might emerge as the right one for you as you go through this exercise.

Planning a trip can be an exercise in nearly blind decision-making, requiring you to project into the future, weighing the merits of little-known places and guessing how much you might like them. And travel is expensive, making mistakes costly and regrettable. By understanding common errors in decision-making, we can learn to keep an eye out for them both before and during a trip, leading to greater satisfaction with where we ultimately end up.

Two

Where in the World? Why Knowing Your Travel Personality Is Essential to Happy Travel

Travel is very subjective. What one person loves, another loathes.
—Robin Leach

In chapter 1, I laid out some well-documented decision-making habits that interfere with happy travel. These are fundamental emotional and mental processes that we *all* rely upon. None of us can see into the future and no one has perfect knowledge of his or her future wants or needs. As travelers, we are all forced to do some pretty complicated forecasting while also grappling with numerous enticing options. These challenges are practically universal. In this chapter, I will make connections between two seldom-united fields—tourism studies and personality psychology—with a focus on the *differences* between us.

But before we get into that, take a moment and envision your perfect travel day. Exactly where would you be? What kinds of activities would you be doing? Who would you be with? Lay out the specifics, in your mind or on paper, from beginning to end.

While I would be willing to bet that nobody's perfect travel day would include a missed flight, a sick child, or a mugging, there would still be a good amount of variation from person to person. You might imagine a day of urban exploration capped off with dinner at a Michelin-starred French restaurant, while your close friend would savor the notion of a quiet day spent alone in nature. Someone else would envision a sunny day at the beach with family, or of skiing on fresh powder, or of indulgent spa treatments. Your perfect travel day is totally personal.

FINDING YOUR FIT

We all want to travel to a destination that feels right to us. Despite the elusive and difficult-to-verbalize feeling of "fit," of being in a place that simply feels right, there has actually been a good amount of research on benefits of what psychologists call "person-environment fit." Much of it deals with how well people's personalities are compatible with a given activity. Extroverts feel happier in a social situation than introverts do, for example.[1] When it comes to their place of residence, people are happier when their personality is compatible with that of their home—extroverts are happier in a nation of extroverts, those high in openness-to-experience are happier in an area of ethnic and racial diversity and high population density, and highly independent people are happier in a nation that values individualism.[2] Students who report that their college is a strong match for them report higher self-esteem and enhanced academic performance.[3] Employees who feel that their workplace's key values align well with their own report greater workplace satisfaction.[4] Being in a place that feels like you fulfills key psychological needs of security, belonging, and related-ness.[5] You feel safe and accepted there. You speak the language, at least metaphorically.

Much of this research has examined how well people fit into the place they are actually living, rather than briefly visiting on vacation. But fit is also a concern of tourism studies researchers, who are trying to zero in on the match between a particular person and a particular travel destination. This is, without a doubt, incredibly challenging work. Think about your favorite destination, or the best trip you ever took. What unique aspects of *you* made this experience so special? The answer is naturally multilayered and highly idiosyncratic. Some of it cannot even be verbalized, as certain places just strike an inexplicable chord, or we encounter them at the exact right moment of our lives. Why am I enchanted by Florence but not by Paris? Its size? The language? The food? Something more? Something less? I can barely tell you why, but I can feel it. Try studying *that!*

Nevertheless, since the 1970s, tourism researchers have been working to identify specific travel personalities, attitudes, and patterns of traits that will reliably predict travel preferences. A primary aim of this work is to help both travelers and travel professionals identify what sort of experiences would best suit a person, so they can understand what would increase that traveler's satisfaction on a trip. Some researchers have taken the direct route, asking respondents to state their feelings about hypothetical travel scenarios. In one study, for example, participants were asked to imagine taking a trip to a country that "has a warm climate, sandy beaches, rare natural and animal habitats, historic ruins, museums, and an excellent native cuisine" and then indicate specific preferences: Would they prefer locally-owned facilities with few amenities or comforts, international chain hotels, or all-inclusive resort complexes? Also, would they prefer to travel solo, with family, with friends, or with an organized tour group?[6] Assuming respondents possess adequate insight into their preferences (and, as discussed in the previous chapter, this is a big assumption), these measures provide a very direct assessment of one's travel wants and needs. That part is easy. Linking these responses to aspects of the individual—namely, specific personality traits—is much more difficult, but it has been done. In the rest of this chapter, I'll consider two primary ways to assess fit: the personality-trait approach and the motivation approach. But in reality, keep in mind that multiple complex factors interact to influence why a person is drawn to a particular location.

THE CARDINAL TRAITS
OF HAPPY TRAVEL

"Personality" is one of those terms that gets a pretty loose treatment in the vernacular, but it has a very specific meaning to researchers and psychologists. It refers to the differences in how each person thinks, feels, and behaves.[7] You can also think of it as a set of characteristics that are stable across situations and over time. While the situations you're in at any given moment undoubtedly shape your behavior, and while we all grow and develop over time, elements of who we are remain steadfast.[8]

Personality psychologists often focus on specific traits that can be measured reliably and are predictive of important life outcomes. Here is a very brief measure of personality that you can take right now.[9]

Is this you?

1 = No way!

2 = Not really

3 = Maybe

4 = Pretty much

5 = Spot on!

_____ Sociable, outgoing, extroverted

_____ Imaginative, adventurous, open to new experiences

_____ Easily upset, anxious, temperamental

_____ Easygoing, warm, sympathetic

_____ Conscientious, dependable, organized

This is a quick indicator of where you stack up on the Big Five personality traits. Question one is asking about your level of *extroversion*, a sociable and energetic orientation to the world. Question two focuses on *openness to experience*: originality, open-mindedness, and curiosity. Question three taps into *neuroticism*, a tendency toward emotional instability and negative feelings. Question four is assessing *agreeableness*, a tendency to be prosocial, kind, and cooperative. Finally, question five looks at *conscientiousness*, the ability to delay gratification, plan ahead, and be responsible. As suggested by the five-point scale offered here, these traits exist on a continuum—you can be moderately extroverted, for instance—rather than all-or-nothing.

Decades of research have established the Big Five as the master traits, the most fundamental and important building blocks of personality. They are easy to measure, fairly consistent from situation to situation and across the lifespan, and predictive of important life outcomes.[10] And at least two of them—extroversion and openness—suggest which travel experiences will suit you the best.[11]

How to Predict What You'll Most Enjoy

Think about how you generally think, feel, and act when traveling. Consider the following travel-specific questions and answer as honestly as you can on the following scale.

I	2	3	4	5	6	7
strongly disagree			neutral		strongly agree	

1. I prefer to start a trip with no preplanned or definite routes when traveling in a foreign country.
2. I prefer to travel to countries where the culture is different from mine.
3. I prefer to make friends with the local people when traveling in a foreign country.
4. I prefer to travel to countries where they have the same transportation system as in my country.
5. I prefer to travel to countries where there are restaurants familiar to me.
6. I put high priority on familiarity when thinking of destinations.
7. I prefer to be on a guided tour when traveling in a foreign country.

8. I prefer to live the way the people I visit live by sharing their shelter, food, and customs during my stay.[12]

This is an abbreviated measure of the allocentrism-psychocentrism spectrum, a popular indicator of travel personality used by tourism researchers.[13] Allocentric travelers crave adventure and novelty. They are intellectually curious, sociable, and active, and they prefer independent travel to travel with groups.[14] Their ideal vacation might be backpacking with a companion, or visiting an undeveloped and undiscovered part of the world. If they have a guide, it's a local who can teach them more about the culture. They might stay in small guesthouses or hostels where they can get to know the owners, eat authentic local food, and try to pick up the language and customs. The goal of the allocentric traveler is challenge, learning, and pushing boundaries. Rest and relaxation are much less of a priority.

On the other end of the spectrum is psychocentrism. These travelers prioritize familiarity, structure, and security, and crave escape and relaxation. For them, travel is a pleasure-seeking experience rather than one that pushes their limits. Psychocentric travelers might prefer to stay in a comfortable chain hotel that reminds them of home. They would seek out restaurants that cater to tourists, with menus in their native language and food that isn't too exotic. They would prefer their activities to be planned for them, and for those activities to be minimally challenging.

A little more about this trait: scores are unrelated to demographics like age, gender, ethnicity, or relationship status. The exception is income and education level: allocentrics tend to be wealthier and more highly educated.[15] And it's a range—you can be a very strong allocentric, a very strong psychocentric, or somewhere in the middle.[16] While the extremes certainly exist, many travelers fall somewhere in between, craving both challenge and relaxation.

You may have noticed that the trait of allocentrism actually sounds very similar to the Big Five trait of openness to experience. Recall that those high in openness would describe themselves as imaginative, original, insightful, and curious. They think outside the box and enjoy unconventional art, music, and food. As such, you can think of allocentrism as openness to experience, but specifically tailored to travel experiences.

Much of the research on travel personality has focused on this particular dimension. For one, it gives tour providers and marketers some very clear direction for helping clients craft their ideal trip. Point the allocentric toward adventures, exotic local cuisine, and rustic homestays; point the psychocentric toward guided tours, Hard Rock Cafés, and the Marriott. From a research perspective, this dimension is fairly easy to measure. As you saw with the measure provided earlier, comfort with various aspects of travel is generally assessed, and people tend to have a strong sense of where they fall on the continuum.

Interestingly, the best of these measures do quite well at predicting one's *ideal* type of trip, but they fall short when they're used to guess where people have actually gone in the past, or hope to go in the future. So if you score highly on allocentrism, this indicates a *general* preference for unconventional, novel activities, but it won't specify whether you would prefer offal to oxtail, or Mozambique to Montenegro.

A key difference lies in the constraints that hold us back from traveling as we wish we could.[17] A college student may dream of hiking solo through New Zealand, but his limited budget hasn't allowed him to make that happen yet. A fifty-year-old woman may long to take a road trip through the US national parks, yet she uses her vacation days to visit her aging parents. I dream of cycling through Tuscany, but distance cycling aggravates a low-back injury. How can any brief questionnaire dial into something that specific? This drawback technically calls the predictive value of these measures into question, but doesn't necessarily diminish their utility. They can tell you the *kinds* of trips you might like, even if they won't tell you exactly where you should go. They can also be used to pinpoint your travel *ideals*, and you can use that information to craft a trip that comes close to those ideals, even if it's not in your dream destination. If you score highly on allocentrism, you don't need to trek through the Himalayas to experience novelty and challenge. A camping trip just a few hours away could fulfill those needs.

Ain't No Mountain High Enough for an Introvert

While allocentrism is an important—perhaps *the* most important—travel-relevant personality trait, it doesn't fully account for all of the differences in travel personality.[18] It's helpful to consider a second important dimension, one that is unrelated to allocentrism. This dimension is extroversion. Extroverts are generally energetic and sociable. They are sustained by social situations. Introverts, on the other hand, are not necessarily socially anxious, but they find their energy sapped by too much socialization and stimulation.[19] They have a rich inner life, thoroughly enjoying their downtime and their solitude. Loud concerts or crowded parties are unpleasant, while quiet cafes and parks are more their speed. Extroverts, by contrast, thrive in vibrant, bustling settings, and prefer them to a one-on-one conversation or an evening at home with a book. It's not social anxiety driving this difference; it has more to do with how much arousal people seek. The introvert likes less, while the extrovert craves more.

To highlight how extroversion intersects with allocentrism, imagine an allocentric traveler who is also highly extroverted and outgoing. This person most enjoys seeking out challenges and adventures with friends, thrives in places buzzing with activity, and loves chatting with those he meets in backpackers' hostels or on airplanes. But you could just as easily envision an allocentric traveler who is more solitary, quiet, and reflective, who enjoys solo travel and sitting back, quietly observing his surroundings. Both types like novelty and pushing their boundaries, but they seek different amounts of stimulation. The same goes for psychocentric travelers. The extroverted type loves group-based travel, enjoys preplanned tours that center on socializing and activity, and thrives in bustling, crowded places like casinos or cruise ships. The psychocentric introvert may travel with a partner or friend, wants everything planned out to avoid uncertainty, enjoys repeat visits to the same destination, and seeks places of quiet relaxation. In Big Five terminology, openness and extroversion appear to be the two key traits to consider when determining your travel personality.

Recently, personality researcher Shige Oishi and colleagues isolated extroversion and examined its role in enjoyment of different natural locations.[20] They hypothesized that because extroverts seek out greater levels of stimulation, they might be more drawn to the ocean, with its potential for beachside socializing. Introverts, by contrast, enjoy lower levels of stimulation and therefore prefer the serenity and isolation of the mountains. This hypothesis was borne out in several studies. Extroverted college students expressed a preference for the beach, which they equated with fun and socializing, while introverts expressed a preference for the mountains, which they equated with reflection and quiet time. Residents of more mountainous states like Colorado, Alaska, and Idaho were more introverted than were residents of geographically flatter states, even after controlling for individualism, population density, and other potential confounds (in other words, residents of Alaska aren't just introverted because they are living in a place with fewer people).

Causality is difficult to detect from these data. Do introverts really prefer mountains, or might the isolating topography of the mountains foster introversion? To test for possible causality, participants were directed, at random, to either a wide-open, flat area or a more secluded wooded location on their college campus. There, they were instructed to have a conversation with peers. If secluded areas foster introverted tendencies, those in the wooded area might talk less or feel a bit less enthusiastic or chatty.

This was not the case, suggesting the causal arrow may point in the other direction: introverts seek out secluded areas. Indeed, extroverted students felt happier in the open area, introverts in the wooded, secluded area. It was a better fit, plain and simple.

These findings are somewhat limited by the fact that they were conducted on a college campus. Did the open field really create the same psychological effect as the Jersey Shore? Was the wooded, secluded area equivalent to a cabin in the Rockies? Also, participants' exposure to locations was limited to a brief period of time. The researchers suggest caution in applying these findings too broadly. However, the implication that not all environments appeal equally to all people is an important one. Not every destination will call out to every person in the same way. These feelings and preferences may be hard to articulate; that doesn't make them any less real.

Identifying key aspects of your travel personality and giving them weight in your decision-making process will help you narrow your options and pick a trip that is best designed for you. So where do you fall on these dimensions? Do you seem to be an allocentric extrovert? A psychocentric introvert? Smack-dab in the middle? Do your scores seem to be in keeping with your past experiences of travel? Do your upcoming travels align with your results?

NUDGED BY VEGAS

I am, without a doubt, an allocentric introvert. Give me a trail to hike or a new culture to take in from the sidelines of a quiet coffee shop and I'm a happy camper. But put me in a loud, crowded rock concert or dance club and I'm immediately planning my escape. A couple of years ago when I was living near Los Angeles and my friends Hung, Eric, and Shelva approached me with a casual "What are you doing tomorrow? Want to go to Vegas?," these two traits—allocentrism and introversion—were put into direct opposition. I do crave novelty, experiences, and stories. I was only going to be living a short drive from Vegas for a few more months, and I still hadn't gone. So why not spend a Friday night in Sin City with my friends when my only other option was to stay home with Chinese takeout and a few episodes of *Gilmore Girls*? With this in mind, I responded with an enthusiastic yes. I opted for adventure over comfort while also suppressing that nagging little voice in my head, the one that was frantically whispering, "Hey fool, remember how much you hate late nights, loud noises, bright flashing lights, and gambling? You know, all the things that make Vegas *Vegas*?" I hushed the inner voice with an irrefutable "YOLO" and packed my bags.[21]

Thanks to some last-minute ATM runs and other general dawdling, we finally left town around 8 p.m., already so foreign to my highly scheduled, morning-person nature. I took deep breaths to quiet my increasing antsiness (*"It's already so late!"* said the little voice) as we drove four hours through the High Desert. We checked into our last-minute hotel, got gussied up, and hit the town. We ate dinner after midnight, something I'd never done before (because isn't eating after 9 p.m. somehow bad for you?). I spent exactly two dollars on slot machines—not my thing—and then was content to be a member of Hung's entourage, which afforded me all the free scotch I wanted while he lost a small fortune at blackjack. We conked out around 5 a.m., had a decadent late-morning champagne brunch at the Bellagio, and then headed back to California.

Back at home, I was surprised to feel almost *proud* to have been a part of such excess. I had defied my introverted nature and forced myself out of my *Gilmore Girls*-on-Friday-night rut, and it had felt eye-opening and even mildly transformative. I mean, I left for a road trip at 8 p.m.! I actually stayed out all night! I was served free drinks at a blackjack table! And a midnight meal didn't kill me! Hey, look at that.

A deeply edifying experience, this was not. But looking back, I see that without meaning to, I had perfectly nudged myself past my comfort zone, past the type of situation in which I feel secure or in control. Mentally and emotionally speaking, I went to a place where I had to take on a new challenge, open my mind, and stop being so rigid and unsociable. Did I become a regular face on the Strip? Definitely not. I still relish quiet time, 6 p.m. dinners, and early bedtimes. But what happened in Vegas did *not* stay in Vegas. Years later, I look back fondly on these eighteen hours with dear friends and am so grateful that I made the decision to push myself. I learned just a little bit about loosening up, adapting, and defying my introverted nature, which absolutely wouldn't have happened at home on the couch.

Pinpointing Where Life Begins

Life begins at the end of your comfort zone, or so the saying goes. But where, exactly, does your comfort zone end and where, if you buy the adage, does life begin? How do you figure it out, short of putting yourself in an unpleasant or risky situation to see how it feels? Sure, trial and error might be an option, but you might make some costly mistakes, like realizing too late that you're ill-equipped for a lengthy hiking trip, you hate socializing on cruises, or scuba diving activates a latent claustrophobia. Instead, try reflecting from the safe bubble of home. Consider the following comfort-zone continuum:

Bored——Comfortable——Challenged——Uncomfortable——Terrified

Most of us, in our daily lives, hang out in the bored-to-comfortable zone. Work, friends, family, hobbies: say what you will, but there's a certain amount of security, predictability, and routine involved. Occasionally, a challenge or two is thrown into the mix: a tight work deadline, some family drama, or an engaging new pastime. Meanwhile, discomfort and terror are states we usually reserve for the dentist chair or the multiplex.

But what we would label as boring, comfortable, and so on is often very subjective. What I find challenging you might find dull. What is merely uncomfortable to you might be terrifying to your best friend. We each reside in our personalized comfort zones, and in everyday life, we seldom have to push far beyond them. And because the fear of discomfort is more acute than the fear of boredom, we may not *want* to push ourselves more than we have to, so we choose boredom over discomfort much of the time. When trying to make a travel decision, and attempting to gauge how far to push, how can we accurately distinguish challenging from uncomfortable from terrifying? For many of us, this is uncharted emotional territory.

Some experienced travelers would tell you not to worry about such things. Instead, throw caution to the wind. Book the flight. Travel solo. Stay in a hostel and talk to new people. Try that unidentifiable food. Just do it, because you only live once. I get it. I am all for throwing off the constraints and being transformed by travel. But there's a fine line between boundary-pushing and panic-inducing. Go *too* far and you may feel out-of-control and anxious, and that's no way to foster a connection to a place or a deep love of travel. Instead, the key is to pinpoint your sweet spot, the point of optimal challenge.

This idea is reminiscent of the Yerkes-Dodson law, a classic concept in behavioral psychology, which speaks to the relationship between anxiety and performance.[22] With too little anxiety, performance suffers, as people are bored, distracted, or unmotivated by the task at hand. And with too much anxiety, performance also suffers as people are too anxious or self-conscious to perform at their best. Imagine an inverted U. The sweet spot is a moderate amount of anxiety, a zone of productive discomfort.[23]

Of course, productivity and performance are seldom the outcomes you most care about when you travel. You want happiness, escape, perspective, transformation, and rich memories. As such, you might be more curious to hear that travel does indeed promote these outcomes, especially when we push our boundaries. The further a person travels from home, the happier he or she is.[24] And as travel experiences accumulate, motivations change from seeking comfort and familiarity to seeking increasingly more challenge.[25] Traveling abroad, particularly for extended periods of time, tends to encourage increases in the trait of openness to experience. This is especially likely when pushing beyond your comfort zone to make friends with people from the country you're visiting.[26] This is a developmental process: as confidence grows, so do the limits of what is considered possible, and the desire for familiarity and stability may slowly give rise to a heightened craving for novelty and immersion.

Travel is self-reinforcing, in that it acts as its own reward. The more you do it, the less frightening and more gratifying it becomes. Consider a study done on a group of inexperienced Belgian travelers taking part in "social tourism," a subsidized program offering budget-friendly vacations to the financially struggling.[27] Many of these participants reported high levels of anxiety related to the uncertainties of travel like packing, navigating local transportation, and checking into a hotel. When asked about her feelings about an upcoming trip, one focus-group participant said, "What should I take with me? What will happen when I arrive? Where should I go? All things that are somewhat unknown and that I think are the cause of considerable stress."[28] Many of these novices stated a strong preference to travel in a group and to stick relatively close to home, choices believed to allay some of their anxiety. But for others, the anxiety ran so high that they ultimately decided to just stay home.

On the upside, novice travelers became more comfortable with making complex travel decisions as their experience grew. Things that were once overwhelming sources of anxiety, such as navigating busy airports, talking to strangers, and dealing in foreign currencies, simply become less intimidating with experience. More experienced travelers find the process less fraught with uncertainty, and, as a result, less scary.[29] Author Manoj Arora nails it: "Coming out of your comfort zone is tough in the beginning, chaotic in the middle, and awesome in the end . . . because in the end, it shows you a whole new world."

What's Your Comfort Zone?

In order to assess yourself and *your* current comfort zone, first consider the allocentrism trait we discussed early in this chapter. Are you the type of traveler who craves adventure and novelty? Then you likely have a naturally higher comfort zone than the psychocentric traveler, who may feel uncomfortable more easily. Think too about your level of extroversion. This can help you zero in on what level of social interaction and stimulation may suit you.

You can also try out a comfort zone calculator (www.whatismycomfortzone.com) to assess your comfort in three realms: adrenaline (Would you skydive? Climb a mountain? Scuba dive?), professional (Would you start your own business? Attend a networking event alone? Start a job in a foreign country?), and lifestyle (Would you travel alone? Quit a job that you hate? Learn a new language?). The three categories are related, touching on a general, underlying tendency to seek stimulation and take risks, but they can also be thought of as distinct (for example, I am very low on adrenaline-junkie tendencies, but very high on the other two). Naturally, being drawn to challenges—especially in the adrenaline and lifestyle categories—suggests that you might just have a naturally high comfort zone for new and challenging travel experiences.

Think back to past travels. Were you ever pushed in a way that took away from your experience? In a way that, even now, you regret? Alternatively, have you ever felt bored or understimulated on a trip? Hungry for more? Do an honest assessment. Let yourself think about the times you struggled or felt uncomfortable.[30] Focusing only on the seamless, fun, easy times might lead to overconfidence, a sense of "oh, sure—I can handle anything!"

Use the continuum reiterated here to help you:

Bored——Comfortable——Challenged——Uncomfortable——Terrified

Choose one aspect of travel—such as food, lodging, physical activity, or socializing—and then break it down, locating an example for each point on the continuum.

For example, in the context of lodging, I might label a familiar chain as boring, while a slightly more upmarket hotel might be quite comfortable. But I would guess that a private room in a small bed and breakfast would be challenging, as it would likely push me to socialize with the innkeepers and my fellow travelers at breakfast or in the common areas. Sleeping in a communal area, such as a hostel dormitory, would make me pretty uncomfortable, as I learned from my years traveling as a poor graduate student. Finally, thanks to *The Blair Witch Project*, camping alone in the woods would, to me, be pretty terrifying.

Armed with this insight, I might be convinced to go with the B&B. Staying there would push me a little, but not in a way that is so uncomfortable or unsafe that my all-important sleep is impaired. You might look at my breakdown and think that a hostel dormitory or camping in the woods alone sounds right up your alley, and that's fine. There is no one-size-fits-all here. The key is finding what is optimally challenging for you, and then taking the plunge.

PUSHED FROM THE OFFICE,
PULLED TO TUSCANY

Think about your next trip. It may be one you already have planned, one you're starting to think about, or the dream trip that's been fueling your travel fantasies for years. What makes you want to take this trip?

On the surface, perhaps you were seduced by a brochure, by a beloved novel or film set in the location, or by a friend's compelling tale of her time there. But if you look harder, you might be able to associate this location with some deeper psychological need or motive.

Because of their practical value to both travelers and to those in the travel industry, tourism researchers have proposed several models of travel motivation. Consider the push-and-pull model, which posits that there are two families of forces motivating us to travel.[31] "Push" factors are the things that make you want to get away from it all. These tend to be internal, psychological factors and include stress, boredom, or needing a break from routine. Or as journalist Earl Wilson put it, "A vacation is what you take when you can no longer take what you've been taking." From this perspective, the actual destination is relatively unimportant; the point is simply to get away.

Push factors can be identified with some basic self-reflection. What about your current state is making you want to cash in your vacation days? If you're bored with the day-to-day, well, pretty much anywhere different should suffice. If you're stressed or want to reconnect with family, you might choose someplace that isn't going to be too overstimulating. If city life is making your head spin, you may long to get back to nature. And if there's really nothing but a desire to get away or to use your vacation time before you lose it, there might not be a lot to analyze here. While push factors are important to assess—if you're trying to escape stress, Times Square might not be the best choice, for instance—pull factors are arguably more interesting.

"Pull" factors reveal why you might be attracted to a particular type of destination: *why this place?* To zero in on this, take a moment and jot down the next trip on your travel agenda (ideally, this would be a pleasure trip, one that you are electing to take). Next, take a moment to list the reasons you're going. What do you want to get out of it? You might also do this with your dream trip. As you think about it, what are the reasons you want to take this one? What feelings, thoughts, and experiences are part of the appeal here?

Next, you might look at the reasons for your upcoming trip in contrast to those underlying your dream trip. Are they similar? If so, that's good news, suggesting that your real-life choices are well-aligned with your ideals.

But if they are highly discrepant, consider why that might be. If it's a matter of money or time, consider whether you might be able to work some of those travel ideals, the elements of your dream trip, into your next one.

Let me illustrate. For the past, oh, ten years, my dream trip has been a cycling tour through some scenic part of Europe, preferably Tuscany. I would pay someone to haul my bags and, after a long day of cycling through the rolling countryside in the sunshine, I'd take a hot shower and sit down at a long wooden table on a terrace, maybe overlooking a vineyard. A small group of my fellow cyclists would enjoy a well-earned dinner with copious amounts of red wine, laughing and chatting late into the night. It would be *Under the Tuscan Sun* meets the Giro d'Italia. I'd fall asleep to the sounds of nature, wake up rested, eat a hearty breakfast, sip strong coffee, happily pass my bags off to my porter, and set out again.

Every year, I find some reason to put off this trip. Time, money, fitness, you name it. But fortunately, I've been able to unearth the features that make this trip my dream, and I can work them into most, if not all, of my other travels. There's physical activity, sunshine, beautiful scenery, some time to socialize (but not too much), great local food and wine, getting off the beaten path, and a strong sense of accomplishment. These broad needs are somewhat easy to fulfill, even if I'm not cruising through the hillsides of Chianti. They are, in fact, the things that make me happy in my everyday life, just ratcheted up and set against a breathtaking backdrop.

These kinds of needs and motivations are generally more dynamic and flexible than personality traits. And assuming travelers have accurate insight into their true motives for travel, they are fairly easy to assess. It's often as straightforward as asking people to describe a perfect travel day, just like I asked you to do. One investigation of a group of study abroad participants revealed common themes of relationship/belonging, curiosity/mental stimulation, self-development and safety/comfort.[32] In some of my own research, we asked a diverse sample of American adults to simply explain why they are motivated to travel. We found motives similar to those in other studies: adventure, relaxation, escape, connecting with others, new perspective, and challenge.[33] As you look at this list, can you identify the motives most central to you? Have they been consistent over the years, or is there no discernible pattern?

HAPPY TRAVEL TIPS FOR WORKING WITH YOUR TRAVEL PERSONALITY

As you work to figure out who you truly are as a traveler, consider the following:

- Where do you fall on allocentrism? On extroversion? Think back to past travels. Do you see how these traits may have played out in real life?
- What makes you really and truly scared? When have you been uncomfortable? Can you distinguish that from the times you've been merely challenged?
- What needs are you trying to fulfill when you travel?
- Look ahead to an upcoming trip. How can you let your traits, comfort zone, and motivations affect where you go, where you stay, and how you choose to interact with others?

All of this analysis is important, but at the same time, don't forget to also listen to your gut. Browse a guidebook, travel magazine, or Pinterest. What truly excites you? City life? Art? Natural beauty? Cuisine? A culture very different from your own? Gut feelings and instincts can be very informative, even if you can't articulate exactly why you feel as you do. As much as psychologists and tourism researchers break down the elements of travel personality, much of this remains highly personal and ultimately boils down to what feels right to you.

THREE

BUYING FUN: WHAT'S WORTH YOUR
TRAVEL BUCK?

Travel is the only thing you buy that makes you richer.

—Anonymous

A journey of a thousand miles begins with a cash advance.

—bumper sticker

Thanks to a three-hour time change and a strong tailwind, I recently arrived in San Diego for my annual psychology conference with an entire day at my disposal. Stepping out of the airport, I was met with a gorgeous January morning and the decision of what to do with all of this free time. After a quick scroll through TripAdvisor, I decided that the famed San Diego Zoo would be the perfect way to spend the day. But then I checked the ticket prices and saw that general admission was a whopping fifty dollars. I almost decided not to go. The thought of dropping that much cash on something so frivolous made me feel guilty. Fifty dollars to walk around a zoo, alone? I could walk along the beach for free, read a novel in my comfortable hotel room, or get some work done in a coffee shop.

But a certain now-or-never motivation took hold, forcing me to suppress my guilt and open my wallet. I dropped my bags at the hotel, grabbed a bike from a bike-share stand, and zipped over to Balboa Park. The four hours I spent wandering around the zoo were a delight. I had a moment of awe when a massive grey rock shifted, revealing itself to be a giant tortoise, then found myself laughing gleefully when I turned a corner and came upon a family of giraffes. I couldn't stop smiling as I watched a giant panda, one of only twelve in the United States, sit back and contentedly munch on stalks of bamboo, seemingly unfazed by the endless crowd of gawkers. I was shocked to see a sleek cheetah and an extremely ordinary dog casually sharing the same living space and was tickled to learn that they were raised together and are the best of friends. All of this was experienced against a backdrop of palm trees and in perfect 70-degree sunshine. I biked back to my hotel deeply contented and actually kind of proud, certain that I had spent my free day in the best way possible.

Fast-forward to later that evening. Back at the hotel, with a few hours to kill before my friends arrived, I mindlessly racked up a fifty-dollar tab at the hotel restaurant without even batting an eye. The meal and the ambience were both utterly forgettable. The entire experience took less than an hour. I was bored sitting there alone and idled away the time scrolling through Facebook. Yet that was a cost I was willing to incur without a shred of internal debate.

In other words, I would willingly drop fifty dollars to pass an hour experiencing mediocrity, but I thought twice before spending the same amount on multiple hours of glee, awe, wonder, fun memories, and California sunshine. Laid out like this, it seems insane. At the time, though, it somehow made perfect sense.

THE TEN-THOUSAND-DOLLAR CHALLENGE

I am not alone in my failure to translate money into good feelings. Imagine that your boss announced that you were to receive a ten thousand dollar bonus in your next paycheck, the only stipulation being that you're required to spend this money in a way that makes you happy. You are not permitted to save it or use it on bills. Your whoop of joy and happy dance should be followed by some real soul-searching as you consider what you should do with this windfall. How, exactly, will you translate cash into happiness? A remodeled kitchen or home theatre might spring to mind. Or maybe you'd love to blow it all on a diamond tennis bracelet. Despite your intuitions, if you're like thousands of participants in the growing body of research on financial decision-making, you would likely make some poor choices. Your new granite countertops, surround-sound living room, or wrist bling probably would fail to translate into the happiness you (and your generous boss) seek.

This fact partly explains the Easterlin paradox: the idea that once personal income reaches a threshold that allows for security and comfort, extra income doesn't result in commensurate gains in happiness.[1] Many of us have heard this fact, supported by years of data, and yet it's hard to believe. After all, true love and perfect health aside, money can be readily exchanged for pretty much anything we want. Given this, researchers have proposed the very reasonable possibility that the problem lies with *us*. We might just be really bad at directing our income toward those things that reliably promote happiness.[2] Personally, I don't need to consult the academic literature for evidence of this. The proof is in my closet, full of shoes and clothes that I bought with the expectation that they would bring me some small amount of pleasure. Yet some of them still have tags on. Some of them I've forgotten that I own. Each of these purchases was made in good faith, with the belief that it would do something to enhance my life. When a purchase fails to deliver, it's easy to chalk it up to the item ("I guess that dress wasn't as cute as I thought it was") rather than to the workings of my emotional system ("I guess it's hard to stay excited about new clothes"), and the cycle of unsatisfying spending continues.[3]

BUYING HAPPINESS
ON THE ROAD

While doing the ten-thousand dollar thought experiment, you might have thought, "Easy! I would spend the money on a really nice trip." You would book a flight to some dream destination and sit back, satisfied at having executed your boss's instruction. But have you? You're clearly off to a good start, spending on an experience rather than on a home remodel, jewelry, or clothing.[4] However, you will still face many small challenges—where to stay, what to do, eat, and buy—when deciding how best to translate your money into happiness while on the road.

If spending-for-happiness is challenging in everyday life, with all of its predictability, it can be overwhelming while traveling. After all, we're faced with so many options and we're relatively unpracticed at much of the process.[5] For example, when booking a hotel sight-unseen, how do we select one over the other? Is paying for a spectacular view worth the splurge? And once we arrive, how do we decide what activities are worth the money? Do we want to buy bulky souvenirs if it means we have to lug them around for days or weeks?

Decisions like these lie around every corner because—forgive my cynicism—travel is, really, a process of trading money for pleasure. In fact, the travel and tourism industry is one of the most lucrative in the world, creating 3 billion dollars in revenue *per day*, a number that has been steadily rising in the past century.[6] As much as we romanticize travel, with its singular ability to open our minds, reignite romance, spark joy, and create rich memories, for the millions of people working in the tourism industry, travelers mean money. Lots and lots of money. And a central goal of any commercial industry is to make *more* money—or get all of us to spend more.

To the savvy traveler, this motive is evident everywhere. From the moment you arrive at the airport, with its high-end shops and tempting snack bars, people are vying for your dollar. Tourist-rich areas teem with rows of seemingly identical souvenir shops, sightseeing bus rides, overpriced restaurants with menus in multiple languages, and more.[7] Hotels and cruise ships contain shops with all of the standard souvenirs but also pricier goods like designer sunglasses, jewelry, and electronics, hoping to take advantage of bored, lazy, or captive potential shoppers. There is even a cost for moments of transcendence, as many churches, museums, and natural areas charge a fee. And in some impoverished parts of the world, tourism provides a sizable chunk of the GDP, making the pressure to spend even stronger.

As a result, your relaxing vacation will inevitably contain annoying, unexpected, and sometimes high-pressure sales pitches; some subtle, some very much in-your-face. You will be forced to quantify moments of pleasure, of relaxation, of experiences marketed as being "once-in-a-lifetime." Trying to hang on to your money, to not be foolhardy or seduced by glossy brochures or professional salespeople, requires a surprising degree of forethought and vigilance. And, on top of it all, you may be doing your mental accounting in a currency you don't understand. Nothing takes away from carefree vacation fun like phrases such as "exchange rate" or, for that matter, "value-added tax." Document every penny, euro, or peso spent and you might not have nearly as much carefree fun as you'd hoped. However, treat it like a plaything, like Monopoly money, and you may come home broke.

This all sounds a bit depressing, but all is not lost. Recall that one well-established piece of happiness advice is to buy experiences over material possessions. So by directing your discretionary income toward travel rather than toward acquiring more stuff, you are already on the path to translating your money into good feelings. However, travel is rife with spending decisions, from hotel rooms to meals to tours to souvenirs, and many of these under-the-radar decisions can make or break your enjoyment. Throughout this chapter, I will apply research from the new science of spending to offer advice—some of which will be counterintuitive—on how to best spend your travel bucks.[8]

A CHEAPSKATE ABROAD

Time out for some soul-searching. Does thinking about spending money pain you a bit? Do your friends and family think you're a little stingy? Would you call yourself a budget traveler? If you're not sure, here's a quick assessment of where you might fall on the cheapskate-spendthrift continuum. Using the scale provided, how much do you agree with the following?

1	2	3	4	5	6	7
strongly disagree			neutral		strongly agree	

If you take good care of your possessions, you will definitely save money in the long run.

There are many things that are normally thrown away that are still quite useful.

Making better use of my resources makes me feel good.

If you can re-use an item you already have, there's no sense in buying something new.

I believe in being careful how I spend my money.

I discipline myself to get the most from my money.

I am willing to wait on a purchase I want so that I can save money.

There are things I resist buying today so I can save for tomorrow.[9]

If you find yourself agreeing with many of these, you're probably on the thrifty side. Heck, I'll confess to leaning toward cheapskate. My car has over 200,000 miles on it. Much of my furniture is second-hand, found on Craigslist or inherited from friends eager for an upgrade. I jump on free samples and delight in a bargain. For a long time, I figured that this was just a function of my stage in life. Turns out, though, that on the path from poor graduate student to tenured professor, my frugality has stayed with me. And yet I have a burning desire to travel. These clashing desires—to avoid spending too much money while also seeing the world in some degree of comfort—have always been a struggle.

And I am not alone in this. The travel section of the bookstore is chockfull of titles like *How to Travel the World on $50 a Day, Southeast Asia on a Shoestring,* and even *How to Live in a Car, Van, or RV.*[10] This is not a new trend. The first guidebook to really take off was Arthur Frommer's *Europe on $5 a Day*, originally published in 1957.[11] Many people, it turns out, are looking for the loophole, the secret that will allow them to see the world without breaking the bank.

While there is no one secret to traveling happily on a budget, I do know that, for the cheapskate in all of us, it requires knowledge: Knowledge of where to find deals, yes, but also knowledge of the psychology of spending. While the Internet and bookstores abound with specific cost-cutting strategies and hacks for finding cheap flights, hotels, and so forth, I offer a few lesser known and more general tips from recent research on the curious and often puzzling relationship between happiness and money.

WHAT'S YOUR TIME WORTH?

Many travel decisions amount to trade-offs. When you choose the beach, you immediately rule out the mountains. When you decide on a family vacation, carefree romance will probably take a backseat. When you opt for dinner at the French bistro, you have no stomach space left for the lobster shack. Less often appreciated is the frequent trade-off between two of our most precious resources: time and money.

The act of getting from point A to point B is one obvious example. Search for a flight to your dream destination and you might notice that even for a standard coach fare, the options you're met with will likely vary in price by hundreds of dollars. Why? Many factors surely play into this baffling array of options, and while I do not claim to understand all of the intricacies of airfare pricing, I do know one thing: convenience costs. That direct flight is often—certainly not always, but often—more expensive than one that has you hopping from airport to airport with long layovers. Those who set the fares are smart; they know that some people are willing to pay a premium to avoid such drudgery.

Another clear airport-related trade-off is the new option to spend a bit extra for TSA PreCheck or Global Entry, two programs that allow expedited clearance for preapproved, low-risk travelers at many airports within the United States. Pending a background check, these fliers can skip some of the time- and soul-sucking lines that many of us endure at airports. This particular time-money trade-off doesn't stop there. Visitors to popular tourist sites from Disney World to the Vatican can buy more expensive tickets that allow them to skip the lines. LineGenie.com offers a prepaid front-of-line service to well-heeled nightclubbers, or you can out-source the misery of waiting in line by hiring a "tasker" on TaskRabbit. com.

My boyfriend and I recently attempted to eat at an insanely popular restaurant in Washington, DC. They don't take reservations, so would-be diners simply line up outside, waiting for the 5:00 opening. We arrived at 4:30, thinking that would be plenty of time to get seated. We could not have been more wrong. To our amazement, the line stretched down the block. Turns out, those at the front of the line had arrived at 3 p.m.! Who in the world would do this? How good could any meal possibly be? Later, we learned that many of these early birds were actually hired taskers, paid upward of twenty dollars an hour to hold a diner's place. Forty dollars to avoid a two-hour line? As we stood there in the cold, this suddenly seemed like money well-spent.[12]

Lodging provides another opportunity to trade money for time. Centrally located hotels know they have a good thing going. Sure, you can save money—sometimes substantial amounts—by staying in the sticks and spending a chunk of your day commuting to where you *really* want to be. Or, you can plunk down more money upfront and be right in the heart of the action, able to amble out your door to a cute café, pop back to your room midday for a nap or to grab the sweater you forgot, and stay out late at night without worrying about when the buses stop running. Location, location, location.

But even considering all of these conveniences, the fact remains that we do like to save a buck, and the trade-off between time and money doesn't always have a clear winner. After all, we can rationalize our money-saving choices. Long airport layovers mean more time to read that engrossing novel. A hotel in the sticks means seeing a new side of the place you're visiting, maybe one that's off the well-worn tourist path. You might meet someone interesting while standing in that endless restaurant line. True, but these seemingly economical choices do often come with unforeseen costs. Multiple layovers mean multiple opportunities to buy overpriced airport food. The inconveniently located hotel may require bus or taxi fare. These hidden costs may not have been apparent to you when you so virtuously booked the money-saving option months earlier, but they can quickly obscure the savings you thought you were gaining.

Time-saving decisions also tend to reduce stress and inconvenience. The more layovers you have, the more chances there are to miss a flight, for a flight to be cancelled, or to have your luggage lost. If you're one of the lucky few who can sleep soundly on planes, you're more likely to enjoy long, uninterrupted sleep on a nonstop flight, too. This may be even more important when traveling with children. A friend of mine, who has two small children, mentioned that he is almost always willing to pay a bit more for a nonstop flight so he doesn't have to wake the kids, schlep them and their many belongings through a busy airport, and get them all resettled once again.

We don't always think about these seemingly minor nuisances when planning flights, hotels, and the like, especially when it's done far in advance. Seduced by a bargain, we book that discounted flight or cheap hotel room, only to have the downsides revealed later. This can explain a multitude of regrettable decisions. Recall how we think big-picture when a decision exists far out in time.[13] Months in advance, saving a few bucks is central. But when you're actually sitting in that airport on a lengthy layover, trudging back to a faraway hotel after an exhausting day, or waiting in an endless line in crippling heat, you realize that you would have happily spent more money to avoid such unpleasantries.

Finally, research by University of British Columbia social psychologists found that people who have a general tendency to prioritize time over money are happier than those who prioritize money over time.[14] This was measured by having participants indicate which of the following sounds more like them:

> Tina values her time more than her money. She is willing to sacrifice her money to have more time. For example, Tina would rather work fewer hours and make less money, than work more hours and make more money.

> Maggie values her money more than her time. She is willing to sacrifice her time to have more money. For example, Maggie would rather work more hours and make more money, than work fewer hours and have more time.

Those who related more to Tina were also happier people in general. This was true even when holding things like income and employment constant, suggesting that prioritizing time over money isn't just a luxury enjoyed by the wealthy. These studies are correlational and therefore we can't conclude that valuing time *causes* happiness. Surely, the connection is complex. However, previous research suggests that valuing money is related to materialistic values, working extra hours, devaluing social connections and exercise, and commuting, all things that detract from happiness. On the other hand, prioritizing time over money encourages the kinds of everyday decisions that strongly relate to happiness, such as spending time fostering connections with others, engaging in meaningful hobbies, and, yes, taking vacations.

In the context of travel, this research provides another sound reason why we might do well to spend more—if it's not prohibitively more—for time-saving conveniences. Time is always a precious commodity, but we often fail to appreciate this in daily life. Its value is likely to be much more apparent as you spend your fourth hour in O'Hare, thinking about the sunshine and piña coladas you could already be enjoying if you hadn't been so intent on saving a few bucks on that cheaper flight.

Of course, it's not always easy to know when buying time is going to be a worthwhile investment. One trick is to try hard to envision what it might really feel like to be in the actual experience you are planning for. Try your best to project into the future. How will it really feel to have all of those layovers, to stay in that faraway hotel, or to wait in a long line in the hot sun? If you can direct some attention to these possible outcomes, you may just decide to spend a little more money to buy a little more time and convenience.

BEWARE THE OCEAN VIEW

Travel is, if nothing else, unique in its ability to immerse us in novelty. It disorients us, unsteadies us, forces us to consider and make space for so many deviations from everyday life. These range from the massive—languages, architecture, and cultural practices—to the mundane—street signs, shampoo options, and brands of chewing gum. So much is brand-new, worth noticing and questioning. Given this, it may seem odd for me to emphasize the importance of keeping travel fresh. But this is exactly why it's so critical: we can completely fail to realize that we actually adapt to our travel experiences. The sad fact is, day one of a trip can feel fresh and new, with so much to soak up and be wowed by, but day five or six can start to feel depressingly ordinary.

This is especially true if you're staying in the same place for a while. Each day of a week-long trip may become increasingly ho-hum. That ocean-front view that so captivated you upon arrival at your hotel? Chances are, soon it will recede into the background, mentally and emotionally. Instead of an automatic "wow" as you take it in, you might have to remind yourself to go look at it, to get your money's worth, dammit! As you do, it might feel like work to direct and hold your attention on it.

By no means does this make you an ungrateful person; no, you're just a sense-maker. You have unconsciously transformed the extraordinary into something comprehensible and, unfortunately, something quite ordinary. Now there is no need to step back in wonder, trying to accommodate this new sensory information. You did that already. You walked into your hotel room for the first time, drew the curtains, and were met with a patch of white sand and the band of blue beyond. You stopped, gasped, and took a moment, because—whoa—this is different! You spent a few minutes taking ownership of this new reality, where your bedroom doesn't overlook a suburban street but instead an endless sea. Accompanying this were thoughts along the lines of "Wow!" or "How did I get so lucky?" and a feeling of awe or gratitude. *This* is the feeling you were so craving as you decided to treat yourself to an ocean view.

However, after a few hushed and grateful moments, your brain wants to move on to more demanding tasks. Your brain is bored. But wait! Another part of you, the part that is shelling out mucho bucks for this view, wants more. More wow, more wonder, more gratitude. Nope. Your brain is done. From here on out, it's going to take some real mental work to notice and appreciate that view, and your ability to get your money's worth is, sadly, called into question.

When it comes to appreciation of the static, unchanging present, your internal psychological makeup is working against you. It's in your nature to adapt to your surroundings. It's actually good for you. Imagine how distracted you would be if you were constantly marveling at all the nice but unimportant things in your environment, like the pretty photo on the wall, the perfect temperature of the room, or the hardwood floors polished to a glossy shine. It's just not feasible, practical, or wise.[15] Yet we fail to realize the extent to which it happens, especially when we're in a new and exotic place. When it comes to travel, if you don't at least give a nod to the inevitability of hedonic adaptation, you might make some poor financial investments, ones that don't deliver the good feelings you were expecting.

The fact of adaptation isn't one we like to acknowledge, especially when it comes to remarkable experiences like travel. I get it. It's a bit depressing. The expectation of constant delight is a reasonable way to justify the exorbitant expense of a vacation. Plus, when you see those Pinterest photos of beaches, mountains, or cathedrals, you can't quite believe that they could be anything but breathtaking. But adaptation is an important consideration because, upon honest reflection, your money (and time) can then be directed toward the kinds of things that keep an experience fresh, things that keep you guessing and marveling.

With some awareness and reflection, you can actually use the inevitable fact of adaptation to your advantage. One piece of advice is to consider how *selective deprivation* can inhibit adaptation, keeping even life's small pleasures from losing their emotional impact. In one study, students attended an initial experimental session and were asked to taste and rate some Belgian chocolates.[16] Afterward, half were instructed to return in a week, and to please refrain from eating chocolate until then. The other half were simply asked to return in a week; no instructions were given about their chocolate consumption. When they all returned a week later, they were again asked to taste and rate chocolates. Those who had been deprived of chocolate for a week rated these chocolates as significantly tastier than the students who had free rein, and the effect was driven by the fact that they were savoring the chocolate more. Specifically, they said that they were mindfully attending to the taste and texture of the chocolate, were thinking about eating the chocolate in the future, and were even imagining telling their friends about it. In that week of self-imposed deprivation, chocolate—which is readily available to college students—had become transformed from something ordinary into a treat worth savoring.

Consider using this to your advantage on your next trip. As much as you hate to acknowledge it, an ocean view *will* become ordinary if you have constant exposure to it. Why not draw the curtains for part of the day, to foster a moment of wonder and appreciation when you strategically decide to expose yourself to the blue ocean outside?

Wait a minute, you might say. Hold on. You're telling me to deprive myself of this rare and precious view that I paid a lot of money for? To close the curtains and intentionally *not look at it*? Yep, that's right! Think of the "wow!" that you'll experience each time you dare to take a peek.

If this doesn't sit well, then perhaps a more logical, cost-cutting strategy is to forgo the ocean view altogether. Get a cheaper room with a view of the parking lot. Heck, you're not going to enjoy that ever-present view for too long anyway. But when you do see the ocean—on morning jogs, when lounging with a cocktail, on romantic sunset walks—it will be much more impactful than if you have access to it 24/7. You're like those chocolate-deprived students, but instead of saving calories, you're saving money. Self-denial promotes savoring and does so in a financially savvy way.

The same principle applies to other aspects of travel. Space out your special, pricey meals with cheaper food found at bakeries, cafés, and grocery stores. Not only can this be a money-saver, but it exposes you to a different, perhaps more authentic, side of a place. And then when you do experience a fancy restaurant meal, it will be something worth savoring instead of just another nice but forgettable dinner. Another tip: in a day of sightseeing, insert breaks for downtime. Or spread your sightseeing out over several days rather than packing it all into one. Not only will this help you maintain your stamina, but it will encourage a sense of wonder at each new site.

A key factor here is novelty. Build it into your travels yourself, strategically. Be sure to see something new or do something different every day. Decidedly inconvenient as it may be, traveling to several different places in one trip might help keep things fresh. But be wise in striking a balance between novelty and exhaustion. Moving to a new hotel every day to keep things fresh may be too annoying to bring benefits. At the same time, a week in the same hotel might get dull. There's no perfect amount of time. Most importantly, don't assume novelty and appreciation will be ever-present just because you're in a new place. You are still you, a sense-maker, a novelty-seeker. As aptly noted by food writer and activist Michael Pollan, "The banquet is in the first bite."[17] Plan to give yourself as many first bites as you possibly can.

MORE TOURS, FEWER TRIVETS

Travel is itself the ultimate experiential investment. However, your trip can pack even more experiential punch if you're willing to pay for fun and broadening side trips, language lessons, wine tours, guided hikes, museum visits, or cooking classes. Although immersing yourself in a new place is the focus of chapter 5, as you plan your trip, be sure to allocate some funds for rich, challenging, and memorable activities. Again, remember adaptation. Don't overestimate your ability to sit on the beach or lie on the cruise ship deck, staring out at the ocean and feeling happy and grateful. Unless you have the attentional resources of a Buddhist monk, this *will* get dull.

Consider, too, the downsides of excessive spending on souvenirs. Because so many of the items that you encounter possess that seductive now-or-never pull, temptation to buy may be overwhelming. I shake my head at the items that I've accumulated in my travels—a wooly snowflake sweater from Norway, a seashell necklace from Thailand, cheaply tailored clothing from Vietnam, a Basque trivet from Spain. What unites these items, apart from the fact that they are all shoved in the way-back of a drawer, is the fact that I knew that I only had one chance to make them mine. The cost of *not* acting, the fear of future regret, rather than actual desire, drove my purchasing.

Robert Cialdini, researcher and author of the classic book *Influence*, wouldn't be at all surprised by this behavior. He names scarcity as one of the most powerful tools of marketers.[18] And you don't need to travel to see it play out. Slogans like "limited time only," "three-day sale," or "only ten remaining!" are incredibly effective at getting us to act immediately and impulsively. Scarcity confers value. When there isn't a lot of something in the marketplace, you can't help but conclude, "Everybody wants this!" or "This thing must be really special!" Think of Cabbage Patch Kids, Furbies, Wiis, and others treasures from holidays past. These items aren't inherently valuable, but they became so because they were so hard to come by. Sales pitches that make use of scarcity effectively play to our need to possess the sought-after and the rare.

And scarcity is acutely felt when traveling. Many destinations are known for a particular item—something you can only get there—and souvenir shops are more than happy to deliver them to us. Maple syrup in Canada. Tequila in Mexico. Masks in Africa. Nesting dolls in Russia. Straw hats in Vietnam. Leis in Hawaii. In addition to the unique specialties of a region are the more general signifiers of our presence there: place-specific t-shirts, shot glasses, keychains, magnets, and other tchotchkes. A critical consumer will pick up on the absurdity of some of these items, such as a bottle opener with an engraving of the pope or "canned fog" from San Francisco, but practically all of us are vulnerable to the lure of the now-or-never object.

Do these items confer whatever psychological benefit we might expect? I've learned the hard way that, much of the time, they weren't worth the suitcase space they took up. But the souvenirs that *have* made a lasting impact on me are those that are closely tied to fond memories. Last summer, I unexpectedly faced a crippling fear of heights when hiking in Norway's breathtaking Jotunheimen National Park. My boyfriend Joe and I were ambling along the popular eight-mile Besseggen trail and had to unexpectedly scale what was—to me—an exposed, rocky area far above ground. Realistically, it was pretty safe ("If you fall, you'd probably break something, but you wouldn't die," Joe said). But for me, a person who feels shaky on a four-foot ladder, utter panic set in. I was frozen on the side of the rock face, unable to go up or down, seriously wondering if a helicopter might be able to swoop in and snatch me up. Slowly, painfully, with Joe's guidance, and only because I had no other choice, I made progress to the top of the climb, while the badass Norwegians bounded up and down all around me. Finally at the top, legs shaking, I picked up a small rock and mindlessly palmed it as my breathing slowed and my panic gave way to pride. I pocketed the rock, which now sits on my bedside table, a reminder of how I rose above my fear. It is utterly ordinary, yet it evokes rich memories of a peak experience in an indescribably gorgeous and remote place. Now *that* is a meaningful souvenir.[19]

Before spending money on (and having to transport) souvenirs, particularly those that are heavy, fragile, or expensive, ask yourself the following:

- Is this item tied to any special memories or unique emotions?
- Am I only buying it because I might not have the chance later?
- Is this item mass-produced or is it made by local artisans? (Skip the former and, if the latter, get the backstory to make the item more meaningful.)
- Will I actually use this or wear this when I get home? Specifically, how and when?

I don't mean to suggest that buying souvenirs is always a bad financial move.[20] Many conjure up vivid memories and deep feelings. But I do want to stress that you will almost definitely feel an irresistible pressure to shop. Don't let your sound judgment be clouded by the powerful lure of scarcity. And know that if you're gripped by indecision, chances are, if you hold off, you can probably find the item at the airport.

ANCHORS AWEIGH

I spend several weeks each summer teaching in Sweden and Denmark, two of the world's happiest, most progressive, most beautiful, and most ridiculously expensive countries. As much as I adore Scandinavia, I exist in a near-constant state of sticker-shock. Every time I whip out my currency converter app and see that my very ordinary glass of wine and sandwich cost upward of thirty dollars, I feel a pang of guilt, a sense of waste, and a strong pressure to really, really get my money's worth. Thoughts of spending are ever-present, and I feel like a pauper as I think long and hard about whether I really need a refill of coffee or a side salad. It's a real buzzkill.

But last year, after teaching in Scandinavia, I met my friend Kate in San Sebastian, Spain and I couldn't get over how utterly inexpensive everything was by contrast. A bottle of Rioja for the equivalent of 12 dollars (in a restaurant, no less)? Yes, please. A second helping of *pintxos y jamon*? Bring it. Apart from the fact that San Sebastian's food and wine are famously exquisite, I was able to finally enjoy myself simply because I wasn't mentally tallying up each overpriced bite and sip. This cheapskate could enjoy some unbridled hedonism and savor every moment of it. The sharp contrast with Scandinavian prices made the experience even better. However, if I had visited Scandinavia *after* experiencing the comparatively low prices of Spain, it would have stung even more than it already had.

What's happening here is that the initial costs are serving as an anchor, essentially setting the bar for what sorts of prices I should expect.[21] And because Scandinavia had set such an extremely high bar, Spain felt amazingly cheap. Overnight, I had gone from pauper to princess, and I have to admit that it felt great.

So if you're planning the kind of trip that has you hopping from location to location, notice if any wildly expensive places are on your agenda.

For example, as a very general rule, urban areas are often pricier, so by this logic, it might make sense to visit them first. San Francisco before Yosemite, Manhattan before the Catskills, London before the Cotswolds. And, certainly, Scandinavia before almost anywhere else. Then, with the anchor set high, you will have the enhanced enjoyment of a cheaper place second. Doing it the other way around, with the anchor set low, will be far less fun.

STEP AWAY FROM THE WALLET

Imagine that you and your partner are splurging on a week at a hotel that is well-known for being luxurious and relaxing. You wake up hungry and spend $16 for a breakfast buffet. A round of midmorning golf runs you $140, followed by a light $25 lunch. Later, you meet up with your partner, who has arranged for the two of you to have an hour-long couples' massage. There goes another two hundred, and then another $150 for dinner and drinks. Ouch.

You took this trip to relax, to get away from the stressful work schedules that have been leaving you both exhausted and disconnected from one another. And while you can't argue that the resort lives up to its reputation for luxury, you feel a growing unease at the amount of money you're hemorrhaging. After a few days of this, you're not having much fun anymore. Every indulgence comes with an exorbitant price tag, and you can't help thinking, "Is this massage *really* worth what I'm paying?" and "I could have made this cocktail at home for a fraction of the price," instead of kicking back and enjoying being pampered.

Constantly tabulating your vacation spending is no fun. But thinking about money also has other, less obvious, psychological costs. Given the centrality of money in our daily lives, researchers have rigorously examined the role it might play in our mental and emotional worlds.[22] They have consistently found that even when the concept of money is subtly primed—say, by unscrambling sentences that have money-related words in them, seeing images of money on a computer screen, or walking past an ATM machine—people go into a kind of mental business-mode. They are more willing to work longer and harder and to persist at a difficult task, which is certainly good sometimes. But the downside is that they tend to behave in a self-interested way. They are less concerned with others, express a greater desire to spend time alone, and even sit further away from an interaction partner. They are less generous and demonstrate lower levels of compassion and empathy. It seems like people kind of become self-absorbed jerks when they have money on their minds. Other research has found that when subtly primed with the concept of money, people savor simple pleasures, such as chocolate, less.[23]

These effects, demonstrated in over 165 studies to date, are the exact opposite of what we want to experience while on vacation. We don't want to be in a cold problem-solving, business-minded mode, disinterested in those around us and unable to delight in small pleasures. And yet when thoughts of money are ever-present, this is exactly the mindset we are setting into motion. The evidence is clear: don't think too much about finances when you travel. However, when we travel, we choose to engage with an industry of experts who are skilled at convincing us to part with our money. That can make this easier said than done.

Pay It and Forget It

One wonderful way to reduce money-focus and the unpleasantness it brings is to pay for a trip in advance. The idea here is that you are decoupling spending from experience. If you pay up front, you're less likely to calculate whether that massage is worth a hundred dollars or if that cocktail is worth ten, the sort of mental calculus that is almost guaranteed to detract from your enjoyment. Because, hey, it's already paid for! Your only job is to sit back and enjoy.

The simplest way to do this is to book an all-inclusive vacation. Resorts like Club Med and Sandals spring to mind as the classic examples, but many, many others exist. Here, you often have unlimited access to all the food, drink, and entertainment you desire. If you want an extra cocktail or dessert, you might worry about the resulting hangover or weight gain, but certainly not an empty bank account.[24]

Of course, not everyone loves these kinds of indulgent, lounge-around vacations. If you crave something more active or adventurous, it's still possible to pay up front. For example, you can buy a package deal to outdoorsy places like Costa Rica or Belize. In addition to prepaying for your hotel and flight, you can also book (and pay up front for) a variety of guided hikes, zip-lining, white-water rafting, scuba diving, and other adventures. Many ski lodges offer packages that include hotel, ski lessons, lift tickets, and some meals. My boyfriend goes to San Francisco Giants' fantasy baseball camp every January, and the flat fee he pays includes lodging, most meals, local transportation, a uniform, giveaways, memorabilia, special guests, autographs, workouts with the trainers, and the experience of playing baseball where his beloved Giants have spring training.

When all expenses are tallied up to reveal the bottom line, these all-inclusive trips may seem shockingly expensive. To be sure it's a good move, you might break down what each individual item—hotel, dinner, excursions—would cost on its own to determine whether this is worth the splurge. But don't forget that it's hard to put a price tag on the simple pleasure of not having to worry about money while you're supposed to be having fun.

These sorts of preplanned trips may reduce some of the spontaneity, so you should consider how much committed booking you do in advance. Allow yourself *some* free time and flexibility for that cool thing that will inevitably pop up. But the more you can pay for up front, the more you will enjoy yourself. Plus, booking far in advance can give you a lot of material for your travel daydreams.

HOW VACATIONS ARE LIKE
COLONOSCOPIES

Vacations and colonoscopies could hardly be more different, but bear with me. The Nobel Prize-winning researcher Daniel Kahneman was examining how, when remembering a positive or negative experience, our memory is unduly influenced by its emotional peak, or its intensely best or worst moment, and also how the experience ended.[25] For what is possibly the most famous in a series of carefully designed experiments, Kahneman teamed up with physicians to examine the peak-end rule in a sample of men who were undergoing, yes, a colonoscopy.[26] While the entire episode was pretty unpleasant for all, a subset of the men were given a slightly longer colonoscopy, but with a slightly lower degree of unpleasantness in those last few minutes. In other words, they withstood a significantly longer period of discomfort than the other men did, but those last few minutes were slightly less uncomfortable than the rest of the procedure.

If given your choice of colonoscopy, you could certainly make a case for just getting the thing over with as quickly as possible and, in some sense, you would be correct. Longer durations of discomfort seem objectively worse than shorter durations. Rip the Band-Aid off, already. However, in another sense, you would be wrong. Kahneman found that the way the procedure ended colored the men's recall of the procedure as a whole. When it ended slightly better than the other men's, they reported the *entire experience* as being better, and—importantly, from a health perspective—were more likely to say they'd be willing to go through it again in the future. The surprise here is that the length of time they were undergoing the procedure didn't seem to matter, a phenomenon so pervasive that it came to be known as *duration neglect*.

Kahneman found similar results for other negative experiences such as dental work, loud noises, and a cold-pressor task (submerging your hand in uncomfortably cold water).[27] A few extra minutes of slightly-less-bad exposure at the end made the entire thing seem better when looking back on it later. And, again, length of time was far less important than we might guess.

The peak-end rule doesn't only apply to negative events. Consider the common experience of gift-giving. Imagine you have a really killer gift to give your friend on his birthday, say, a cashmere sweater. But because the one gift, however extravagant, just didn't seem like enough, you also picked up some nice chocolate. As you present him with these two thoughtfully wrapped packages, should you care which one he opens first? Research suggests that, actually, you should.[28] In two studies, one in which college students won DVDs, and a second where Halloween trick-or-treaters received candy, the most overall pleasure was derived when the best item—either a top-rated DVD or a full-sized chocolate bar—was given *last*. In fact, tacking on a just-okay item at the end (a less-desirable DVD or a piece of bubble gum) provided no extra pleasure. You might as well stick with the sweater and forget the chocolate, or at least give him the chocolate first. How the experience *ended* was most critical for satisfaction.

For practical reasons, peak-end studies have examined instances that exist rather briefly in time.[29] And for the sake of drawing conclusions with some degree of scientific certainty, the procedures tend to be tightly controlled and not always reminiscent of real life. So the question remains: does the peak-end rule equally apply to a longer-term and unconstrained experience, like a vacation?

To some extent, yes. Simon Kemp and colleagues recruited a sample of students taking a vacation over a holiday break that lasted, on average, seven days.[30] When prompted via text message, they were asked to respond as soon as possible and tell the researchers how happy they were feeling in that moment, how they felt during the best and worst moments of that day, how memorable and unique those particular moments were, and how they felt that day in general. Because they did this every day of their trip, researchers could assess how these ratings changed over time, as the end of the trip approached. They also completed follow-up measures about a week after and about a month after the trip had ended. In these measures, they rated their overall happiness on the trip, the best and worst moments, and how memorable and unusual the trip was.

First, they found evidence for duration neglect, confirming the finding that longer vacations were not rated as better (although the span of time was somewhat limited, from four to fourteen days). Second, and more to the point, when the participants returned home, settled back into normal life, and recalled how pleasant their trip was, they apparently were not basing this judgment on an average of all the highs, lows, and neutral moments they experienced. Comparing this recall to the daily evaluations they provided while traveling, certain moments did indeed carry more weight. Recalled overall happiness of the trip was predicted by how it *ended*, so that a positive ending predicted an overall positive recall, while a negative ending predicted lower overall positive recall. Findings were less clear for the peak (or, for that matter, the trough or lowest point) of the trip.[31]

Go Out with a Bang

The point is that, before you come home from your vacation, consider making the last day or night really special. Applying the peak-end rule and the concept of duration neglect, it's likely you're not actually going to be giving each moment of the trip equal weight and averaging these moments together to make your judgment. So if your trip ends with a cancelled flight, a sick child, or—heck—a colonoscopy, you might recall the entire trip as unpleasant, even if the bulk of it was actually quite enjoyable. On the other hand, if your last night involves a really special meal or a romantic evening on your luxurious private balcony overlooking the ocean, you may just have a more positive memory of your trip as a whole than you otherwise would. And since one of the delights of travel is the rich memories it provides, why not make choices that help ensure them?

Need further convincing? There are several other areas of research that explain why you'd be best off indulging at the *end* of your trip.

Again, consider adaptation. Earlier, I suggested that you save some money by foregoing a hotel room with a spectacular view, because you're probably going to stop appreciating it pretty quickly. You may find, then, that an expensive week in a fancy hotel starts to seem rather ordinary by day four or five, perhaps making it a regrettable investment. But when it's one special night that follows a string of mediocre hotel experiences, it's likely to bring you a boost of appreciation and enjoyment that is well worth the money.

Putting your splurges off also gives you the benefit of anticipation. Knowing that your final evening of vacation will be spent at a great restaurant or a fancy hotel gives you something to look forward to, even as your trip nears its end and your return to everyday life draws depressingly closer. One study of Dutch vacationers found that the period of time leading up to a vacation is often as pleasant as the vacation itself.[32] Continue to capitalize on the power of anticipation even while traveling by putting something special off until the end.

Also, keep in mind the idea of anchoring mentioned earlier.[33] That fancy hotel on the first night of the trip will naturally make the midrange places you've booked for the rest of the week seem pretty lackluster. Save it for the end and you will naturally compare it to what was experienced right before it, making it seem even better than it may have otherwise.

Finally, note that going out with a bang can actually save you money! If you're on a budget, know that you don't need an entire week of indulgences in order to recall having an amazing time. Just a strategically placed one can make your entire trip seem better than it otherwise might have been. In short, then, end on a high note. It's a simple, economical way to enhance your trip, both in the moment and in hindsight.

HAPPY TRAVEL TIPS
FOR SUCCESSFUL SPENDING

Smart travel spending goes way beyond tracking airfares and scouting out discount hotel rooms. It requires a consideration of human psychology: decision-making, hedonic adaptation, and the power of persuasion. As you plan, ask yourself the essential specific questions:

- *What will I adapt to? What will stop bringing me happiness after a few days (or even a few hours)?* This can be a tough one. For one, you might not know exactly what you'll be experiencing. Second, the inclination is to assume a constant state of wonder. Dispense with this belief and simply ask yourself what aspects of your trip will be ever-present. Those are the things you will get used to quickly. Adjust your spending accordingly.

- *Will choosing-cheap cost me time and stress later on? If so, is the trade-off worth it?* Look at the layovers you'll have to deal with on that discounted flight and think of all the money you might end up spending to amuse yourself. Consider the time, money, and hassle involved when choosing a hotel on the outskirts. Try your best to project into the future, and decide if the savings are worth it.

- *What can I pay for up front, before the trip even begins?* Beyond flights and lodging, are there activities that you know you want to do? Museums you're sure you want to visit? To decouple spending from experience, go online and see if it makes sense to book in advance.

- *What kinds of souvenirs do they sell in these locations? Would I really appreciate or use that item?* Consider thinking about what purchases you might want to make *before* you're put into a high-pressure, now-or-never spending situation. At home, relaxed, logical, and in tune with the habits of ordinary life, you might easily conclude that you'd never wear a wooly Norwegian sweater with snowflakes on it, for instance. Ideally, that can influence your decision when you're in the heat of the moment. You can extend this same line of questioning to the friends and family you feel pressured to shop for. And keep in mind, as novelist Anatole France noted, "It is good to collect things, but it is better to go on walks."

• *How should I arrange my experiences over the course of my trip?* Keep in mind both the concept of anchoring and the peak-end rule. Visit pricey places first, if possible, and be sure to have an amazing last day or night.

"When preparing to travel, lay out all your clothes and all your money. Then take half the clothes and twice the money." Author Susan Heller's sound advice hits the mark. Travel contains so many hidden costs (and, of course, an overstuffed suitcase is a huge nuisance), and many people are making a living off of your travel buck. Failing to plan how you will manage the pressure to spend can be one of the biggest spoilers of an otherwise well-crafted trip. Spend begrudgingly and you may detract from your own good time. But do it with reckless abandon and you may come home to an empty bank account and serious guilt.

FOUR

THE COUNTDOWN IS ON: AN UNEXPECTED WAY TO BOOST YOUR ENJOYMENT OF A TRIP BEFORE YOU EVEN LEAVE HOME

Travel is about the gorgeous feeling of teetering in the unknown.
—Gaby Basora

When I was growing up in Southeastern Pennsylvania, my grandmother and her friends liked to occasionally jazz things up by hopping aboard a bus for a "mystery tour," a short trip with an unknown destination. Arranged by a local bus company, these tours often ended up centering on fall foliage, casinos, or the Amish. She recalls one October tour when she and her companions—my grandfather, great-aunts, some church friends, and a bunch of strangers—were told only how many days their trip would be (two) and what kind of clothes to pack (bring a jacket). Armed with that scant knowledge, their bus headed west on the Pennsylvania Turnpike, immediately ruling out Philadelphia, Baltimore, the Jersey Shore, and other points east as their destination but opening up, quite literally, a world of other possibilities. She and her companions were never at a loss for conversation as the miles ticked by. Looking out the window and trying to piece together where they might end up, they tossed out various possibilities. Gettysburg? Pittsburgh? The Alleghany Mountains? The Grand Canyon of Pennsylvania? (Yes, it exists.)

They ended up crossing into Ohio, taking a small dinner cruise on Lake Erie, and exploring some lakeside towns, but that hardly matters. Because there was a puzzle to be solved, instead of reading a magazine or napping the bus ride away, the journey was as exciting as the destination. Each mile traveled was a clue; each slowing or turning of the bus brought a jolt of excitement. No one seemed to mind that they might end up somewhere they had been before, or somewhere they may not like. The process of getting there, of sleuthing it out, and of having their curiosity satisfied as the bus arrived was the real fun.

Are you as adventurous as my grandmother? Would you elect to take a brief day or weekend trip to an unknown destination? What about a longer, big-ticket adventure—would you leave that up to chance? If so, Washington, DC-based Magical Mystery Tours specializes in exactly that sort of experience. After you provide some basics (budgets, dates, and general preferences), one of their agents will craft a trip just for you, but only they will know where you'll be going. You'll be told what to pack and what kind of weather you're likely to experience . . . and that's about it. A week or so before you're slated to depart, you'll be given a sealed envelope with the specifics of your journey inside. They'll suggest that you quell what must be an overwhelming need-to-know and put off opening the envelope for as long as possible. Some travelers even have the immense willpower to wait until they arrive at the airport. As you imagine this moment of unveiling, the nervous excitement is palpable. It would be the adult version of a kid on Christmas morning, waiting to tear into a pile of gifts, if that pile of gifts was really expensive and potentially life-changing.[1]

Some people, especially seasoned travelers looking to mix it up or those who are overwhelmed by the process of choosing a destination, might relish this kind of experience. For others, it seems like too big a gamble. Our precious travel time is something that many of us are just not willing to leave in the hands of others. As discussed in chapter 1, we are confident that we know our tastes and preferences best, even when compared to those who hold special expertise on the topic.[2] We have strong intuitions about where we do and most definitely do *not* want to go. Plus, the risk of disappointment when opening that envelope can feel too high to take this gamble. But is our intuition here correct?

THE MADDENING MAGNETISM OF THE UNKNOWN

Travel always has some degree of mystery surrounding it. Its allure, in fact, lies in the act of willingly plunging into a vast unknown. As we plan a trip, we often let our minds simulate all of the possibilities we might encounter. We envision the vast array of delicious and exotic foods we'll be served at charming restaurants, the unique treasures we'll unearth in a flea market, or the awe-inspiring landscapes we'll behold on a hike or scenic drive. We also wonder about who we might become in these new and unfamiliar locations. Will we transform into someone calmer, kinder, less neurotic, or more adventurous? Will the ocean breezes be as soothing to our office-weary bodies as we imagine? Will it be terrifying or will it be exhilarating to step out of our comfort zones? Will we experience awe as we behold the grandeur of a sweeping mountain vista, and if so, what might that really feel like? And how will we get along with our families in all of this time together?

We can question all we want, but we inevitably dwell in uncertainty until the days of our trip arrive. And we wouldn't want it any other way. If offered a glimpse into a crystal ball that would tell you how every moment of your trip would unfold, how every bite of food would taste and how every ocean breeze would feel, would you take a peek? My sense is that, no, you wouldn't. I wouldn't. The not-knowing is exciting. It's energizing and inspiring to envision a future awash in possibilities for fun and engagement, romance and relaxation. As author Clarice Lispector remarks, "I do not know much. But there are certain advantages in not knowing. Like virgin territory, the mind is free from preconceptions." And absent any preconceptions, the mind is left to wander, and our vacation becomes a canvas on which to project our deepest wishes.

Uncertainty in the Lab

Studies show that an element of uncertainty can amplify our emotional reactions, sometimes in a way that we fail to fully realize. When I began graduate school at the University of Virginia, my research lab was investigating the surprising pleasures of being uncertain. To be clear, we were interested in experiences in which a person lacks the critical information needed to tie a story together; the why's and how's that allow one to label something "explained" in his or her mind.

In my favorite study from this series, undergraduate participants were told that they would be taking part in an online chat to get to know students at other universities.[3] (These "students" were actually the handiwork of a clever computer programmer. The participants were not actually talking to real people.) At the end of the chat session, participants were to indicate who, to them, was their "best potential friend." Ostensibly, all of the other chat-participants were doing the same. Lo and behold, it was then revealed that everyone in the chat picked the participant! It was essential to stage an event that would really make people happy, and glowing personal feedback absolutely does the trick. The real question is, given how quickly we adapt to life's joys, how long would this period of happiness last? Here is where uncertainty was put to the test.

At this point, participants were randomly divided into two conditions. Some had their curiosity satisfied and were told which chat-participant said what about them. This way, they could understand exactly why everyone liked them so much, thereby reducing their uncertainty. They may have concluded, "Okay, Sam thought we had similar music tastes. And Sally is a fellow baseball fan. That makes sense." The other group was *not* told who said what, and they were left to dwell in uncertainty, perhaps thinking, "*Why* does everyone like me so darn much? I just can't figure it out."

If given your choice of condition, which would you prefer? Would you want the puzzle of your newfound popularity solved? If you're like most people, you would. In fact, another group of students was asked to simply *imagine* being in the study described, and to indicate whether they would rather know who said what about them, or to remain uncertain. *Every single one* of them said they would really prefer certainty, and estimated that this would make them feel happier than not knowing would. Because, yes, in many cases not knowing can be utterly maddening.

And herein lies the great paradox of uncertainty. Whether it's waiting on pins and needles to open a gift, wondering whether that seemingly magical first date will lead to another, or even seeing those three dots on the screen of your iPhone as you await a text message, the conclusion is clear. We long to have our uncertainty quenched, even if it does rob us of some pleasure. This is partly why the idea of a mystery tour doesn't sit well. How can a person be expected to concentrate on the stuff of everyday life when this huge unknown is lying ahead? The wait would be, at best, distracting and, at worst, unbearable. You may even need to devise a strategy on how to distract yourself from obsessively thinking about your vacation, and who wants to do that?

Strikingly, then, we don't appear to realize the upsides of uncertainty, at least when it comes to positive outcomes. Because guess what: contrary to people's best guesses and deepest intuitions, those chat-room participants who didn't know why they were everyone's favorite *actually felt happier longer*. After they received the good news, they were left alone for fifteen minutes to complete some questionnaires. While doing these tasks, which were designed not to be *too* demanding, their minds were wandering back to what had just happened in the chat room. *WHY does everyone like me so darn much? I just can't figure it out!* They had this happy event to linger on, play around with in their minds, and attempt to explain to themselves. *Was it my sparkling wit? My impeccable taste in music? My dazzling good looks?* As a result of playing through all of these flattering possibilities, their positive moods were maintained over the next fifteen minutes of the study. Meanwhile, those who could explain why they were so well-liked came down from their emotional highs quickly, returning to baseline-levels of mood as they concluded, *Yeah, that all makes sense. Now, on to these questionnaires.*

Let me be clear: This effect applies to *positive* uncertainty, when there are no real downsides in the realm of likely possibilities. There are few pure examples of this in the real world, which became readily apparent to us as we tried to design realistic, involving studies on the topic.[4] Much of the uncertainty we grapple with in everyday life is actually between a positive and a negative outcome. The medical test reveals that I am healthy, or I am not. I got into grad school, or I was rejected. He loves me, he loves me not.

Vacation destinations, though, may be another rare example of mostly positive uncertainty. In fact, a mystery tour would provide an excellent real-world, longer-term test of its benefits, and if someone wanted to provide the funding, I would gladly carry it out. Until then, it remains a hypothetical. But imagine that a hundred lucky participants got to go on a trip to Hawaii in exchange for being in my study. Half would be randomly assigned to the certain condition, which mimics the typical vacation experience. They are told six months in advance that they will be going to Hawaii to enjoy luaus, hiking, surfing, and relaxing in a four-star beachfront resort. A second group is left with uncertainty, and are merely told that in six months, they're going to be going on a really nice trip someplace warm; essentially, a mystery tour. The research team would track participants' daily mood and how much they are thinking about the trip in the six-month lead-up period.

Which trip would *you* choose? Does knowing what you now know about the pleasures of uncertainty make you think twice? If lab-based experiments are any indication, we might find that those going on the mystery tour are thinking about the trip more. They might be feeling happier. But in this complex, long-term scenario, something critical is absent.

ADDING VALUE
THROUGH ANTICIPATION

Uncertainty plays an important role in our emotional lives and its presence is complex and confusing. We crave *some* uncertainty. We don't wish to know how each day will turn out; that would be incredibly dull. We hate when the ending of a suspenseful novel or TV series is prematurely made known. The fact that these infuriating giveaways are called *spoilers* indicates just how much our enjoyment hinges on having our curiosity piqued, intensified, and then satisfied. But we also have strong negative reactions toward *too much* uncertainty, or uncertainty that takes too long to resolve. When a TV show ends on a cliffhanger or when you have to put your novel down just as a key plot twist is about to be revealed, it's a little crazy-making. You can't put the nagging questions out of your mind. You long to have your curiosity satisfied, to find closure, and to move on. Even if the outcome is likely to be negative, you just *want to know*.[5] Indeed, scientist Linus Pauling remarked that "satisfaction of one's curiosity is one of the greatest sources of happiness in life."

Too much uncertainty can drive us bananas. It can distract and even annoy. As much as we may try to think of anything else, our minds inevitably return to the big unknown that lies ahead as we long to have it explained. Even when the potential outcomes are all amazing, this can exert a psychological cost. But there's another reason why your intuition may advise against massive amounts of uncertainty, say, a mystery tour. Aside from the small likelihood that you might hate where you end up (also a distinct possibility when planning your own trip!), when you take a mystery tour, you sacrifice one of the best aspects of travel: the planning, the daydreaming, the excited conversations with companions. Surely, you will be thinking a lot about where you'll be going, but it runs the risk of being obsessive, ruminative, or maddening rather than exciting.

In a few months, I get to travel to the coast of Maine at the peak of autumn to give a couple of talks on happiness. I was there once before, about fifteen years ago, and didn't have nearly enough time to experience the fall colors, the hiking opportunities, and the lobster (oh, the lobster). When I learned that I was being sent there, my heart actually raced. I've already begun investigating unique hotels and looking at the map to scout out daytrips. Friends have made restaurant recommendations, often with a tone of jealousy in their voices that, I admit, only adds to my excitement. In the upcoming weeks, I'll make a playlist of songs suitable for cruising along the seaside. I'll look at photos of idyllic New England towns on Pinterest. I'll scout out the most interesting day hikes, and you better believe that I'll be making a lengthy list of lobster shacks to try. I'll thoughtfully choose outfits appropriate for hiking, for nice dinners out and, oh right, for work, and carefully pack everything I need for a reasonably comfortable flight.

This process is just plain fun. When I hit a lull in my day, I might read a glowing review of a new Portland restaurant or do a Google image search of "Acadia National Park hiking." I'll bask in a small moment of wonder and excitement before resuming my work. The day feels a little brighter. There is something to look forward to. Given this, I am not at all surprised by the research finding that much of the joy of travel lies in the anticipation. A sample of Dutch vacationers was asked to carefully track their momentary mood in the time before, during, and after a trip. Findings indicated that the time leading up to travel was just as pleasant as the time they were actually traveling.[6] In another study, participants were asked to "please try to imagine, in the most precise way, four positive events that could reasonably happen to you tomorrow. You can imagine all kinds of positive events, from simple everyday pleasures to very important positive events."[7] Participants imagined things like eating their favorite foods, having a successful job interview, or spending time with friends. After engaging in this activity for fifteen consecutive days, participants showed greater increases in happiness than those asked to imagine negative or neutral things. This study suggests that imagining positive future outcomes may make one feel better in the present.

And this is unique to positive life *experiences*. The anticipation period leading up to an experience is more pleasant, exciting, and less consumed by impatience than the period before acquiring a new material possession.[8] Waiting for a vacation (or a special meal, or a concert) feels much better than waiting for a material item of similar value, be it a new stereo or the latest smartphone. Even waiting in line, something that no one enjoys, is reported as being more pleasant when the line is leading to an experience like a movie or an amusement park ride. Waiting in line to buy stuff is related to more impatience and frustration, perhaps because there is less emotional payoff to compensate for the inconvenience.

And as the days of your trip unfold, there naturally *will* be ordinary moments where you find yourself standing in line, waiting for your family to get ready for the day, or paging through a magazine. There likely will be unpleasant moments, too: jet lag, rain, grumpy children, a disappointing meal. But that's not what you think about as you browse Pinterest or page through your guidebook. In your imagination, you are encountering only the most pleasant of experiences, embarking on a mental vacation that is, most likely, too good to be true.

Do we recognize the importance of anticipation? Yes, sometimes. In one study, participants were asked to imagine getting to kiss their favorite movie star, and believed that the experience would be more valuable if they could delay it a few days.[9] They didn't want to wait a year, but they also didn't want to do it immediately or even in twenty-four hours. Of the options provided, three days was the sweet spot. Intuition told them that as nice as that brief kiss might be, a key component of its value was the exciting period where they could let their minds simulate the experience. The same is true for other life experiences, like vacations and meals out.[10] We have a sense that some of the value of a special life experience lies in the waiting, the anticipating, the fantasizing.

On the other hand, when offered material possessions like clothing or electronic gizmos, people more often opt to have these things right away, thank you very much.[11] Often, it's because there is little added value in waiting. We pretty much know what a pair of jeans or a TV is like; there is little to anticipate. Sometimes, the waiting even produces anxiety. People wonder if they made the right decision, if they could have done better, if it will have been worth the money, if the jeans will flatter, or if the TV is as fancy as their friend's. Experiences, which are more abstract in our imaginations, are less prone to these sorts of judgments, social comparisons, and anxieties. So whether it's kissing George Clooney, dining at Chez Panisse, or visiting the Louvre, the advice is clear: let the excitement build and revel in the possibilities.

Looking Ahead Trumps Looking Back

Researchers have also investigated the power of anticipation, particularly in contrast to retrospection.[12] Over five studies on experiences both good and bad, familiar and novel, they found that looking ahead to a given experience was more powerful than looking back on it.[13] This was true even for experiences that contain very little uncertainty. In the study most relevant to travel, they asked students to envision winning an all-expense-paid ski vacation for two. To make sure all students were creating the same mental image, they were given a detailed description of what this trip would be like: how long it would last, what kind of lodge they would stay in, and all of the free lift tickets, ski lessons, and specific amenities they would enjoy.

Importantly, half of the participants were told that this trip was to be happening six months in the future, creating a sense of anticipation. Others read an identical account of the vacation, but it was described as one that had already happened, six months ago, thereby evoking a sense of reminiscence. After shaking them out of their reveries, researchers asked them all to report how happy they felt thinking about the trip and how much thinking about it had affected their current mood. They were also asked to indicate how enjoyable the trip sounded, independent of their actual feelings toward it.

While most students enjoyed thinking about winning this fabulous vacation and reported that it sounded pretty incredible, those who were told it was still to come, who had that sense of anticipation, reported more intense positive feelings than those who were reflecting back on it. Note that the actual ratings of the trip were high for both scenarios. Both looking forward and looking backward, winning a fancy ski trip sounds incredible. It was the intensity of the emotional experience toward it that differed. This basic pattern, where anticipation evokes more intense feelings than retrospection, was found across all five studies.

The authors suggest a number of plausible reasons for this asymmetry. First, looking ahead elicits a number of what-ifs. Possibilities abound, because an event can unfold in so many different ways. Secondly, there may be more extreme expectations for something still to come than something that has already happened. However, careful analysis of underlying psychological processes suggests that the most probable explanation is the degree of mental work we are willing to do for something still-to-come, which can contribute to a more intense emotional reaction. It feels closer in time than something in the past.[14] When something lies ahead, we tend to think about it much more than if it had already unfolded. And the more you effortfully think about some emotion-laden event, the more likely it is that strong emotions will result.[15]

Try it yourself. Think about your dream trip, the one you've always wanted to take but, for whatever reason, you haven't made happen yet. Think about a typical day on this trip, six months from now. My dream trip is, of course, the Tuscany bike tour. The thought of pedaling easily through the rolling hills with some newfound friends, surrounded by vineyards and olive trees, knowing that a local Chianti awaits me at the end of the day, fills me with a palpable excitement. Even as I sit here, I feel my heart rate pick up. Now I imagine looking back on it, playing through the memories. Instead of excited, I feel more serene, satisfied, and pensive. Pleasant feelings, to be sure, but far less intense. This is the case even for a hypothetical trip. There is just something deeply exciting about anticipation.[16]

The Swedes even have a word—*resferber*—that translates to a kind of "travel fever," the joint feeling of nervous excitement that you may experience when thinking about an upcoming trip. It might arise when browsing through images of your destination, paging through a guidebook, or purchasing plane tickets. At least in Swedish, this singular experience is powerful enough to warrant its very own word.

Free Happiness!

Imagine that you are deciding when to use a week of vacation time. As you scan your calendar, two feasible blocks of time pop out at you. One is next week, the other is three months from now. Which do you choose?

As much as you might be dying to get out of town as soon as possible, if you keep in mind the benefits of the build-up, the answer should be clear. All else being equal, delaying your trip a bit gives you more time to get excited.[17] You're not spending any extra money (and, in fact, booking in advance could actually *save* you money, as sometimes you can get deals by committing early). Yet the total pleasure derived from travel will probably be so much greater. Elizabeth Dunn and Michael Norton, social psychologists who study how spending money can promote happiness, argue that this delay will provide you with "free happiness."[18]

This idea also has interpersonal implications, suggesting that you should think twice before surprising someone with a trip or some other special experience. While the surprise factor would be intense, the person is deprived of the build-up. A friend's husband once told her, "Pack your bags!" and jetted her off for a weekend that was punctuated by dinner at a world-famous restaurant that she'd always dreamed of trying. The meal was exquisite, the weekend unforgettable, and yet she was a bit disappointed to have missed out on the anticipation. It is a key component of a special life experience.

The Calculus of Distributed Anticipation

I have a vague recollection of my 8 a.m. college calculus class when, bleary-eyed and under-caffeinated, I learned how to calculate the area under a curve. Fuzzy as the details are now, believe it or not, this abstract concept has much application to how we might think about our happiness over time. It may even have some travel advice to offer. Consider the happiness experienced over the course of two months leading up to a hypothetical vacation (see Figures 1 and 2).

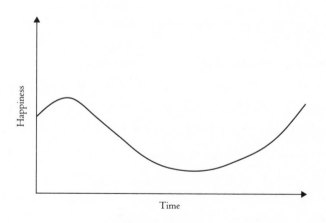

Figure 1. Traveler A, with time to anticipate, but with few moments of surprise.

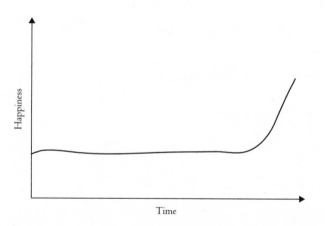

Figure 2. Traveler B, with little time to anticipate, but with a great degree of surprise.

Traveler A typifies the hedonic experience of a vacationer who has clearly made plans. There is a period of anticipation, perhaps marked with some peaks—maybe the moment the tickets are booked, or as she excitedly discusses the trip with friends. But because most of the key details are well-known, there are few big moments of surprise for her to enjoy. As work and family life consume her, she finds that she barely thinks about her upcoming trip.

Traveler B was given a last-minute surprise trip. Up to the moment of the reveal— "pack your bags!"—life was going on as usual, thus we would expect no big happiness boosts. However, while she may have missed out on

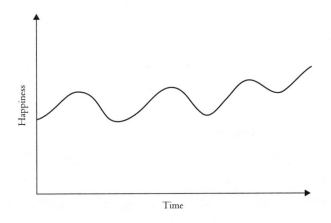

Figure 3. Traveler C, with a combination of both anticipation and surprise.

the slow build of Traveler A, notice the big happiness spike at the end, when she learns the details of her travels.

Which is preferable? The slow build or the intense peak? I defer to the logic and clarity of mathematics for this stumper. If we were to calculate the area under these two curves, the sum total of happiness experienced would be higher in Figure 1. This, to me, makes a strong case for knowing where you are going and getting pumped. But there is something desirable and enviable about the intense peak of Traveler B. Daily life brings so few exciting jolts. Call me greedy, but I want that, too.

Are A and B our only options? Is there really an inherent and necessary trade-off here? Can't we have the best of both? I think that we can (see Figure 3).

Consider, if you will, Traveler C. This vacationer has strategically made some clear plans. The destination has been chosen and plane tickets purchased. A delightful Airbnb apartment in a lively neighborhood has been reserved. She has clear things to get excited about. But . . . it's not *all* planned. She's consciously delaying looking into restaurants, museums, activities, and events, thinking that she'll do some of that here and there, maybe after a stressful day at work or on a lazy Saturday. Pinterest boards have yet to be made, the guidebook has barely been cracked. When she heard that the Food Network was going to be profiling the restaurant scene there, she programmed her DVR and is going to watch it a couple of weeks before departure. In effect, she is giving herself mini-surprises and boosts along the way. Thanks to these small choices, the area under her happiness curve is the largest.

This is the key: a balance of anticipation and surprise. Call it *strategic, distributed anticipation*. Know enough to get excited, maintain that excitement by distributing your exposure to information about your location, and consider how and when you might insert a few moments of surprise and excitement into your waiting period.

There are some travel companies who play upon this idea quite nicely. Consider the clever approach of CheapCaribbean.com. This discount web-based tour provider often features the "Deal of Fortune," where travelers do know where they are going—say, Jamaica, Cancun, or Belize—but are willing to leave their fancy, all-inclusive hotel up to chance in exchange for a bargain. A week in advance, they do find out exactly where they will be staying and can then Google and Pinterest their hearts out. So the general destination is always known, but one of the key details is left a mystery.

Would you take this gamble to save a few bucks? I would, and the discount wouldn't be the only reason why. I would be forced to distribute my anticipation. Knowing the entire time that I was going to Jamaica, I could start researching the weather (perfect), activities (many), local culture (fun and fascinating), and food (can you say jerk chicken and fried plantains?). As departure approaches, there's a chance that I could run out of things to research, or shift my focus to the stresses of travel. But suddenly, one more piece of the puzzle is revealed: the fancy place I'm staying! My excitement spikes again as I behold photos of my luxury suite with beachfront balcony and drool over the swim-up bars, golf courses, massage rooms, and vast buffets. Distributing your anticipation, either on your own or with the help of a clever travel company, will help you maintain your excitement in the period before your departure.

THE "HOW" OF MENTAL
TIME TRAVEL

While the exact details of how any trip will unfold remain a happy mystery, we actually have a good amount of personal control over the level of uncertainty we inject into our travels. How, exactly, can you make the most of all the free happiness that is to be gained before a trip? Here are some tips that will help you build and maintain the anticipation.

Savor the Images

Block off a few hours and bury yourself in the vast fantasyland that is the bookstore travel section. Or go high-tech and bask in the glory of the Internet. Travelers love sharing their experiences, and websites like Pinterest and Instagram abound with awe-inspiring images. Sure, they may be excessively filtered and cropped. Who cares? Go ahead and revel in these images: the food, the architecture, the landscapes. Let yourself savor what is to come. Imagine eating that delectable food, stepping into that cathedral, or reaching that mountaintop. You earned that right when you bought your ticket.

Get the Backstory

Enjoy the glossy images, sure, but also consider going deeper, delving into the history and culture of the place you are visiting. If you're not a history buff, even a novel set in the location you plan to visit can help set the stage. A cookbook dedicated to the local cuisine can give you mouth-watering images and information on what's to come. Have any movies or television shows been shot there? Think *Roman Holiday, Under the Tuscan Sun*, or *A Room with a View* for Italy; *When Harry Met Sally, Sex and the City*, or most anything Woody Allen for New York City. I recently saw the excellent film *The Danish Girl*, shot partially in Copenhagen, and kept excitedly whispering to my mother things like, "My students and

I ate dinner at that café!" Seeing your destination used as a backdrop is fun, fascinating, and a bit surreal as it hits you that you will soon be inhabiting that film-worthy space.

If you dig deeper, novels, movies, television and the like might also reveal subtle lessons about the norms and cultural mindset of a place. For the class I teach in Scandinavia, we watched a few episodes of some recent Danish television programs. *The Bridge*, a crime drama, gave us lessons in topics as wide-ranging as the Danes' dry sense of humor, Danish stereotypes of Swedes, and the red tape of their government bureaucracies. Another recent program, *Borgen*, shed light on issues of gender equality and the current political system in Denmark. Of course, some creative license is certainly being taken in these fictionalized programs and that has to be kept in mind. But movies, television shows, and books can't help but be deeply influenced by the culture from which they emerged, giving you an entertaining glimpse into the people and places you'll soon encounter.

Let It Build Together

All of these strategies can also be used interpersonally. Thumbing through a guidebook together, scrolling through images online, watching a movie set in the location you're visiting, or attempting to cook something from the local cuisine can be fun and will help build collective excitement for what is to come. Asking your travel companions what they're most excited about can also be a fun conversation topic. It may even highlight features of your location that you hadn't thought about yet.

THE ULTIMATE IN DISTRIBUTED ANTICIPATION

One implication worth considering is that if the lead-up time really is as pleasurable as the trip itself, then several small vacations spaced out across the year would bring more happiness than a single big one.[19] Imagine constantly having a little getaway on the horizon. There will always be Google-image searches to do and restaurants to read about. As the year rolls on, you'll constantly have so much to talk about, think about, and get excited for. Anticipation will be ever-present.

So if your next year of travel is comprised of a weekend at the beach, Christmas at Dad's, a wedding a few hours away, and a spa weekend with the girls, take heart! While each individual trip may not seem terribly exciting, as the year unfolds, these multiple small adventures might actually bring you more total happiness than one huge blowout trip would.

THE DANGERS OF HIGH EXPECTATIONS

An Oscar-nominated movie. A new restaurant that is getting rave reviews. A book your friend touts as the best thing she has ever read. These recommendations carry with them a huge amount of pressure, as we expect them to be phenomenal. We all have experienced disappointment with things that have been overhyped, and travel is no different. Research has found that first-time tourists are often more disappointed in a destination than are return visitors, suggesting that a dose of reality can help ward off unrealistically high and ultimately disappointing expectations.[20] One real danger of getting extremely excited for a trip, of letting your mind create so many possible moments of wonder and adventure, is that you might just be setting yourself up for disappointment.

This is a tricky conundrum. We want to anticipate our travels. It's one of the most fun and rewarding parts. But how do we do that while also avoiding setting ourselves up for disappointment?

Say you're taking a trip to Costa Rica and have been thinking only on a Pinterest level. You might arrive with high expectations of seeing howler monkeys, toucans, and the resplendent quetzal (Costa Rica's most beautiful and elusive bird) at every turn. Because the Internet is much more likely to deliver images of the extraordinary than of the mundane, it's natural to have these unrealistic, inflated expectations. It's what travelers want to share, it's how marketers draw us in, it's what travel writers are paid to glorify. I have yet to glimpse an image of a birdless tree captioned, "Been standing here for four hours. No birds" or of a hotel that is photographed from the angle that allows me to see the dingy gas station or construction site next door.

It's Not All Resplendent Quetzals

Given all of this, how can we manage our expectations and avoid fantasizing our enjoyment away? One dose of reality can come from your fellow travelers, those who aren't incentivized to glorify a location. Sites like TripAdvisor and Yelp don't merely offer glowing portrayals of restaurants and hotels. People share their horror stories, too. People rely heavily on these sites often when choosing a hotel or restaurant in a new city, but could they also be a tool for managing expectations?

The prospective diary mentioned in chapter 1, in which you look ahead and lay out how a day of your vacation may actually unfold, can also be an effective antidote to starry-eyed anticipation.[21] Think ahead and make your best guess of how a day might actually go. If you're really honest with yourself, you might end up with something like:

Costa Rica, Day 1

4 a.m.: Wide-awake due to jet lag, staring at ceiling.

8 a.m.: Husband finally wakes up. I hunt for the coffee, make it, start to feel awake.

8:30 a.m.: Discuss what to do today, decide on a well-known hike. We argue a little (he wants to do a guided hike, I want us to do our own thing) but ultimately I win. We have a pretty good hotel breakfast and get ready to go out.

10 a.m.: Got a little lost on the drive but finally arrive at the hiking trail. It's way more crowded than we expected, but we set out anyway.

11 a.m.: Spot a colorful toucan in a tree!!

11:30 a.m.: Reach the summit! It's gorgeous, even better than the photos
we saw online. We have a snack, snap some pictures, hang out a little,
then start to get annoyed by the crowds. We decide to head back.

3 p.m.: Back at the hotel. He reads, I try to nap.

5 p.m.: Start talking about dinner and how to spend the evening.

You get the idea. While there are some high points in this day, which
are well-worth getting excited about, reality can't help but take center
stage in this exercise. You simply *have* to do ordinary things even while you
travel: coordinating schedules, compromising, dealing with crowds, having
downtime. It can't all be resplendent quetzals.

By prioritizing travel, you are investing your hard-earned dollars in
a way that is likely to bring you more pleasure than would a new material possession. But buying a ticket and booking a hotel isn't enough. By
capitalizing on the complementary forces of anticipation and uncertainty,
your excitement can be maintained from the moment you first whip out
your credit card to the point of lift-off. As author Vivien Swift notes, "In
love and travel, getting there is half the fun. The lustful impatience, the
passionate daydreams, the nerve-wracking waiting . . . lovers and travelers
are all alike when they find themselves on the brink of a new adventure."
Embrace the daydreams, the waiting, and the free happiness that comes
with anticipating your upcoming adventure, and—of course—balance
them with the occasional reality check.

BEYOND PINTEREST: A NOD
TO THE NEGATIVE

One reason why the time leading up to a trip is so enjoyable is because
we are living in a world of fantasy. We possess an inherent optimistic bias
when visualizing our futures.[22] Our minds play through an anticipated
highlight reel. It is far less fun to imagine worst-case scenarios—the lost

luggage, cancelled flights, horrible weather, or stomach bugs that can easily arise as we venture into the unknown.

But let's face it: travel has gotten increasingly stressful, starting at the airport. Flights are commonly overbooked and cancelled. Bag fees are a burden. Security checkpoints are high-drama and inefficient, what with their draconian rules on shoe removal and liquids and gels. Legroom is constantly shrinking, and even the armrest is personal space worth fighting for. Travelers have, not surprisingly, become increasingly hostile, as the whole experience brings out the worst in people.[23] What was a luxury to relish just a few decades ago has become something to endure with gritted teeth. And getting there is only the beginning.

Starry-eyed anticipation protects us from these sad facts. But if we don't spend a little time considering the potential stresses and problems of travel, we're setting ourselves up for a lousy experience.[24] More than that, we run the risk of missing out on a key benefit of travel: coming home refreshed, energized, and happy. One study actually found a strong inverse relationship between travel stress and happiness, both during and after a trip. Excessive travel stress totally counteracts the potential emotional benefits of vacationing.[25]

No, we can't foresee every challenge we'll face, but without some attention and thoughtful planning, we might find ourselves grumpy and exhausted before we even reach our destination. Not a good start. Thankfully, there are some strategies we can employ to anticipate and effectively cope with travel's challenges.

WOOP It Up

Researcher Gabriele Oettingen offers a four-step sequence, known as WOOP—wish, outcome, obstacles, planning—that lets you bask in the positive but also strategize about the possible problems that might interfere with your getting what you want. This problem-focused approach to planning has been effective when dealing with real-life challenges like eating healthily, exercising, managing anxiety, and studying. It works for kids who are struggling academically, for medical patients who need to change their health behaviors, for those dealing with relationship insecurities, and others.[26] Its utility is far-reaching and it's easy to implement. There's even a smartphone app.[27]

Consider how WOOP—also known as mental contrasting—can help you maintain your travel excitement while also making you aware of possible challenges. First, identify and articulate your wish. It can be a small thing. In the case of an upcoming family beach trip, you might say, "My wish is for the kids to get along with one another and to give my husband and me some peace and quiet while we're at the beach." Next, envision a specific positive outcome. What will it look like and how will it feel to achieve this goal? You might imagine your kids laughing and playing in the sand while you read a trashy novel and bask in the warm sunshine. After dinner, they pass out, exhausted, and you and your husband open a perfectly chilled prosecco and sit on the deck, listening to the crashing waves. You feel relaxed, loved, grateful, and just plain happy.

So far, this sounds a lot like mere positive thinking, right? But the key is that you don't stop here. Next, think of the likely obstacles that may get in the way of this outcome. The possibilities abound: Your children constantly argue. They won't go to sleep and give you peace. It rains and you spend the day cooped up in the hotel. You get a sunburn that leaves you grumpy. Instead of the relaxing sound of crashing waves, you have a constant stream of bass-thumping music from the guests next door. While this list may seem depressingly endless, try to identify some of the most likely candidates. To assist you, reflect on your previous travel experiences. What went poorly? What were you ill-prepared for?

Finally, plan exactly what you will do if or when each obstacle arises. "If it rains, I will . . ." and insert a concrete action. "I will be prepared to go to the movies" or "I will be armed with books and games for the kids." You might not be thrilled with these alternatives, but you will be less overwhelmed and more clear on what to do if you've done this sort of mental work in advance.

Planning also allows you to make choices ahead of time to prevent a negative outcome. In the case of the family beach vacation, anticipating negative possibilities might nudge you to take precautions and do a little extra research to facilitate a plan B. Ideally, you won't need it. But if you do, you will be prepared rather than blindsided and overwhelmed.

Using myself as example, as I think about my upcoming trip to Maine, my wish is that I can relax, get some writing done and carve out some time to hike. I also really wish to savor lots of buttery lobster. Seems pretty manageable. I next envision myself sitting in a cute café with my laptop, focused and in the flow of things. After a few solid hours, I feel satisfied with my progress and am able to put work aside to fully indulge in some vacation pleasures. I'll drive out to Acadia National Park for a hike, and then find a great restaurant where I can enjoy some fresh seafood.

Laying this out feels great. It makes me excited. I could stop here and be quite pleased with myself. But in the spirit of WOOP, I consider the possible pitfalls. For one thing, in my daily life, I am actually kind of terrible at relaxing. I'm antsy, I fret about work and constantly worry about all of the more productive things I should be doing. I remember the fact that I will still be me, even in a new place. Given my wishes and desired outcomes on this trip, I specifically worry that I might get too anxious about work to allow myself the presence of mind to bask in the simple pleasures afforded to me. I also expect that, since I will be on my own, I will spend too much time looking at Facebook, attempting to fulfill a social need but effectively removing myself from the moment while I'm at it. And wouldn't it be a waste to be stressing on a scenic drive or scarfing down lobster without really appreciating it?

Okay, so how can I overcome these challenges to turn my wishes into reality? Here is where the strategizing starts. First and foremost, I will work for three solid hours in the mornings. Experience has taught me that if I accomplish something early in the day, I am far more able to relax later. I will go for a run or a hike to use up some of my restless energy, so maybe I'll be better able to unwind later. At mealtimes, I will leave my phone behind so I have to tune into the deliciousness before me. Simple things, to be sure, but things I might not recognize as problems without the directed forethought encouraged by WOOP.

I share this personal example for several reasons. First off, I needed to work through that, so thanks. But I also want to stress that some of the obstacles we experience while we travel are of our own creation. The habits that we carry with us in daily life are often the things we seek to escape when we leave home. Without thoughtful consideration of how they might impact our travels, these habits are all but guaranteed to come with us, no matter how far away from home we go.

As your next vacation approaches, inject some realism into your planning. Consider laying out how a full day might actually unfold. Note the challenges you may face and acknowledge that not every moment will be Pinterest-worthy. Pinpoint specific challenges—let history be your guide—and use WOOP to help you make a clear plan. If the challenges you identify are specific things about yourself—anxiety, antsiness, unrealistic expectations—you can even start practicing how to keep them in check before you leave.

Of course, there is only so much you can do to prevent travel stresses. One might even argue that the lack of predictability is a major reason why travel stress is so unbearable. The plane will take off . . . at some point. Your luggage will be returned . . . eventually. Research tells us that one key component of a stressful experience is lack of predictability.[28] Despite this, travel planning is not the time for mere fantasy and blind optimism. Smiling, shrugging, and assuming everything will go your way is no recipe for success when mishaps are so likely. Allow yourself the fantastical, magical thinking, but don't let it be at the expense of realistic planning and preemptive damage control.

SCHEDULING THE RETURN

You don't want to think about this right now. I know you don't. But as you plan your trip, it will probably dawn on you that, at some point, you will need to come home. I've been there. Okay, I'm there right now: trying to plan this trip to Maine and wondering how long I should stay in my destination. I could fly home Saturday and give myself a buffer in case my flight gets delayed or cancelled. Even if my travel goes smoothly, this way I'd have the chance to do laundry, grocery shop, and otherwise ease back into real life before heading back to work on Monday.

But . . . I could also eke out one more precious vacation day if I take my chances and travel on Sunday! I have the rest of my life to do laundry and grocery shop, don't I?

Research has something to say here, and the message is loud and clear: ease back in to real life. Most people return from vacation feeling happier, but those who return home and jump immediately back into work tend to lose that happiness boost quickly.[29] So don't arrive home at 10 p.m. and plan to dive back into work the next morning. Returning home and immediately feeling overwhelmed can completely counteract the serenity and perspective you may have gained on your trip. Leave yourself a little time to ease back in. In fact, one study's findings suggest that a weekend at home immediately following a vacation actually prolongs its benefits.[30]

LEAVE IT ALL BEHIND

The stage is set. The important planning has been done, you've been getting pumped, and you've done all the troubleshooting you reasonably can do. You've thoughtfully balanced anticipation with uncertainty, Pinterest with WOOP. Now it's time to detach, to leave home not only physically, but mentally.

Because unfinished business tends to occupy our minds, tie up loose ends at home and at work.[31] There are no dirty dishes in the sink. The bills have been paid. The mail has been stopped. Work projects are as wrapped up as can be expected. Key people know you're checking out. Don't underestimate the power of the email vacation message. Let everyone know that you are out of the office, away from email, and they should not expect a reply until a specified date. Even if you do plan to hop on email a time or two, the world doesn't need to know that.

HAPPY TRAVEL TIPS
FOR BUILDING ANTICIPATION

To help maximize the build-up period, reflect on the following:

- *Have I allowed some time between booking and departure? How can I best use that time?* Research your destination and revel in the fantasies, while also injecting a dose of reality by considering and planning for any challenges you might face.
- *What should I leave uncertain?* Leave some elements of your trip a mystery, so that your mind may more easily wander to all of the exciting possibilities that exist..
- *Have I left a buffer?* Plan to have some downtime after the trip, so you won't have to jump immediately back into work.
- *How can I exit real-life as completely as possible?* Give yourself permission to step away from work and home life by tying up loose ends and letting your absence be known.

Now that you've set the stage for a pleasurable, engaging, and meaningful travel adventure, let's turn our attention to how you can make the most of your trip in-the-moment, as it unfolds.

FIVE

STEP OFF THE TOUR BUS: HOW TO PEEL BACK THE LAYERS AND *REALLY* SEE THE WORLD

It's never the Eiffel Tower and Louvre you remember for the rest of your life.
—Anthony Bourdain

The man had been waiting in my hotel lobby for almost two hours, armed with a book of photos and written testimonials from scores of satisfied customers. I'd met him earlier that day, when my bus had arrived in lush, mountainous Dalat, Vietnam. As was the local tradition, motorbike riders were at the bus depot waiting for the day's onslaught of tired tourists arriving with heavy bags, sagging spirits, and relatively deep pockets. I was more than happy to let one of them take me to my hotel.

Minh was a balding fifty-something with a wide smile and surprisingly good English. When he asked me what I planned to do in Dalat, I replied honestly: after three weeks in the noisy inferno that was Saigon in summertime, I really had no plans beyond casually wandering around and enjoying the cool mountain temperatures. As we pulled up to my hotel, he suggested that I book him as my personal guide for the next day. My instant reaction was my standard: introverted unease. While this man seemed completely unthreatening, I was nervous about committing to hang out with *anyone* for an entire day, much less a stranger. I mumbled that I would think about it, paid him for the ride, and checked into my hotel.

I unpacked, Skyped with my mom, puttered around the room, and eventually decided to head out for some exploration. I was so struck with guilt at finding Minh still waiting for me in the hotel lobby—I *did* say I'd think about it, after all—that I dutifully listened to his sales pitch (*"See the real Dalat!"*), read the glowing testimonials from his former clients, and found myself agreeing to let him drive me around the countryside on the back of his motorbike the next day. He left smiling and I walked out into the night air, feeling both nervous and emboldened. What had I just done? What was I in for?

Nine a.m. sharp the next day, we were off. And for the first time in my life (not counting the previous day's three-block hop to my hotel), I was riding on a motorbike. While clinging to a stranger. On some back road, near some little town. In Vietnam.

My unease morphed into exhilaration as we left the crowded city streets for open country roads. Throughout the day, we would pull up to nondescript shacks and I would follow Minh inside, clueless of what I was about to experience. In one, I saw a young woman making thin sheets of rice paper with one arm while holding her newborn baby with the other. Later, in a dimly lit garden shed, I met a man making rice wine in glass jars and was offered a generous sample. I saw tea plantations, pineapple fields, and a greenhouse growing gerbera daisies by the thousands. We visited the ethnic minority village of Lanh Dinh An, best known for a statue of a massive concrete chicken but also home to skilled artisans and spirited children. At one point, we stopped for lunch at an unmarked hut in the countryside. My stomach turned at the uncleared tables and the floor littered with napkins but Minh nodded approvingly. "A dirty restaurant is a good sign: they are too busy to clean," he told me. This logic was lost on me until I realized that, yes, in a restaurant that lacks refrigeration, fast turnover is essential for food safety.

At least to my uninformed eye, Minh made good on his promise: I had seen the real Dalat. Without him and his motorbike, I would probably have spent the day wandering aimlessly, snapping photos, and eating pho. Pleasant, sure, but little to write home about. So basking in the afterglow of a day well spent, when he dropped me off at my hotel I shocked myself by hiring him to take me—on the motorbike, with all my luggage—on a two-day journey north to Nha Trang, the next city on my docket.

Was this a risky move? You bet. Thinking back now, I shake my head at some of the things I did while alone, on the other side of the world. But travel requires calculated risks. As author Leigh Ann Henion says, "Foolish acts and bold adventures almost always appear, especially in the beginning, to be the absolute same thing."[1] We are often faced with the choice of doing the safe, easy, and comfortable thing or pushing further, daring to eat that bizarre food, venture into that little art gallery, or climb onto the motorbike. These are the things that, without a doubt, make traveling so eye-opening and memorable, even when there is some discomfort to contend with. As Seth Kugel, former *New York Times'* "Frugal Traveler" columnist advises, when assessing risk, "draw the line at physical danger, not social awkwardness."[2]

ZOOMING IN

Imagine you've chosen your next travel destination. You decide to scope the place out on Google Earth, that mind-blowing tool that allows you to glimpse details of practically anyplace on the planet. You scroll and zoom and scroll some more until you locate the city or country you plan to visit. On your screen now lies an expansive panorama, allowing you to view the topography—look at that coastline! that mountain range! the layout of that ancient city!—but it's necessarily broad and lacking in detail. So you zoom in further, to the level of individual streets, buildings, rivers, and mountains. You might even switch your perspective to "street view," virtually walking the streets until you locate your hotel, a famed cathedral, the town square, or the trailhead to a hike you'd like to take.[3]

You can do all of this from the comfort of your couch. Really, you can travel the world with the click of a mouse. So if it's this easy and inexpensive to see the world, why do we bother traveling at all?

We travel because we want to zoom in far further than Google Earth could ever allow. We want to zoom into the heart and soul of a place. We are deeply curious about what other people's lives are like, about what makes them tick. We also crave personal experiences unique to our chosen destination. We want to indulge our senses in ocean breezes, savor exotic foods, connect with locals, climb new mountains, stand amidst ancient ruins. We don't just want to sit on the sidelines and look on; we want to be transported, physically, emotionally, and spiritually. No reasonable person would equate a Google Earth tour of a place with the experience of actually going there.

This chapter will highlight the differences between these virtual and actual worlds, with a particular emphasis on cultural connection and active immersion. First, I will lay out how to attain these broader goals of immersion by discussing different realms of potential exploration. I will also argue why—despite the passive sort of relaxation we may sometimes crave—stepping off of the sidelines and immersing ourselves in these kinds of experiences will promote discovery, personal growth, positive feelings, and rich memories.

IMMERSION: IS IT EVEN POSSIBLE?

I'll say up front that "immersion" is a tough term to define. It means different things to different people, for one. Referring back to chapter 2, psychocentric travelers, those who seek predictability and comfort, will naturally seek out less immersive experiences than will the novelty-seeking allocentric travelers. To some, immersion means sampling foreign foods and using local transportation. To others, it means living like the locals do, perhaps in an extended homestay. We might all agree on what it *isn't*, though: Immersion cannot be achieved if we only interact with our travel companions, eat all the same foods we eat back home, and stay only in highly touristy areas. While this may be a perfectly pleasant vacation, it doesn't equate to an immersive travel experience.

When *I* say immersion, I'm also referring to an active process of exposing ourselves to the people, places, activities, and customs of a place. It requires an open mind and curious spirit. It demands that we suppress the little voice in our head that wants to say, "That's so *weird!*" when encountering something outside the realm of our own experiences. And it requires remembering author Clifton Fadiman's words: "When you travel, remember that a foreign country is not designed to make you comfortable. It is designed to make its own people comfortable."

The idea of immersive travel dates back at least eighty years, to the Experiment in International Living.[4] The program, geared toward late-teens and young adults, was developed with a mission of fostering peace and understanding through communication and cooperation with people of vastly different cultural backgrounds. They were trendsetters then, and still are today, in all aspects of what people generally refer to as immersion. Students in the program were among the first to reside in homestays and engage in international community service programs and cross-cultural education. Today the program still operates, with a focus on teaching empathy, sustainability, leadership, and human rights.

Recently, other opportunities to immerse oneself in a place have mushroomed, most recently thanks to the emergence of the sharing, or peer-to-peer, economy: Airbnb, Uber, Homeaway, and more. Instead of keeping locals at a distance, perhaps viewed from the balcony of a resort or a subway car, the sharing economy encourages interaction and under-standing. However, lest we conclude that we're living in an immersion golden age, it's also true that connecting with home has never been easier and increasing globalization has made it all too easy to find a McDonalds or Starbucks in parts of the world that, a generation ago, contained only local eateries.

In addition to the irresistible pull of Facebook, a Big Mac, or a Venti White Chocolate Mocha Frappuccino, another very real challenge to immersion is simply *time*. According to the US Travel Association, the average American takes sixteen vacation days a year, and the average vacation lasts about four days.[5] Researchers have found that to really start to feel at home in a place, to get acculturated, takes around six months, maybe even longer if you have yet to master the language. Therefore, the typical brief vacation is hardly long enough for anything remotely resembling true immersion.

So maybe few of us are likely to be mistaken for locals. That's no excuse to sit on the sidelines, missing out on rich experiences. We can expose ourselves to brief moments, a sort of microimmersion, which are highly valuable in their own right. Michelle Bell of Grasshopper Adventures, a bicycling tour company in Southeast Asia, describes elements of immersion like this: "I think it starts with the place you choose to stay. Choose local, not some international chain hotel that looks the same everywhere. Eat in local restaurants. Do your research—try the local foods, shop for items made locally, including local handicrafts. Best of all, head off the beaten path. In additional to the Paris-es of the world, there are also a lot of tiny little villages that make their own local wine that you wouldn't get anywhere else and that tourists don't frequent because there's no airport there. Most importantly, learn at least a few words in the local language and talk to the people who live there!" Notice that none of this advice requires an abundance of time, just a sense of curiosity, an open mind, and a little background research.

MOOSE MEATBALLS AND CHOCOLATE RAVIOLI

When I ask people how they immerse themselves in a new place, they often say something about food. Sure. We all have to eat, most of us love to eat, some of us even live to eat. Enjoyment of food is associated with happiness.[6] And trying new foods is a low-risk and high-reward activity: cheap, quick, Instagram-worthy, and often highly pleasurable (and if you try something truly gross, at least it's a good story!). Plus, a few meals at well-chosen restaurants, cafes, food stalls, or even grocery stores can offer some real insight into a new place while also creating a memorable experience. When I look back on my travels with friends, we often talk about the things we ate. Maine lobsters cooked over a campfire in Bar Harbor. Making moose meatballs in Sweden with my students. This indescribable chocolate ravioli on Lake Como. Pho for breakfast in Vietnam. This fried breakfast cheese in Costa Rica that my boyfriend and I tried in vain to recreate at home. Even foreign types of candy bars and potato chip flavors. Eating the local food is a quintessential microimmersion experience.

Finding the Local Gems

Unfortunately, particularly in touristy areas, we can miss out on the local food culture in favor of readily available restaurants catering to tourists. It's easy to see why. You may have just spent the morning sightseeing in a foreign city and are wandering down a crowded street looking for a lunch spot. Tired, hot, and longing for a break, an oasis in the form of a shady café appears before you. The menu is in English! And to top it off, there's even a charismatic host out front, beckoning you in with a wide smile and charmingly accented English. It's almost like he's been waiting there just for you.

Don't go there. Not only are these restaurants overpriced, they are also probably inauthentic, catering to what tourists supposedly want as opposed to what local people actually eat. If you want a more local experience, move on. Walk mere blocks off the tourist strip and see what you find. Or do your research and have a plan, so you aren't seduced by the easy tourist trap when you're feeling tired and desperate.

And don't forget grocery shopping! Or even grocery window-shopping. As one frequently traveling friend of mine stresses, "Go to the supermarket! More interesting than any museum to me!" Chef and television personality Anthony Bourdain, well-known for his worldwide culinary adventurers on his series, *Parts Unknown*, echoes my friend's claim. When asked what he does upon arrival in a new city, he says, "I go to the central market, very early in the morning. I like to see what's in season, what they're selling. The little businesses that pop up in those places to feed the merchants from the market are pretty helpful. I get an immediate sense of what's going on in a town and what the food's like."[7]

Or be more direct and simply ask the locals where they like to eat. Your taxi driver, Airbnb host, or hotel staff likely know the local hotspots, the places the tourists don't go. Another friend of mine remarks, "I've gone to small, local neighborhood restaurants, ate at the bar, chatted up servers, then asked about the 'must do' things I might not know about."

Finally, you can arrange to have a meal with someone in their own home. The sharing economy has recently expanded beyond sharing someone's house or car to include meal-sharing. A few years ago, on a trip to Denmark, a friend and I signed up for a program called "Dine with the Danes." It's a simple concept: you supply the company with a few details and they match you with a Danish family whose house you are to go to at an appointed time. After some get-to-know-you talk, the family will feed you a three-course meal with beer. Works for me! The couple we were paired with, Pia and Lars, lived in a suburb of Copenhagen, in an area we never would have seen had we not been going there to eat. Lars was a reserved computer programmer who opened up after a few beers. Pia was an outgoing attorney who took great pride in her garden. The food was pretty basic; they didn't seem interested in impressing us but really just wanted to share a normal meal, a slice of ordinary life. That night, over baked chicken, rice, and Carlsberg beer, I learned much more about everyday life for the residents of Copenhagen than I ever could have in a restaurant.

SORRY, MOM: WHY YOU SHOULD TALK TO STRANGERS

Let's say that you find some hidden gem of a restaurant or café and take a seat at the bar. It's a slow night and the bartender is chatting and laughing with the other patrons. What do you do? Find a way to join in? Or stay to yourself, burying your nose in your novel or keeping your eyes locked on your partner?

Travel is rife with what psychologists term approach-avoidance conflicts, where one goal has both positive and negative qualities.[8] A classic example is talking to strangers. Social connection is simply essential for well-being.[9] But striking up conversations is a risky move. On the one extreme, we can be rebuffed or outright rejected, which feels terrible, and on the other, we can get trapped in an interaction we're unable to gracefully escape. As a result, apprehension often wins out and we shy away, content with a book and a beer, or a cappuccino and a newspaper.

Researchers would have something to say here, probably a more polite version of, "Oh, get over yourself." Turns out, conversing with strangers—with all the rules of safety firmly in mind—brings unexpected emotional payoff. In one series of studies, Chicago-area commuters on public transportation were instructed to strike up a conversation with a stranger standing near them on their respective buses and trains.[10] At the end of their ride, these conversational risk-takers felt happier than those who were instructed to stand or sit in silence. Delving further, the researchers found that when we do shy away from casual conversation with strangers, it is often due to a misplaced anxiety that others might not want to talk to *us*. This belief, much of the time, is false. Many people are actually eager to talk, the researchers found. So that cab driver, bartender, airplane seatmate, or fellow solo diner? They might be more game for a chat than you realize.

But what about *us*, as the initiators? What if we're on the reserved side? Surprisingly, the emotional benefits of connecting with strangers hold even for the introverts among us. When introverted participants were essentially told to "act extroverted," they found that doing so actually felt pretty great.[11] This confirmed a novel hypothesis: introverts underestimate the pleasure they can gain from social interaction. Outside of the confines of the research lab, there is likely a limit to this effect—at some point, the truly introverted will feel exhausted and disingenuous. But every now and then, there are gains to be made by donning your game face, being brave, and taking that social risk.

If we're traveling with family or friends, we might not see the benefits of reaching out any further. "I'm here for some quality time with my family. I don't need to make some shallow chitchat with a stranger!" We are certain that close others are our biggest source of connection, laughter, and warmth. While that may well be true, researchers have recently found that interacting with "weak ties"—people that we don't know well—actually brings an unexpected boost in mood and feelings of belonging.[12] That casual chat with a classmate, making small talk with someone on the subway—these things provide a pick-me-up that we can fail to realize.

In fact, interacting with strangers carries a *unique* benefit, particularly if we're feeling low. It forces us to cheer up. Of course, with really big problems and profound sadness, we may need advice and a sympathetic ear from someone we deeply trust. No doubt. But sometimes, if we're just mildly mopey, our dearest friends and romantic partners will put up with our wallowing. This can just keep us stuck in a sad or low place. On the other hand, if we know we have to interact with a stranger, social norms dictate that we pull ourselves up. The end result? Your game face can turn into something real, and there can be times when talking to a stranger can actually make you feel better than interacting with a loved one![13]

This happened to me last summer. I had just said a last goodbye to my study abroad students in Copenhagen and was feeling unexpectedly sad. Although the night was young, my plan was to buy a bottle of wine and some Danish comfort foods (read: butter cookies) and go back to my hotel room and wallow with a friend via the miracle of Skype. Instead, I unexpectedly met a friendly Scottish guy in the grocery store and had a spontaneous beer with him. I did mention being bummed at my class being over, but I certainly wasn't going to subject this stranger to my weepiness for more than a minute or two. The conversation quickly shifted to lighter topics like our favorite things about Copenhagen and other places we've visited. After an hour or so, the spring was back in my step. This person had distracted me from my sadness to the point where it had all but disappeared. Yes, I would miss my students, but it was a beautiful night in Copenhagen, and I had much more travel to look forward to. It was just the perspective change I needed.[14]

More Unites Us Than Divides Us

Of course, one difference between our daily social interactions and the ones we have while traveling, particularly to foreign destinations, is that the people we meet are, well, foreign. How do we connect with people with whom we share so little? And wouldn't those interactions be strained and unpleasant? And what about the language barrier? Because we naturally fear what's new and different, for many of us, the very idea of venturing into uncharted conversational waters is intimidating enough to keep us silent.

While this sort of reservation makes intuitive sense, it turns out to be misplaced.[15] What happens is that, *before* an interaction takes place, we tend to focus on the differences between ourselves and our interaction partners ("It's going to be really hard to relate to a person from a different race" or "My life in the big city is just so different from this person who lives alone in the mountains"), but when we interact with them, the commonalities naturally reveal themselves, mitigating the potential conversational barriers imposed by differences. You meet a member of a different racial group or nationality, strike up a conversation, and realize, "Hey, this person likes the same beer as me," "She has a teenaged daughter, too," "We find the same things funny," or any number of other similarities.

Remember Minh, my Vietnamese motorbike driver? When I hired him to drive me, I'll admit to being nervous about how we might find topics of conversation. Really, what could we possibly have in common? I'm a single thirty-something college professor from the United States. He's a married fifty-something tour guide from the Vietnamese countryside. But while sharing a meal with him at another too-busy-to-clean restaurant, I learned that we were both fans of early morning runs, a small nugget of information that was enough to fuel our initial conversations and led to more and more revelations. I learned that he has to run extremely early in the morning to get back before his kids wake up. "You have kids? How many?" and so on.

In effect, interactions with members of seemingly different social or cultural groups proves far more pleasant and less intimidating that we tend to predict. Even more importantly, we often learn that we share more similarities than differences, a lesson that is instrumental in breaking down barriers and combatting prejudices.[16] As Mark Twain said, "Travel is fatal to prejudice, bigotry, and narrow-mindedness." But this lesson can go unlearned if we don't put ourselves out there and take a chance.

How to Talk to Strangers

You might be the kind of person who is extroverted and bold enough to simply go up to a stranger and say hello. But if you'd rather have this facilitated, options abound. Couchsurfing.com is thought of as an incredibly budget-minded approach to travel (you join the online community of fellow couchsurfers and can stay with one for free, with the tacit agreement that you'd be willing to return the favor in the future). It can, however, also be used to network with locals. You can message someone in the place you'd like to visit, ask a few questions, and maybe meet up when you arrive. This is especially helpful if you're going to a place where few people speak English. This person, who presumably joined the network because he wished to connect with foreigners, might even invite you out with friends and help facilitate communication.

And don't miss out on small social opportunities. Brief encounters with café employees, rental car agents, cab drivers, housekeepers, and others can provide you with great tips on local hotspots, places the tourists don't go, as well as meaningful, unvarnished insights into the psychology of a place and its people.

Some tour guides also may facilitate conversation. Adam Platt-Hepworth of cycle-tour company Grasshopper Adventures emphasizes the importance of engaging with locals. He says, "If clients are hesitant, the guide or driver might go with them for a walk to get the whole thing rolling. I would say that in most of Southeast Asia, you don't need to try that hard to engage and immerse as long as you aren't in a tourist town."

NOT ALL WHO WANDER ARE LOST

One of my favorite things to do in a new place is simply to go out by myself and wander. When I get lost or disoriented, I'll call up my nascent mental map and if that fails, I'll pull out an old-fashioned paper one and try to get my bearings. Why not my smartphone? Well, for one, I am cheap, and I seldom pay for international data plans. But this one is also an intentional choice. I don't like being so beholden to my phone for navigation. Efficient as it is, it's disempowering, making me feel passive and helpless. Rather than leading, I'm being led.

But it's more than that. It takes away the joy and pride of discovery. One of my all-time favorite travel memories is of wandering the streets of Rome with my friend Marcia. We had both recently taken our first art history course and were beyond excited to stand before the ancient structures we'd spent all year studying. One day, we set out to find the Pantheon. Armed with only a tattered map, we did our best to navigate the labyrinthine streets and alleyways, but at some point we just threw our hands up in frustration. Where *was* it? How could such a massive, celebrated landmark be so hard to find? Wandering aimlessly, we emerged from a narrow alleyway and there it was, no more than a hundred yards away, right in the middle of a busy square. Wide-eyed shock quickly gave rise to awe and then glee. We went inside and toured the building, then grabbed a table at a nearby café, eating pizza while just staring at this famous building that appeared as if by magic, right in the middle of a bustling city.

In the age of smartphones, Marcia and I wouldn't have wasted a minute in our search for the Pantheon. We'd need never experience the frustration of getting lost. We wouldn't have had to question, to pull out the map, to orient ourselves. It's undoubtedly a time- and frustration-saver.

But is there something lost in all of this efficiency? In addition to the shock, delight, and pride at finding it on our own, new research suggests that there's another downside worth considering.[17] On the campus of the University of British Columbia, students were instructed to go out and locate an unfamiliar building. Some were told to use their smartphone's GPS technology to help them, others were left to fend for themselves. As you might imagine, those who let their phones guide them found the task much easier and located their assigned buildings faster. However, with their eyes glued to the screen, they missed out on the opportunity for social connection, smiling at and talking to far fewer people. These students reported feeling less connected to others as a result.

There's also evidence that we don't process locations nearly as deeply when we outsource this mental work to a GPS-device. Evidence of this mindlessness reveals itself in shocking accounts of people driving hundreds of miles out of their way, or even driving off of the edge of a bridge that had been marked as closed, because a malfunctioning GPS told them to. Moving beyond click-bait and anecdote into the realm of research, one study compared a sample of London taxicab drivers with a matched set of London bus drivers. Participants were similar in age, years on the job, and other key variables, and naturally, the two groups do very similar work. And yet they found that London taxicab drivers, lauded as navigational experts of the city's intricate twists and turns, could recognize more London landmarks and could better judge the proximity between landmarks. More impressively, perhaps, they actually showed more gray matter in areas in the brain associated with spatial reasoning and relations, compared to London bus drivers, who follow prescribed and unchanging routes.[18] Also, this gray matter volume was larger in those who had been a taxi driver for longer, but the regions diminished in volume in retired taxi drivers, suggesting a use-it-or-lose-it phenomenon. As cognitive scientist Julia Frankenstein puts it, when we use GPS, "We see the way from A to Z, but we don't see the landmarks along the way. Developing a cognitive map from this reduced information is a bit like trying to get an entire musical piece from a few notes."[19]

How to Get Lost

Some of the advice here is clear. Go analog with paper maps. Ask directions when necessary. Check the position of the sun (I'm serious). But you might also orient yourself by simply walking around aimlessly without a goal and while not under a time-crunch, being open to the idea of getting a little lost. Stephanie Rosenbloom, travel columnist for *The New York Times*, says, "Even a trip to the most touristy spot can feel personal and spontaneous if you forgo turn-by-turn navigation. I advise glancing at a map to determine the general direction you wish to walk, then winging it."[20] Of course, take money for cab fare, just in case things go horribly wrong.

Not much of a walker? Suffering from tired feet? You could also get on a subway or on a local bus and ride it to the end of the line, likely to the places tourists don't go. Notice who gets on and off. Do the demographics change? What new businesses and architecture styles do you see popping up? And how do the city's landmarks and skyscrapers look when viewed from this distance? This can be a fairly easy and effective way to get a flavor for your location beyond the prime tourism areas.

BEYOND THE CITYSCAPE

Given our reliance on smartphone technology and the rapid rise in urban sprawl, it's no wonder that the effects of going "back to nature" have become a topic of great interest to researchers. While it will come as no surprise to dedicated naturalists, it turns out that connectedness to nature carries a wealth of psychological benefits. And, interestingly, at least when it comes to nearby nature—small gardens, urban parks, and the like—these benefits go unappreciated.[21] In one series of studies, when participants were asked to estimate what their mood might be as the result of taking a brief walk along a nearby nature path versus walking the same route through a series of tunnels, they underestimated just how pleasant walking on the path would be, despite the fact that they were familiar with it.[22]

The benefits of being in nature extend beyond a mere mood boost. In one study, participants either spent fifty minutes wandering around a park or around a city. Afterward, those who took the walk through the park showed an increase in positive mood and a decrease in negative mood. But they also showed a decrease in anxiety and rumination, compared to those who walked in the city.[23] Notice that everyone was getting some exercise outdoors. It was being in nature that was key.

Other effects of nature have been documented. Both subtle exposure to nature-related cues—looking at photographs of nature scenes rather than of buildings—as well as first-hand experience of nature—briefly walking outdoors rather than inside—produced increases in subjective vitality, a sense of mental and physical energy.[24] In a longer-term study, participants in a four-day immersive nature experience showed increases in creativity and problem-solving ability.[25] In yet another, women who resided in an area surrounded by greenery actually *lived longer* than those who didn't, although the specific mechanism underlying this effect is difficult to isolate definitively.[26]

Chasing Awe

When have you last felt dwarfed by nature? Can you recall ever needing a moment to comprehend something vast, utterly foreign, or otherwise mind-boggling?

Although it's surely been felt for as long as humans have wandered the earth, only recently have psychologists begun carefully unpacking the complex emotion of awe. Awe is felt when an experience simply doesn't compute. It lies outside of our normal frame of reference, and, because of this, we have to do some quick mental work to make sense of and accommodate the experience. Awe can be part and parcel of a religious experience, but it can also be felt in more secular realms. Many of the moments people describe as peak experiences in life seem to contain an element of awe. Namely, they contain elements of transcendence, humility, loss of self-awareness, feeling disoriented in time and space, and being struck with the sense that the world is beautiful.[27]

In one of the first scientific studies of awe, researchers convincingly distinguished it from garden-variety happiness by demonstrating that, notably, it is brought about by very different experiences. Happiness is often a result of rewarding social connections and goal attainment, but awe is distinctly asocial. Being in nature—particularly exposure to panoramic views—as well as being in the presence of art and music, elicited awe far more than it elicited happiness.[28]

Notice that elicitors of awe are the sorts of things many of us seek out in our travels: nature, art, music. We drive endless miles through the US national parks, chase the Northern Lights, gaze up at the Sistine Chapel ceiling, and go to rock concerts and music festivals, oftentimes tolerating crushing crowds and paying exorbitant sums in order to do so. Why? Maybe without really knowing it, what we're chasing is actually the singular experience of *awe*.

You might well know how awe feels. It's not quite a *happy* feeling, right? There is a sense of smallness, of insignificance. Of being outside of yourself. There is a quick perceptual shift as you struggle to process something utterly foreign. There may be a physical sensation, too: chills, goosebumps, or a lump in the throat.

Awe is often talked about as being transformative. It brings us into the present and pulls focus from the self. Everyday concerns melt away. When grappling with the reality of, say, the Grand Canyon, there are no thoughts of what's for dinner. The argument you just had with your children? As you stand there, contemplating the incomprehensible, it's disappeared. Awe makes people more generous and prosocial, probably because it pulls focus from our own small selves and orients us to the power and scope of the world outside of ourselves.[29] People who feel awe also experience an altered perception of time. Time feels abundant, and they are less impatient as a result.[30] For my money, awe that can be sought—whether from a panoramic view atop a skyscraper or the bottom of a river valley—enriches any kind of journey.

Setting the Stage for Awe

Awe cannot be forced, unfortunately, but we can set the stage for it in our travels.[31] Expose yourself to perceptual vastness and beautiful nature. Look up at the night sky. Drive or walk to a scenic overlook. Stand in the center of a massive Gothic cathedral. Go to the symphony or a rock concert. And, recall that awe arises as you try to make sense of what you're beholding. Maybe don't do a ton of research or look at a number of images before you go (although know that if you do, you're still going to be getting a watered-down version of what awaits). If the potentially awe-inspiring thing is a lengthy drive or climb away, all signs say to proceed toward it anyway. If getting there was a burden, if it was a time-suck, take heart in the knowledge that any annoyance will slip away as you feel awe envelop you.

Author and awe-chaser Leigh Ann Henion lets the quest for wonder dictate her travels. Not only does she seek out experiences of dazzling beauty—the Northern Lights, a volcanic eruption, and a bioluminescent lake, to name a few—she adds complexity to her experience by meeting insiders and experts who share her passion and curiosity. She recalled witnessing—no, being immersed in—a massive butterfly migration deep in the mountains of Mexico:

> The streams of cascading monarchs made the trees' branches look like ever-expanding arms reaching down to embrace me. I was filled with an inexplicable surge of energy that made me want to laugh and cry at the same time. The butterflies were live orange confetti setting the sky ablaze. They were the beauty that cultures try to capture in stained glass windows, the elation people seek in nature.[32]

The spontaneous and intense physical and emotional sensations, the altered perspective of space and time, and the sense of smallness conveyed in this brief passage beautifully express the transcendent power of awe.

LET IT FLOW

So far, I've presented a few tricks to immerse yourself in a new place, even if you have only a few days to spend there. These all have to do with you meeting with something *outside* of yourself: exotic food, local people, foreign neighborhoods, and awe-inspiring places. But there's another way to immerse, and that's through what psychology researchers call active engagement. This is more of an *internal* sort of immersion, one where you meet with a deeply rewarding and challenging activity and find yourself getting fully absorbed.

But before we get into all of that, think about the specific things you typically do, both at work and at play. For instance, I might name teaching classes, writing, surfing the Internet, eating, choir practice, and commuting among my everyday activities.

Next, a harder question: How would you describe your state of mind during this time? That's very broad, so to help you out, pick one of the activities you listed and think about how well these questions describe your state of mind while performing this activity.

Use the following scale:

1	2	3	4	5
not at all true of me		somewhat true of me		extremely true of me

1. My mind isn't wandering. I am totally involved in what I am doing and I am not thinking of anything else.
2. The world seems to be cut off from me.
3. I am less aware of myself and my problems.
4. My concentration is like breathing . . . I never think of it.
5. I am so involved in what I am doing that I don't see myself as separate from what I am doing.
6. I am really quite oblivious to my surroundings after I really get going in this activity. I think that the phone could ring, and the doorbell could ring or the house could burn down and I wouldn't notice.[33]

For me, I seldom feel like this when surfing the web or commuting. My mind is wandering and I am easily distracted, even bored. I'd give myself a lot of

1s and 2s on the scale. But while teaching, I often lose track of time. Lots of 4s and 5s. Occasionally, it happens with writing, if I can discipline myself to turn off social media and email. And when I sing in a choir, I feel it all the time. Stepping back, I see that what unifies teaching, writing, and singing is the amount of attention they require but also the extent to which I enjoy them.

The brief survey taps into the *flow state*, an experience of intense absorption in an intrinsically rewarding and challenging activity.[34] It's commonly reported in people whose work entails a high degree of single-minded focus, like elite athletes and musicians.[35] Flow tends to involve losing sense of time, a feeling of personal control, and a diminished self-consciousness. After experiencing flow, people report things like "being in the zone." Although people in flow states do not report feeling happy in the traditional sense (they are too involved in the task at hand for that kind of self-awareness), flow is highly reinforcing. People who experience flow are often hungry for more. Mihalyi Csikszentmihalyi, the psychologist who was the first to systematically study flow, says that to be a happy person, spend as much time in flow as possible.[36]

Flow is a very unique form of immersion. It is much more internal and personal than the social and cultural immersion described previously. It is you merging with an activity. And it is certainly not unique to travel. You can find flow anytime you encounter and vitally engage with a rewarding and challenging activity. But travel creates an often-overlooked opportunity for flow: new, fun, and challenging activities often present themselves, if we can pull ourselves away from our beach chair (and smartphone) long enough to find them.

How to Find Flow

So how do you find it? There are two main ways to set the stage:

First, choose something engaging to do, something that will likely mesh well with your current skill level. It should be challenging, but not so challenging that you feel self-conscious or anxious. You have to find that sweet spot. Sometimes, it takes experimentation. Secondly, remove distractions: smartphones and cameras, for instance. Nothing will destroy flow more quickly than an incoming text message or the compulsion to digitally capture a moment.[37]

Once, I took a surfing lesson with a group of college students in Southern California. A lifelong swimmer, I feel pretty comfortable in water, and was probably overconfident in my ability to effortlessly ride the waves. My first few attempts to get past the strong breaks left me stunned, coughing up mouthfuls of nasty saltwater. The board was continuously thrown back into my chest and head, naturally instilling anxiety.[38] Meanwhile, the students were getting it, standing up fearlessly, if only for a few seconds before plunging into the water and coming up laughing. Already feeling like an old fogey in this student group, I now also felt clumsy and incompetent. I eventually rode a few waves in on my knees and it was fun. But as a whole, this was a little too challenging and scary to really promote flow. I was anxious and really just wanted the whole thing to be over.

However, a similar experience a few years later hit that sweet spot. I went stand-up paddleboarding in a protected bay in the Outer Banks. I had kayaked and canoed before, so I understood the basic physics of paddling and steering. And, despite the surfing fail, I was still pretty comfortable in water. Balance, however, had never been my strong suit, and because standing up to paddle was a completely new physical action, there was some real challenge involved. I had to focus completely in order to shift from kneeling to standing on the wobbly board, acutely attuned to very subtle bodily cues, slight shifts in the board, and the movement of the water. At first, each paddle required dedicated concentration. But I started to get the hang of it after a while, and could then take in my surroundings and bask in the fact that I was standing on water, which is a very cool sensation. We eventually ventured into some shallow waves, and single-minded focus took over once again as I tried to stay upright.

As Csikszentmihalyi might say, action and awareness were merged as I gained confidence, leaning into each paddlestroke, engaging more and more muscle groups, and making fine adjustments to accommodate the breezes and the light chop of the water. Maybe I looked silly or awkward on the board. I have no idea. It didn't matter. I had transcended self-consciousness in those moments.

After what ended up being three hours on the water (which I had no idea about, because I was unaware of the passage of time!), we called it a day, and then sat down on the beach. Finally, I could dedicate my attention to what I had just done, and I felt like I'd had an optimal experience of challenge and fun. One reason I experienced flow while paddling was because there were really no external distractions. I couldn't take my smartphone or camera with me on the water, so there was little to pull focus from what I was doing. In ordinary life, flow has gotten increasingly elusive as distractions and the pressure to multitask have become ubiquitous.

WHAT IF I JUST WANT TO RELAX?

You may be reading this and thinking, "Lady, I'm *tired*. I don't want to do something challenging. What I want—no, what I *need*—is to get away from it all, quiet my mind, stare out at the beach, and read a trashy novel." And to this I say, "Great. Do it."

But realize that, as exhausted as you are, you will get so much more out of your travels if you also find ways to engage more fully. You don't need to climb mountains, ski a black diamond, live with a host family, or become fluent in the language. But I promise that you will be happier if you combine the rest and relaxation you so crave with the sort of active engagement that promotes flow.

Hear me out. For one, time gets distorted while we're in flow. Usually, it zips by. In looking back on an experience and making a judgment about how fun and pleasurable it was, it turns out that the rate at which time passed provides a useful cue.[39] When we see that time has gone by unexpectedly fast, we rate what we were just doing as being pretty great. "Time flies when you're having fun" is more than a cliché; it's a useful heuristic when making judgments about how we just spent our time.

Also, we tend to stretch our skills and abilities as we experience flow. You're your best self, at least when it comes to performing that activity, when you're in flow. All of your attention and energy is being spent on what you're doing. You can't look back and say, "Oh, if only I had been more focused." Attention-wise, you literally gave it your all. With flow, there are no regrets.

The Challenge of the Fly-and-Flop

In the travel industry, a fly-and-flop vacation is one where you fly to a beach, flop down onto it, and stay put. In many ways, it sounds pretty sweet. But it might not be as perfect as we think. Not because the beach or attached resort will disappoint, but because we're not always so great at, well, flopping. (And flying isn't exactly a bowl of cherries, either). Consider this: you may well be overestimating your ability to just *be*. As I've discussed earlier, we adapt to static, unchanging pleasantries like a comfortable hotel room or a quiet beach. It will probably get old and you'll likely get antsy. In his argument for engaging, flow-type activities, Csikszentmihalyi argues,

> The popular assumption is that no skills are involved in enjoying free time,
> and that anybody can do it. Yet the evidence suggests the opposite: free time
> is more difficult to enjoy than work. Having leisure at one's disposal does
> not improve the quality of life unless one knows how to use it effectively
> . . . without goals and without others to interact with, most people begin to
> lose motivation and concentration. The mind begins to wander, and more
> often than not it will focus on unresolvable problems that cause anxiety.[40]

But also consider the fact that that hotel room and that beach can be made better when supplemented and contrasted with other types of activities.[41] We prefer variety more than we realize, it seems, especially when looking back on our experiences.[42] More variety gives us more distinct material to reminisce on.

It also turns out that we don't like idleness as much as we think we do. Studies reveal that people would rather do tasks that are knowingly pointless, like assembling and reassembling a bracelet or walking an extra distance to deliver a document, rather than using that time to merely sit quietly.[43] They would even prefer to administer mild electrical shocks to themselves, rather than being alone with their own thoughts![44] Funny, then, how sitting idly on a beach consumes many of our travel fantasies.

Remember a cardinal rule of happy travel: You are still yourself, even in a new place. There's no reason to believe idleness aversion won't accompany you on your next trip. Plan for it. Work in some engaging activity, however you define it. A cooking class. A language class. Hiking. Birding. Kite-surfing. Fly-fishing. For other ideas, look on Tripadvisor.com for things to do in your destination. Book it ahead of time. Then let yourself get lost in this activity. Find your flow, lose track of time, let your attention be absorbed in activity. And then that beach chair will be all the more welcoming.

Are We Having Fun Yet?

Idleness creates the opportunity for a certain type of fruitless and harmful self-reflection. To illustrate, recall New Years Eve, 1999, a special day that, for many, had much in common with a highly anticipated vacation.

Y2K-anxiety notwithstanding, it was the dawn of a new millennium, a night for celebration. Inspired by Prince to "party like it's 1999," many people made elaborate plans, spending large sums on travel, champagne, new clothes, cover charges for clubs, and other makings of an unforgettable evening. A creative research team interviewed some of these revelers and uncovered something fascinating: The more time, effort, and money people invested in this evening, the less fun they reported having![45]

Follow-up studies shed light on why: the constant monitoring of emotional states ("Am I happy right now? Is this as fun as I expected?") combined with the pressure to enjoy a once-in-a-lifetime event detracted from the simple pleasure of the moment.

If you consider all the time and money that goes into a trip, plus the knowledge that your time in the place is limited and the general belief that vacation time must be fun time, you have a recipe for incredibly high expectations and a whole lot of pressure.

While this pressure is built in to rare and costly experiences, some of us naturally feel it more acutely. People who agree with statements like, "How happy I am at any given moment says a lot about how worthwhile my life is," "If I don't feel happy, maybe there is something wrong with me," "I am concerned about my happiness even when I feel happy," and "To have a meaningful life, I need to feel happy most of the time" actually tend to be less happy and more prone to depression. This is particularly true in pleasant situations when they, by all accounts, should be feeling happy.[46] Maybe they're feeling pretty good, but it's somehow just *not enough*. While most of this compelling research has been conducted in a tightly controlled laboratory environment, the implications for travel are clear: people who value happiness, who pressure themselves to *be happy, damn it!* are likely to rain on their own parades with excessive self-monitoring.

A secret of happy travel, then, is to learn to turn the internal happiness monitor down or even off and to let happiness emerge as a natural byproduct of cultural immersion, challenge, awe, and interpersonal connection. This is a final reason why active engagement rather than idleness is key for a successful vacation. As Nathaniel Hawthorne said, "Happiness is like a butterfly which, when pursued, is just out of reach, but if you sit quietly, may alight upon you." It cannot be forced, it cannot be bought. This is one of the challenges of happy travel.

HAPPY TRAVEL TIPS FOR IMMERSION AND ENGAGEMENT

Happiness researchers have for a long time broken down "the good life" into two key components: moments of pleasure and moments of engagement and challenge. When traveling, it can be all too easy to focus only on pleasure, although the most meaningful and memorable moments may be ones of challenge.[47]

Before embarking, or early in your trip, ask yourself how you might get off of the metaphorical tour bus, to experience a place more deeply and pursue engagement and challenge. Consider the following:

- *What level of immersion feels right to me?* Everyone has his or her own comfort level, as we discussed previously. Perhaps trying new foods feels all right, but talking to locals makes you nervous. Can you identify why? Can you strategize on how to make this easier?

- *Where might I experience awe?* Are there any natural wonders, sweeping panoramas, or ancient majestic buildings in the vicinity of where you're going? Awe cannot be forced or guaranteed, but putting yourself in the presence of vastness can certainly set the stage.

- *How can I find flow?* Look for an intriguing activity that may be challenging enough to absorb your attention, but not so challenging that you feel unsafe or anxious.

- *Do I excessively monitor my own happiness?* Do you put pressure on yourself to have fun and be happy, especially in pricey and privileged situations? (If vacations are rare for you, also think about special occasions like holidays, fancy meals out, and weddings.) Realize how counterproductive this is. And realize, too, that immersive activities might be a powerful antidote to this mindset.

Six

Pictures or It Didn't Happen!: The Challenges of Savoring in a Hyperconnected World

He who has seen one cathedral ten times has seen something; he who has seen ten cathedrals once has seen but little; and he who has spent half an hour in each of a hundred cathedrals has seen nothing at all.

—Sinclair Lewis

In 2003, the book *1000 Things to See Before You Die* hit the shelves and quickly became a bestseller. It featured brief descriptions of natural, cultural, and historic must-sees around the world, plus a checklist sightseers could use to tick off their accomplishments. Four years later, the movie *The Bucket List* was released, inspiring people to consider all of the things they wanted to see and do before kicking the proverbial bucket. Web-app developers also jumped on the trend, and now there are countless apps you can download to make your own personal bucket list and chronicle its completion. And recently, the website maploco.com briefly went viral. This site allows you to click on all of the US states or nations in the world that you've visited and then post your achievements on social media. I confess that as a fan of both maps and documentation, I followed suit, proudly ticking off forty-five US states and thirty countries and posting my maps for my Facebook friends to admire and envy.

To be sure, bucket lists have an inherent appeal and there really is nothing wrong with having one. It can be both fun and motivating to prioritize and look ahead to what we most want to do. And when cast in this existential, life-is-short sort of light, making a grand plan, whether it's to see the Northern Lights, road-trip through the Rockies, or sail around the world, isn't frivolous but is actually a mark of a well-lived life.

But a bucket list is just that: a *list*, shallow and impoverished of detail. When it comes to travel, if we don't go beyond ticking things off, opting for quantity over quality, have we really seen anything? The checklist mentality reinforced by the bucket list encourages seeing things *just* to say we've seen them. Also, it encourages us to pack as much as we possibly can into a trip: "The Taj Mahal—check. Next?" They encourage us to frame travel as a project, as work, as a series of goals devoid of any deeper meaning.

Another approach has also sprung up, and it lies in direct contrast to this travel-as-conquest mentality. "Slow travel" is an extension of the slow food movement, which maligns mass-produced and fast food and encourages education and appreciation of local and sustainable cuisine. In the context of travel, slowness involves, first off, choosing to stay put rather than sprinting through as many cities and countries as your itinerary and energy level will allow. Slow travelers might opt to bike or walk instead of driving to allow time to see more details of their location. They might take the time to get acquainted with the language of the region, attempting to use it when possible.

Slow travel is not about hitting as many guidebook-mandated places as possible; it's about seeing more by seeing less, going deeper, and maybe even starting to feel at home in this new place.[1] It also encourages immersion and connection—much of what we discussed in the previous chapter—getting to know the authentic local culture rather than ticking off numerous prescribed attractions.

To get a feel for what a day of slow travel might look like, imagine renting a cottage in a small town in the European countryside. While charming and exotic in its own right, the town gets little attention from the guidebooks and certainly didn't make the cut for *1000 Things to See*

Before You Die. When describing your trip, your friends are likely to say, "You're going *where?*"

During your time there, you establish a few comfortable routines. Each morning, you rise without an alarm and walk to a café in the town square. You greet your server and some of the other patrons in the native language and sip your coffee on the patio while paging through the local newspaper or one of your backlogged issues of the *New Yorker* (because who has time to read it in daily life?). Or maybe you just engage your senses, noticing everything from the latticework on a nearby building to the buttery goodness of your morning croissant to the conversations of the café's other patrons. Later on you might bike to the next town over, buy some fresh fruit at the local market, visit a nearby chateau, or just walk through town, stopping to check out whatever appeals. Dinner would be a leisurely affair, with locally sourced food and wine at a nearby restaurant without another tourist in sight. Your days are occupied and engaging but not stressful nor exhausting.

However, it's less a particular itinerary than a *mindset* that matters. Country versus city, car versus bike versus train, one week in a place versus two—these details aren't as relevant as you might think. To really be a slow traveler you have to attend to and savor your surroundings, being in the present moment rather than dwelling on what comes next. It could also mean skipping the major tourist attractions in favor of a more relaxed pace and a more authentic experience (no one goes to Times Square or Hollywood to see the "real" America, right?). To really be a slow traveler, you have to quiet the inner Energizer Bunny, the one telling you to go, go, go. You have to dispense with the checklist mentality and realize how much more you can see when you're not rushed, when you're mindful and appreciative.

Sound nice? In theory, absolutely. Sound easy? For many of us, well-practiced at maintaining the rapid pace of daily life, no. If we're going to be really honest with ourselves, it does not.

SLOWING DOWN AND BEING
WHERE YOU ARE

Most of us do want to learn the art of slowing down, of being present and appreciative.[2] As a result, in the past decade or so, the concept of *mindfulness* has gone from new-age to mainstream. From meditation classes now being offered in schools, hospitals, and gyms, to the increasing academic interest in mindfulness and meditation, to the recent trend of mindfulness coloring books for adults, everyone seems to grasp the importance of unplugging and quieting the mind. And it's much more than just a fad. Mindfulness—a nonjudgmental, open awareness of the present—carries numerous benefits, including lower levels of anxiety and depression and higher levels of happiness, energy, optimism, and self-esteem.[3]

Closely related to mindfulness is the ability to translate what we are witnessing into good feelings, going beyond mere awareness and actually savoring or appreciating our internal states and outward experiences.[4] You might think of *savoring* as a specific type of mindfulness. While you can be mindful of the good, the bad, and the ugly, savoring is focused specifically on the *positive* aspects of an experience. When you savor you are actively and deliberately attending to, appreciating, and enhancing your positive feelings.[5] You aren't just passively taking in sensory information; you're translating it into something pleasant through an active direction of attention.

Savoring Your Experience

Let's say you've recently decided to try out a new restaurant that's been getting rave reviews from friends and critics alike. You're excited to really, fully experience the food you're going to be served. But how, exactly, do you do this?[6] You might learn a little of the backstory of the cuisine. If locally sourced, where does it come from? And what is the story of the restaurant? Is it family owned? Historically interesting? With more to the story, you have more to think about when you're there, and you'll have fewer places for your ever-wandering mind to drift. Once seated, you might do something to mark the meal as special. Some do it by saying grace, but you can also just take a moment, perhaps with your partner, to share your good fortune or express how excited you are for the experience. You might ask a few questions of the server or staff to learn more about the food and wine you're about to experience. When you're finally served, you can deploy your attention to the food in front of you. You take your first bite of handmade gnocchi, or sashimi, or warm, crusty baguette and delight in the taste and texture. Naturally, magazines, books, screens, and other distractors have no place here. Attention should be reserved for the experience at hand.[7]

Savoring is often discussed as a focused orientation to the present, but it can also take place in advance of an upcoming event, perhaps through anticipation. When you book your reservation for that special restaurant, you can begin the savoring process by imagining what the experience will be like and how it will feel to be there. And it can happen retrospectively as well, via reminiscence.[8] Afterward, you can look back on the meal, recalling the taste of the food and the fun time you had talking to your server, sipping wine, and sharing a special meal with your partner.

We all have some sense of what it means to savor, but it's actually quite a complex mental and emotional experience. When you close your eyes and focus on the complex, delicate taste of an Oregon pinot noir, when you marvel at a mountain vista or bask in the warmth of the sun, you are savoring. When you try to tune out distractions so that you can be fully engaged in a present experience, you are savoring. When you try to look closely at what is before you, trying to remembering details of it so you can relive it later, you are savoring. And when you turn to your companion to talk about your enjoyment, you're probably savoring as well.

For all of its breadth and complexity, one thing is certain: savoring and slow travel go hand in hand. It's difficult to imagine a person having the luxury of stepping back and really appreciating when in the midst of a whirlwind tour. But an open itinerary only sets the stage for savoring; it is no guarantee. Remember the challenge of the fly-and-flop?

Why Enjoying the Sunset is Harder Than Riding the Waves

The opportunity for savoring is one reason why we travel. We seem to believe that *if only* we could get away—from work, from extended family, from rush-hour traffic, from our never-ending list of errands—*then* we could find the mental quietude and single-minded appreciation that we so desire. However, being mindful and appreciative has more to do with our own ability to quiet our minds than with any particular location.

While both are positive, savoring is, in some ways, the exact opposite of the flow state we discussed previously. Many things are optimally experienced in a flow state, which is characterized by absorption, losing sense of time, and a diminished self-focus. Those in flow states are so immersed in the task at hand that they are not focused on how they feel about it. They often recall these kinds of states as incredibly enjoyable and rewarding, but they are not aware of this enjoyment in the moment. But when you're savoring, you're mentally shining a spotlight on the positive things around you. You're fully attuned to *your experience* of pleasure and you're taking conscious steps to prolong that pleasure.

Both states—savoring and flow—are highly desirable, but there is a time and place for each. If you mentally step back to savor your first time stand-up paddleboarding, for example, you may quickly end up in the water. And savoring rock-climbing or downhill single-track mountain biking? Not advisable. Experiences that would be enhanced by savoring are the kinds of things that seldom involve direct, stimulating interaction or challenge, but rather, they allow us the luxury of mentally stepping out of the experience to mark it as special.

It's impossible to discuss savoring without also revisiting that pesky tendency we all have to get used to the things around us. Flow activities are practically immune to these forces. So long as we keep adding challenge to what we are doing, the gratifying experience of flow should still result.

Because savoring is seldom discussed in the context of challenge, it certainly *seems* easier. Lazily sitting back and appreciating a glass of wine or a scenic panorama seems far easier than mastering stand-up paddleboarding. Physically, this is certainty true. But mentally and emotionally, a savoring mindset is actually harder to sustain. It often involves experiences we easily disengage from, because they *don't* demand single-minded attention. Examples abound and include delicious food, beautiful views, works of art and music, and bustling cities—so much of what we long for when we plan our travels. These things wow us initially, but thanks to adaptation, it becomes almost tragically easy to eat mindlessly, browse a magazine instead of marveling at the view, tune out the music, and take for granted the cultural richness of city life. Without stimulation or challenge, it's all too easy to be distracted and miss the present moment. As a result, it's these sorts of positive but nonchallenging experiences that can go unappreciated and are therefore enhanced by learning the art of slowing down and savoring.

Plus, the challenges and concerns that accompany travel can also detract from savoring. Even benign shifts in attention—say, wondering what your next meal will be or where that little art gallery is—can pull focus.[9] And, because savoring is unlikely to happen when we're unfocused and preoccupied, it's getting harder as our attention is increasingly divided between what lies before us and what our technology demands.[10] As we will get into shortly, technology—smartphones, social media, cameras—poses a serious challenge as well.

Finally, the positive aspects of travel often are overwhelmed by its inevitably stressful or annoying downsides. Problems demand attention and solutions.[11] Good things, not so much. So we naturally zero in on challenges and frustrations instead of on pleasures and successes. As neuroscientist Rick Hanson says, "The brain is like Velcro for negative information, but Teflon for positive." Practically speaking, it's tough to marvel at a gorgeous cityscape when you're figuring out how you're going to reunite with your lost luggage or worrying about where you might sleep that night. If you want to enjoy your travels, it is critically important to know how to push back against the negative things that naturally are going to demand your attention.

How Good Are You at Savoring Your Experiences?

Some of us have a leg up and are naturally better at savoring than others. How do you fare? Read each of the following statements and indicate how much each of them applies to what you thought and did the last time you went on vacation.[12] You might choose to focus on a specific experience in which savoring might have been an appropriate response, like eating a special meal or standing at a scenic overlook. Or you might think of your vacation as a whole.

Use the following scale:

Not at all		Somewhat		Very Much
1	2	3	4	5

1. I tried to take in every sensory property of the event (sights, sounds, smells, etc.).
2. I thought only about the present and got absorbed in the moment.
3. I tried to slow down and move more slowly (in an effort to stop or slow down time).
4. I reminded myself how long I had waited for this to happen.
5. I took mental photographs.
6. I expressed to other people present how much I valued the moment.

7. I reminded myself how transient this moment was and thought about it ending.
8. I closed my eyes, relaxed, and took in the moment.
9. I consciously reflected on the situation—took in the details, tried to remember them, made comparisons.
10. I tried not to think too much—just relaxed and enjoyed.

If you gave yourself high ratings on many of these items, you may be naturally skilled at tuning out distractions, thinking about the small amount of time you have to experience good things, sharing them with others, and sharpening your senses to try and focus on them more fully. In other words, you use strategies that help you savor and stay present in the moment.

But if you didn't do so well: why? What keeps you from savoring your travels? Do you have the checklist mentality, in which you try to cram in as much activity and sightseeing as possible? Are you always checking and posting to social media sites? Do the stresses of travel tend to loom large in your mind, pulling you out of the present? Or are you always looking ahead to the next big thing?

Building Your Savoring Skillset

We can't completely prevent travel-related annoyances and we can't eliminate the distractions that pull focus, but the good news is that, through practice, we can all become better at savoring. It is a mindset that can be practiced anywhere. But because it does require attention, first, set the stage by minimizing distractors. You're not going to savor that cup of coffee while also answering emails or scrolling through Facebook, so put the smartphone away. Allow yourself the mental quiet required.

Another well-established technique for training yourself to savor is through journaling. And you don't have to wait for vacation to start. What are three good things that happened *today*? Even on a bad day, you can probably come up with three small things. Or, more broadly, what are some things in your life that you appreciate?[13] As you ask yourself this, some obvious things will pop up—family, friends, good health, a secure job. Don't stop there. Expand on why you're grateful for these simple pleasures. How do they make you feel? Learning to find opportunities to savor is a skill that will carry over into other realms of life, including travel.

While you're traveling, employ these same techniques. As you sit in that sidewalk café, what experiences jump out as special and noteworthy? Maybe it's some unique architecture. Maybe it's the loving interaction between a mother and daughter a few tables over. Maybe it's the rich and complex flavor of your coffee. Whatever it is, because your ability to focus on it and make vague attributions like "That is really special and cool and beautiful" may last only a few seconds, use the journal to go deeper. Ask yourself, what strikes you in your immediate environment? Maybe it's the features of a major tourist attraction—a grand cathedral, a massive waterfall—or maybe it's more subtle: exotic spices used in the local dishes, the apparent joie de vivre of the locals, the clean mountain air. We can all develop an eye for these things, mark them as special, and share them with others.

An alternative to journaling in-the-moment is to take time at the end of the day. You might think about the best thing that happened that day. Write about it in depth, expanding on why it was so great and how you felt in this moment. Or add an interpersonal component by casually bringing the moment up over dinner and ask your companions to describe their favorite moments, too. Don't be afraid to go deep. Why exactly were these moments so special? How did they make you feel, physically and emotionally? These kinds of expressions actively and effectively remind us of the subtle pleasantries that can easily be neglected or even forgotten.

S-A-V-O-R

Finally, because savoring is a complex and multistep process, it's helped me to break it down like this:

S—*slow down*. Take the time to sit, look, listen, and just *be*.

A—*attend*. With distractions minimized, focus your attention on the sensory experience before you. Take in all of that rich information that is so often filtered out and ignored.

V—*value*. Go beyond just attending. Take an extra moment to mark your experience as special, meaningful, or beautiful.

O—*open up and out*. Expand on what you just experienced to further amplify your feelings. This is where journaling might come in, or talking about it with the people around you, or even a few of the techniques I'll describe later in this chapter.

R—*reflect*. Savoring doesn't have to stop just because the mountain, the meal, or the merlot is physically gone. Mentally revisit it, recalling the thoughts and feelings you had in the experience, to extend your feelings of pleasure.

TICK-TOCK

While she was in college, poet and author Sylvia Plath was spending the summer with a family in a New England beach town. She was enjoying herself, taking care of the children, sunning herself, and making new friends, but she wasn't exactly savoring every moment. Then one day, as the end of summer was drawing near, she glanced at the calendar and was shocked to see that only three days of summer remained. In her personal diary, she writes,

And so I leave the two streetlights at the end of Beach Bluff Avenue which shone in crosses of light through my door every night. And the crickets chirping on the wind. And the blue of Preston Beach water. Good-bye Castle Rock ... and my quaint, crooked streets of Marblehead, with hollyhocks springing tall from the narrow dooryards ... I want to stay awake for the next three days and nights, drawing the threads of my summer cocoon neatly around me, to savor until dying of the last wave, the last dawn, this place, the leaving of which means leaving a great space of living.[14]

Notice how Plath is newly aware of her surroundings, expressing appreciation for subtleties that she's probably adapted to, the sorts of things that are very easy to take for granted. The crickets, the flowers, and the quaint, crooked streets suddenly shift from the background to the forefront of her attention. She is savoring these things in the same way she may have done when first arriving in the town. Importantly, she is motivated to capitalize on the short amount of time she has left in Marblehead. She doesn't want to squander any more time, but rather, she wants to stay awake and make the most of every minute that remains. Savoring is, suddenly and overwhelmingly, her default mindset.

This counterintuitive notion, that focusing on something sad can motivate us to make the most of it, so fascinated and resonated with me that, back in graduate school, I made it into my dissertation. The idea first came to me at the end of a truly epic summer study abroad trip. Before I'd left, my mother had told me numerous times, *"This is a once-in-a-lifetime experience. Once in a lifetime!!"* Her words ran through my head as I stared out at the Arno River on my last morning in Florence, Italy (which was and maybe still is my favorite place in the world). Really, when would I *ever* get back here? At the time, as a senior in college, international travel just was not something my family and friends did, nor was it something I could I see in my soon-to-be-poor-graduate-student future. I viewed this trip as a complete aberration, a blip of good fortune that would not soon be repeated. I just stared, trying my best to take it all in, grateful and yet so sad to be feeling the time slipping away, uncontrollably.

As affecting as this was, as an aspiring emotion researcher, I also filed the moment away as a bittersweet experience. I became obsessed by the complex emotion of bittersweetness, in which sadness and appreciation are inextricably linked, and began seeing examples of such experiences, large and small, everywhere. Spending time with friends or family you seldom see. The intense joys and sorrows of a long-distance relationship. Watching your children grow up before your eyes. Spending time with aging loved ones. The cherry blossoms in spring or the maple trees in autumn. Even the last piece of chocolate.[15] These things are inherently meaningful, beautiful, or delicious on their own, but adding in a clear expiration date cranks up the intensity, making them much more powerful and poignant: *You need to appreciate this now! Not tomorrow, not next week, but NOW.*

The travel industry knows the value of scarcity and capitalizes on it with "doom tourism," last-chance excursions to places that may not exist in their present form for much longer.[16] Here, travelers may exquisitely sense the passage of time while also beholding places of fragile beauty. It's a perfect recipe for bittersweetness. Sites of doom tourism include the Galapagos Islands, the Patagonian ice fields, polar bear habitats in the Arctic, the Amazon rain forests, and the sinking Pacific island of Tuvalu, all of which are threatened by global warming. According to Ken Shapiro, editor-in-chief of *TravelAge West*, a magazine for travel agents, "It's not just about going to an exotic place. It's about going someplace they expect will be gone in a generation."[17] Based on what psychologists know about scarcity, telling people that it may just be their last chance to see a place can be a brilliant marketing strategy, motivating them to pay a premium for the opportunity.

Building on Bittersweetness

You don't need to shell out tens of thousands of dollars to see the polar icecaps or visit a sinking island to feel the bittersweet passage of time. Scarcity is what travel is all about; when we have only a few precious days to experience a place, and if it's a place we love, we can't help but feel happy to be there while also being saddened by the short amount of time we have to experience it.

In fact, as we discussed in chapter 3 with regards to the irresistible lure of souvenirs, scarcity makes most anything increase in value. And when *time* is scarce, we are motivated to make the most of what we have left. One somewhat counterintuitive strategy based on my own research is that— even though it may seem like a buzzkill—reminding yourself about the impending ending of your trip may motivate you to be in the moment and appreciate what lies before you.

In one study, I recruited a group of college seniors about six weeks before graduation.[18] Admittedly, as anyone in the throes of final exams and job-search anxiety will tell you, college graduation and vacation are vastly different experiences. But they are similar *psychologically* in some key ways. For both a vacationer and a soon-to-be graduate, a happy and treasured life experience will soon reach its inevitable end, never to be repeated. When graduation day actually comes, the intense happy–sad feelings hit hard, not unlike Sylvia Plath's experience of her last few days in her treasured beachside town.[19] But I found that we could back this awareness up a bit so that students could reap the benefits of bittersweetness in advance of the end date. By encouraging them to think about the fact that graduation was going to happen very soon, they were more motivated to make the most of their remaining weeks in college, and were happier as a result.[20] Time takes on new value when it's in short supply, and we want to make extra-sure to use it well.[21] In light of this, while you're traveling, you might try to remind yourself of how fast it's going and how little time you have left. Don't do this to such an extreme that it spoils the moment, but let the emotionally rich, messy bittersweetness of it all come into your consciousness and enrich the experience.

When I travel, I have a countdown app on my phone that tells me how many more days I have left on my trip.[22] Given that I look at my phone far more than I care to admit, thoughts of time's scarcity are never far from my mind. I also work it into my journaling, thinking not only about why I'm enjoying a particular thing, but also the fact that my time to enjoy it is so brief. So not only is this gelato *amazing*, but it might be my very last chance to eat it!

I'M IN IOWA!

While most everyone can become better at savoring their travel experiences, it can be naturally more difficult for those who have seen a lot. One danger of having remarkable life experiences is that you are inadvertently, unknowingly, raising the bar for the future. After all, what is the Jersey Shore compared to the French Riviera? How can you enjoy a local nature trail after you've trekked through the Alps?

In 2006, I was gearing up to drive from Pennsylvania to California to start a new phase of life, with my mom coming along for the ride. We had barely passed Pittsburgh and I was already looking forward to my very first glimpse of Colorado's Rocky Mountains. All that stuff in between—Ohio, Indiana, Iowa, Nebraska—although I'd never been to any of these states, I was eager to just zip through them. After all, I'd seen Paris, Rome, Barcelona! It was going to take a lot to wow *me*!

Mom, on the other hand, would be the first to say that she was no great traveler. Not coincidentally, she was also an open and grateful recipient of all that the Great Plains had to offer. I distinctly remember the two of us driving across Iowa on pancake-flat, cornfield-lined Interstate 80, clearly residing in two distinctly different emotional worlds. Nothing against Iowa, but I just couldn't wait to get through that seemingly endless state. Mom, on the other hand, was taking it all in—the flatness, the corn, the miles we'd just put between ourselves and Pennsylvania. At one point, she said, with a sense of hushed wonder, "Jaime, I'm in IOWA!"

That moment has come back to me time and time again, and I've come to realize how I longed to see everything like Mom saw Iowa. For those of us who travel often, maintaining that kind of wonder can be tough and the ability to do so is enviable. But our standards can't help but shift due to the experiences we have. In the litany of travel risks, this one—the increasingly blasé attitude that gradually takes hold as we see more and more—is seldom mentioned, but it's very real.

Some fascinating new research by Jordi Quoidbach and colleagues supports what I call the "ho-hum effect." They surveyed visitors to the Old North Church, a well-known Boston landmark. While it holds architectural and historical appeal, it's a far cry from Angkor Wat or the Sistine Chapel. Researchers found that after asking visitors to list the most exotic places they'd previously visited, *they spent less time in the church and savored it less*, compared to those who'd brought more ordinary places to mind. It's almost as if they were reminding themselves that they had fried bigger fish than this.

This is a fascinating addition to the established research on hedonic adaptation. Most of this research has been done with things that are experienced constantly or in fairly rapid succession: The tenth piece of chocolate in a row is less enjoyable than the first, for instance. But this study suggests that even after much time has passed, your outstanding travel experiences stay with you, making the subsequent ones less enthralling.

On the surface, this is a pretty depressing finding. Really, how do frequent travelers maintain a sense of wonder? Will the white sand and turquoise water of the Caribbean inevitably detract from our enjoyment of the local beach? Does a Michelin-starred restaurant spoil us for a local taco stand? Should we *avoid* extraordinary experiences, lest they ruin us for the more ordinary pleasures that pervade daily life?

Don't Raise the Bar?

I don't think ever-increasing expectations are inevitable, although fighting against them requires some strategizing. First, note that while Quoidbach's participants savored less after thinking about their wealth of prior experiences, doing the opposite tended to enhance savoring.[23] In other words, even if you've seen and done a lot, remind yourself of all that you still want to experience.

Along these lines, gratitude can be a powerful antidote to an increasing sense of ho-hum, particularly if that ho-humness is accompanied by the belief that your extraordinary experiences are the sorts of things you *deserve*. Expressing gratitude may directly counteract this effect. One study found that writing a gratitude letter instilled a greater sense of humility compared to a neutral writing prompt, and a similar effect was seen when gratitude was expressed daily over a two-week period.[24] Gratitude expressions—telling someone else why you are so thankful for them—removes self-focus and shines a spotlight on the key role others play in our lives. By extension, taking time out to reflect on your travels, focusing specifically on how fortunate you are to be having them, might help foster a perspective of wonder and gratitude.

Also, any given location contains multitudes of layers. The first time I visited Florence I was wowed by the David, the Ponte Vecchio, and the Uffizi: all the art and architecture that tourists naturally seek out. The next time I visited, I spent more time wandering through less touristy neighborhoods and the outlying countryside, in more of a slow-travel kind of way. It was a vastly different experience—special in its own way. One piece of advice to maintain the wonder is to go deeper. Immerse. Learning more about the history or culture of the place you're visiting can assist in this, too.

Finally, travel with someone who has seen less, and let his or her enjoyment be contagious. My mother helped me appreciate Iowa far more than I would have on my own, even as I longed for the Rockies.

TO SAVOR, TO PRESERVE, OR TO SHARE?

Savoring is admittedly a broad concept, an umbrella term that encapsulates multiple ways of attending to and amplifying our positive feelings. But whether you're savoring a meal, a scenic view, or even a conversation, one thing is required—focus. Our ability to savor is severely compromised when our attention is divided. Maybe this is why we long to get away from it all: so that we might find the single-minded focus needed to examine, appreciate, and be present.

Funny, then, how we have this uncanny knack of removing ourselves from the moments that might be the most worthy of savoring. When something beautiful or noteworthy presents itself, we are faced with some conflicting desires: First, we want to be there, in that moment, mentally, emotionally, even spiritually, wholly focused on what lies before us. Second, we want to hold on to that moment, to preserve it, to make it ours. And third, we want to share it with others who aren't there to witness it.

Until very recently, these goals rarely came into direct conflict. You might have seen a perfect coastal sunset, the sky varying shades of pink, orange, and yellow, the reflection glistening on the ocean. You took out your camera, composed a few shots, and—for most amateur photographers—went back to the business of watching the sun go down. You would look forward to getting the film developed once you got home—maybe the photos would be good, maybe not—and then you could share them with friends and family first-hand, reliving the experience as you did.

But now, the needs to savor, preserve, and share exist concurrently and seldom harmoniously. You might be initially wowed by the sunset, but instead of simply and quietly basking in its beauty, your smartphone almost reflexively comes out of your pocket. After taking a few shots, it's all too easy to crop, filter, and Instagram them for all the world to see (and then keep logging in to see who has liked the photo). By the time all this fumbling is done, the sun has gone down. Perhaps the moment may live on digitally, but your first-hand experience of it has been dramatically altered in the process.

These three goals—savoring, preserving, and sharing—are all very well-intentioned. But while savoring is related to a number of positive outcomes, such as optimism, resilience, emotional stability, and happiness, the effects of preserving special moments and sharing them on social media are more questionable.[25]

THE HIGH PRICE OF PRESERVATION

We have a deep need to preserve beautiful but fleeting moments such as those encountered while traveling, because the fact that they exist only in time is just too sad to face. Isn't this what drives a tourist in Paris to videotape his visit to Notre Dame, take selfies in front of the Arc de Triomphe, and buy a miniature Eiffel Tower to put on his knick-knack shelf back home? It's a means of coping, along the lines of, "No, this experience isn't *really* over! Look at all the reminders I'm going to have!"

I once traveled in Europe with a friend who refused to take photographs, claiming it took her out of the moment. She said not to worry, that she was taking "mental photographs." It was back in the days of bulky film cameras, and she was happily unencumbered by all of the equipment the rest of us were toting around. She was just looking, taking it all in. Yet it made me uncomfortable, almost sad for her. Didn't she want to *keep* these precious moments?

What flawed logic this was: that capturing an image on film—particularly as mindlessly as I was doing it—was somehow making it *mine*. Why were her mental photographs inferior? Might they actually be better, somehow?

While these nagging thoughts didn't keep me from loading rolls of film and clicking the shutter, I started noticing the behavior of the tourists around me as we roamed Paris. I wondered about a guy filming the interior of Notre Dame with a massive camcorder. Was he really seeing it, or was he missing it even as he preserved it for later? (And would he even watch it later?) Was there a downside to turning away from the Arc de Triomphe and posing for a picture in front of it, as opposed to just standing before it and taking it all in?

Given the rapid rise of digital photography, these questions have become even more pertinent. We can take a seemingly infinite number of pictures, capturing a vista or building from every angle—maybe even recruiting a drone to hover above and do the work for us—and subjecting the resulting images to various filters, fun borders, and cropping tools. Even amateur photographers can now take gorgeous, creative shots. It is undoubtedly fun, but what does it do for our experience of a moment? Does preserving it for the future do something to detract from it in the present?

In some respects, yes. One recent study found that those who took photographs of the works they viewed in an art museum showed poorer recall of those works compared to people who didn't take photographs.[26] Essentially, when used without conscious intent, a camera can serve as an external hard drive for our memories. But, interestingly, those who were asked to hone in on and photograph a specific detail of an artwork—a brushstroke or a specific part of an object, say—showed *better* recall of the works, presumably because they weren't just mindlessly snapping but were actually processing much more deeply.

Also consider a recent series of nine studies, conducted both in the field and in the laboratory, that found that while photography does tend to enhance enjoyment of positive experiences, it's actually more complicated than that.[27] If a person is already fully engaged in a particular activity—in a flow state, for instance—then photographing it doesn't seem to add anything. Plus, if photography actually interferes with the ability to engage with an activity—by breaking the flow—it can actually *reduce* enjoyment. In short, some experiences are so physically, mentally, or emotionally involving that photography can only detract from their extraordinary nature. It's really the more mundane, everyday experiences that are most enhanced by photography. So perhaps taking that photo of your delicious morning bagel might make it seem more special, but repeatedly interrupting your ski run or kayaking trip to snap photos might just spoil the fun.

Preserving moments can even encourage a special type of procrastination, where the hard work of savoring is put off for a later time, maybe never to come at all. A student in my research lab recently relayed her experience during a summer study abroad trip in Italy when "church fatigue" had begun to set in: "The first few churches we toured had me in awe—I couldn't get enough of the intricate detail, the beautiful stained glass, and the feeling that the building struck in me. However, after seeing what felt like the hundredth church in the span of three days, I wasn't feeling that sense of awe anymore. The buildings were just as breathtaking as the first few I had seen, but I just couldn't appreciate them anymore. I was still taking a million pictures of every church we went into, but only because it felt like 'the thing to do' and not because I was captivated by the beauty. At the time, I thought I'd go back and look at the pictures and be able to appreciate them when I wasn't used to seeing churches on every corner, but I don't. Now, looking back through my pictures, I scroll through the album and all I see is church after church after church." Both research and personal experience suggest that preserving moments for the future doesn't always provide the emotional payoff we think it will.

Preservation Recommendation

We're not going to stop taking photos. The need to hang on to the brief, precious, and privileged moments of life runs deep. How can we do it better?

One trick is to engage in *mindful* photography, using the camera not as your eyes or your memory bank, but as a tool that helps you hone in on what around you is worth capturing. To test this idea, I've done several experiments instructing college students to take mindful photographs in their everyday lives.[28] Some were told, "Try to make your pictures creative, beautiful, and meaningful to you. Try to capture the best view of the subject matter. Do not rush through this exercise. Instead, try to take everything in and take the best pictures that you can."

I found that over the course of two weeks, these students reported higher levels of appreciation, motivation, and vitality than those who were asked to take more neutral, informative photographs of places that weren't as meaningful to them. They also enjoyed the activity more. In glimpsing the photographs they took, I could see why. The mindful-photo group had captured moments of friends laughing, of notable buildings on campus, of gardens, and of favorite foods. Rather ordinary experiences, yes, but they didn't seem to be mindlessly snapping at any old thing. In fact, I'd like to think that many of their photos were creative and thoughtful enough to go on the admissions office webpage. Mindful photography seems to facilitate savoring, teaching us to see what is around us with a more careful and appreciative eye. Ask yourself: what about your experience is *most* worth capturing?

Another way to practice mindful photography is to intentionally limit the number of photographs you allow yourself to take, instead of capitalizing on a seemingly limitless amount of digital memory. This can be especially useful with those extraordinary experiences that photography seems to diminish.[29] There is no magic number, but what about ten photos of a hike, or three of a famous building, or just one of your meal? Set the number ahead of time, so you know to be selective. It may help you balance the need to preserve with the upsides of being present and in the moment. A similar tip is to try and take all your photos early in an experience, and then be done with it. This way, you don't have to manage the anxiety of not capturing a meaningful experience, but once the job is done, you might be better able to relax and appreciate. I've found this especially useful at historic sites, famous buildings, and on out-and-back hikes.

A different technique involves putting the camera away completely, and finding a more thoughtful way to commemorate what you see. Author Alain de Botton argues that while the need to hold on to these beautiful, fleeting moments is exceedingly powerful, taking pictures—at least for the casual photographer—is an inferior way of doing so.[30] It's all too easy to point and shoot mindlessly, mentally glossing over key details, perhaps thinking you'll attend to all of them later. Other preservation techniques, while more effortful, force us to go deeper.

Rather than taking photographs, how about some word painting, in which you do a vivid written description of a particular scene? Imagine the sunset, with the multicolored sky, the clouds, the reflection on the water. Try your best to bring it to life for someone who isn't witnessing it. Or, draw the scene before you. This doesn't require an easel and a palette of pastels. It only takes a sheet of paper and a pencil.

This summer, I took my study abroad students out to the waterfront in Stockholm, Sweden. I randomly assigned them to either verbally describe or draw out some aspect of what was before them. There was definitely some reluctance, especially for those asked to draw. And I completely get it. Aside from dancing, there is nothing I'm worse at than drawing. I stressed the fact that the final product is of very little importance. It's true! The drawing is simply an exercise to encourage deeper processing. Some reactions from the students a few weeks later included, "The drawing activity helped me to notice details that I took for granted. Since I've gotten home, it's helped me to better remember what it was like to be in Stockholm"; "Later, during my solo travels, I started taking fewer pictures and instead wrote down the things I saw in an attempt to appreciate all the details in the moment"; "I realized I was noticing information coming from all of my senses, not just sight alone. I took note of the smells and sounds as well as the scenery around me"; and "After coming home, I realized that the word painting assignment is one of my most vivid memories . . . I feel like I can still smell the cinnamon buns I wrote about coming out of the oven, hear the friendly conversation of people passing by, and remember the feeling of the warm morning sun on my skin."

SOCIAL MEDIA: THIEF OF JOY?

Let's say you've taken that sunset photograph. Come on. I know you did. The need to preserve is irresistible. Now, do you upload it to Facebook or Instagram and wait for the "likes" and expressions of wonder and jealousy to pour in? Again, it's a surprisingly complicated decision.

On the upside, you might feel proud of your photo and truly want to put it out there.[31] And you may get a heightened burst of appreciation upon hearing people's positive responses. Or you might experience a moment of connection with the people you miss back home, which is especially nice when you're traveling alone and wish you could share the experience with someone.

But the downside is that all of that cropping, filtering, and posting of the perfect travel photograph takes time and pulls focus from what's around you. Being preoccupied by your friends' reactions—or the lack thereof—will likely pull you out of the present moment. It might make you appreciate your good fortune, but through an indirect route: "Hey, my cousin Tony just liked my picture! Yeah . . . he's back home in Toledo while I'm here in Bali relaxing. I really am lucky." Contrast that with the purer form of appreciation you might feel by just taking in the sunset, savoring it quietly and with focused attention. Both are nice, yes. But savoring-by-proxy just feels inferior. It's happening through the pathway of social comparison.[32] Even when you're decidedly better off than those around you—in person or online—there can be an emotional cost to checking out what everyone else is up to. Comparing your life to Cousin Tony's, even if he looks like a chump in contrast, is negatively related to happiness.[33] Research shows that comparison, as Theodore Roosevelt said, truly is the thief of joy.

And there are other risks of social media overuse. You might casually log on to share an update, and, as you mindlessly scroll through your feed, you can't help but notice all the fun your friends back home are having, which is an even more insidious type of social comparison. Nothing can beat the sunsets of Bali, of course, but . . . they sure do look happy at that baby shower or that pub crawl. Homesickness can be an inadvertent result of social media logins. One study found that, at least for college students spending a month abroad, social media use related to FOMO—fear of missing out—even as it also effectively kept students connected with home.[34]

Additionally, and maybe more importantly, recent research has found that sharing extraordinary experiences has a surprising social cost, creating a divide between you and those who don't share your experiences.[35] Imagine you post that photograph, with some brief commentary about how incredible Bali is. To you, you're simply sharing this happy moment with others, hoping to make your joy contagious, maybe even virtually transporting the less fortunate to the tropics. Turns out, though, this isn't what's happening back in Toledo. The folks back home don't really share your joy to the degree you expect. When we self-promote—and let's face it, sharing vacation photos on social media does contain an element of this—we underestimate how annoying we are.

In one study, participants were asked to construct a hypothetical social media profile containing five facts about themselves.[36] Some were given the explicit goal of making others like them. Naturally, then, they opted to share impressive things about themselves—accomplishments and exciting life events, for instance. But their approach backfired. When raters viewed these profiles, they rated their authors as less likeable and more conceited, but no more successful or interesting, than authors of more neutral profiles. Although the judges did not know the owners of the profiles they were viewing, the implication is that the messages we put out on social media, as well-intentioned as they may be, might fail to transmit the positive messages we're trying our best to convey.

These possible downsides don't stop us from sharing—or maybe even amping up—our travel adventures for the viewing public. A recent *New York Times* article featured tourists behaving badly—jumping out of hotel windows into dangerously shallow swimming pools, climbing onto ancient Greek sculptures, posing naked in front of religious sites—all in pursuit of the perfect, unique travel photo to share on social media.[37]

For some travelers, photography has become less about the place and more about oneself in this place, doing something remarkable for the world to see. Indeed, a colleague recently told me about a conversation he had overheard among students while leading a study abroad trip. They were scrutinizing their choice of outfit for the next day's sightseeing tour (and apparent photo shoot), which seemed to trump the historical and cultural significance of what they were about to see, or at least pose in front of. A recent piece in the *Chronicle of Higher Education* concluded with, "Navigating the new digital environment is perhaps the thorniest challenge facing the study-abroad profession, given the complexity of the relationships and trade-offs inherent in every choice we make—but the stakes are too high for us to simply ignore it."[38]

Finding a Healthy Middle Ground

Indeed, these seemingly simple decisions—exactly what is photo-worthy, what picture should be shared on social media, and how attractive one looks in said photo—can add distraction and even stress to a trip. It can also fly in the face of savoring.[39] There is starting to be some industry pushback. Selfie sticks, those extendable devices that you can attach to your phone to take better self-portraits, have become so ubiquitous and irritating that museums and theme parks are banning them. High-end hotels have begun creating technology-free zones, with no wifi and no televisions.[40]

But perhaps we can take the reins and impose some limits on ourselves, keeping in mind the simple yet hard-to-follow rule of "everything in moderation." The *occasional* email check, the *occasional* Facebook post. Allowing yourself to take, say, five photographs of a location, so that you're forced to really hone in on what is special about what lies before you. Checking email sparingly (a wise move even while you're *not* traveling, as more daily email-checks are related to worse moods).[41] Giving yourself one social media check-in per day or so, which might actually help you identify and appreciate your favorite moments as you thoughtfully debate exactly what you'd like to share with the world.

With 70 million photos being shared on Instagram every month, photo-sharing has meaningful consequences for both the poster and the audience alike.[42] As travel blogger and photographer Sruthi Vijayan argues, "It's fun to show off a bit—the world should know you are in Cabo and that *CABO IS AMAZING.* But if the premise of your vacation rests around checking into places and staring into your phone instead of looking at the person across the table, then why travel at all?"[43]

HAPPY TRAVEL TIPS
FOR SAVORING THE MOMENT

In order to be a present-minded and appreciative traveler, you might ask yourself these questions both before and during your trip.

- *Will my itinerary allow me to slow down, notice, and really appreciate what I'm experiencing?* Especially on a far-flung or once-in-a-lifetime kind of trip, there can be an understandable motivation to pack in as much as possible. If you're flying all the way to Vienna, say, why not also try to squeeze in Prague while you're over there? Ask yourself if you'll still manage to be able to see—*really see*—what you're seeing with the itinerary you've created.

- *What strategies will I use to be present and really savor my experiences?* Chances are, not all of the strategies I mentioned here—from gratitude journaling to word painting to counting down the hours until your trip ends—will appeal to everyone. And that's fine. Research shows that you need to choose and commit to a strategy that suits your unique personality, schedule, and goals.[44] So note which sounded most like you, start doing it, and practice it with regularity. Who knows, you might want to continue it even after your trip ends!
- *Does my technology and social media use detract from my ability to savor? If so, how will I moderate my usage?* This isn't a problem for everyone, but if it is for you (and you'd probably know if it was), exactly how will you keep the temptation to preserve and share moments in check?

SEVEN

THE ULTIMATE RELATIONSHIP TEST: WHAT YOU NEED TO KNOW BEFORE TRAVELING WITH SOMEONE

Never go on trips with anyone you do not love.

—Ernest Hemingway

When traveling with someone, take large doses of patience and tolerance with your morning coffee.

—Helen Hayes

It was August of 2010 and I was taking my first turn around the psychology building at James Madison University as a new faculty member. Classes weren't in session yet so the building was mostly empty, but I saw one faculty office door open. I tentatively approached to introduce myself, and within a few minutes, discovered that my new colleague Jessica and I shared a love of road trips, karaoke, and the romantic comedies of the 1980s. And somehow, in that short conversation, we decided that we simply *had* to take a last-hurrah, end-of-summer trip to the beach. I left thrilled to have connected with someone so quickly. But I couldn't help also thinking, "Yeah right, like *that's* going to happen." I chalked it up to both of us being excited to have found a new potential friend.

I was wrong. We sent a few emails back and forth and within a couple of days, we'd booked a small cottage in North Carolina's Outer Banks for four nights. The following week, we loaded the car up with a cooler, beach chairs, magazines, and snacks, and set out on the five-hour drive.

This was a pretty risky get-to-know-you move, I now realize. Upon hitting the road, we could have come to the awful realization that we had nothing to talk about. Worse yet, we might have discovered some serious incompatibilities that would have all but destroyed our ability to be amiable colleagues, much less good friends.

What happened instead were spirited discussions of topics ranging from our philosophies of teaching to our dating histories to how to get cute clothes for a fraction of the retail price. I got the lowdown on life in Harrisonburg and shared some of my recent adventures living in Los Angeles and Portland. We read magazines on the beach, sang karaoke at a dive bar, bought tacky souvenirs, and chatted late into the night over rum-and-Coke-Zeros. There was no tension, no awkwardness, no drama, and we remain good friends and travel companions to this day.

Would we have this kind of easy, close relationship today had we not taken this trip? Hard to say. My guess is that we'd be cordial, certainly, but it's more likely that we would resemble colleagues much more than we do friends.

NO SURER WAY

Mark Twain was spot-on when he said, "I have found out that there ain't no surer way to find out whether you like people or hate them than to travel with them." What is it about travel that is so telling? First, there's simply the sheer quantity of time we're spending with someone. In real life, we're seldom with *anyone* twenty-four hours a day, seven days a week. Not our family, not our friends, and certainly not our work colleagues. Because of this, we're usually privy to only a thin slice of people's lives: the office, parties, choir practice, or church. This makes our knowledge of them both limited and specific.

Minus our beach trip, I would know only a small bit about Jessica: Jessica-at-work, maybe occasionally Jessica-at-a-restaurant. Both of those contexts are governed by strong rules and norms—dress a certain way, act professionally, mask your bad mood, keep conversation at the appropriate level of disclosure. Naturally, the whole, complicated, real person inside is hard to unearth in these restrictive contexts.

But travel is governed by far fewer rules. I mean, really, how *are* you supposed to act sharing a beach cottage with a virtual stranger? Now *here* we have a situation in which you can quickly get to know many sides of a person. Also, when you travel with others, there comes a point when you have to let your hair down and just be real. As polite and guarded as you set out to be, in all of this time together, the true person inside will either make herself known or implode under the pressure of trying to keep up appearances. At work and at the occasional dinner, happy hour, or office party, it's easy to project the image you want the world to see. You can't keep that up when traveling. It's too exhausting.

While I wasn't explicitly sizing her up at the time, upon looking back, I realize that I was actually learning quite a lot about Jessica. I was getting a chance to see her first thing in the morning, in the middle of an argument with her boyfriend, while we attempted to share the expenses of the trip, and as we had to negotiate which of us would get to sing Reba McIntire's "Fancy" at karaoke after a few drinks. I witnessed how she coped with daily nuisances, like not being able to find a vegetarian-friendly restaurant, as well as new challenges, like stand-up paddleboarding. I also saw how she handled me and my idiosyncrasies, like my 6 a.m. internal alarm clock, early morning running compulsion, and introverted need for "me time." This is a lot of information to gain about someone and a very condensed period of time in which to gain it. As a result, after that week I knew more about Jessica than I do about some people who have been in my life for years.

I've learned some new and wonderful things about my friends as we've traveled together. When I was traveling around Italy with my good friend Kate and the airline lost her luggage for several days, I saw how easily she was able to laugh it off and still have a great time. I'd known her for about ten years at this point, but this period of travel stress revealed something new. When I started traveling with my boyfriend early in our relationship, I saw how easygoing and agreeable he is. He's open to anything I want to do, and if I suggest a restaurant or activity that's disappointing, he doesn't blame me. And when I traveled cross-country with my mother, I saw the sense of wonder she took into every experience (remember Iowa?), which seldom reveals itself in our hometown of Reading, Pennsylvania.

But for every relationship that has been strengthened by travel, there is one that has been fractured. Traveling with someone might reveal things that you simply don't like and never knew before: a fear of new cultural experiences and a general sense of closed-mindedness; excessive rigidity and an inability to compromise or deviate from routines; frugality, grouchiness, clinginess . . . the list goes on and on. Or it can just unearth general incompatibilities that are irrelevant in daily life. Maybe you're a morning person while your friend is a night owl. Perhaps you're bored silly at your friend's cherished art museums, while she in turn despises the nature walks you love. You might never have known this before. You might not have thought to ask or care.

In this chapter, I'll discuss how to determine whether or not you and a potential travel partner are compatible. When I say "travel partner" or "travel companion," I'm referred to anyone you're traveling with. By choice, by chance . . . or under duress. Romantic partners, friends, family members, work colleagues: whomever. And, because even the most well-suited companions are subject to travel's inevitable stresses, I'll offer some tips on how you might deal with them successfully to maintain and even enhance your relationship.

FINDING YOUR MATCH

Many of us don't have the luxury (or the struggle, depending on your point of view) of choosing whom we travel with. When we sign that marriage license or have that child, we're implicitly stating that these people will be the companions of our future travels. But let's say for a moment that you *are* in the position to choose. Maybe you're considering going to a work conference with a colleague you don't know terribly well. Maybe you're putting together a girls' getaway weekend and are trying to decide whom you should invite. Or maybe you're in the passionate throes of a new romance and are spontaneously invited to jet off to Paris together.

In these types of situations, where there are so many unknowns, how do you determine whether traveling together would be a good idea? According to Amy Van Doran, founder of the New York City matchmaking service the Modern Love Club, "Finding someone you travel well with is just as hard, if not harder, than finding a romantic match."

Travel Personalities, Revisited

In chapter 2 I introduced the Big Five, those five broad personality traits that capture most of the key differences among people. Recall that two of them, openness to experience and extroversion, reveal quite a lot about how you are as a traveler, generally speaking. They are also important to consider when planning to travel with someone else. As we discussed, the highly open person gravitates to the novel and the exotic. This might not mesh well with someone extremely low on openness, who has a vastly different comfort zone. One person may want to take chances and immerse herself in local culture, while the other prefers the comfort of the familiar. If these differences are minor, perhaps this pair could complement one another nicely, with the more open person nudging her companion to take more risks and vice versa. But if the differences are extreme, conflict can easily occur.

Differences in extroversion/introversion can play out in a similar way. The extrovert would enjoy group travel and interacting with strangers far more than an introvert would, but introverts and extroverts might actually pair up well. The extrovert would feel more comfortable doing the work of asking directions, chatting up servers and cab drivers, and connecting with locals, while the introvert would be more suited to learning the local history from a guidebook or museum. In her book *No Baggage*, the reflective Clara Bensen finds herself traveling with a textbook extrovert. She remarks, "He pulled me out of my safe observational tower and down into the sparkling chaos of the world, and when the chaos went too far, I pulled him up to consider the view from my tower."[1] Again, assuming neither tendency is too extreme, this might be a great match, but you can easily see the incompatibility between an extrovert who wants to spend every night out clubbing paired with an introvert who never looks up from her novel.

The three other Big Five traits also relate to how you might travel with others. Consider agreeableness, briefly assessed by the extent to which you'd describe yourself as "easygoing, warm, and sympathetic." Naturally, you want your companion to be high on this trait. This person would be willing to compromise, would forgive your quirks, and be receptive to your opinions and preferences. You'd also prefer him to be low on neuroticism, the tendency to be "easily upset, anxious, and temperamental." He wouldn't get too worked up if things didn't work out perfectly. He would be generally even-tempered and emotionally stable. Finally, with all of the forethought and attention to detail that travel requires, at least one person needs to be conscientious, measured by how much a person describes himself as "conscientious, dependable, and organized."[2] This person would be naturally inclined to double-check for passports, ensure you're at the airport on time, remember to bring the map, and so many other unexciting yet critically important tasks.

Most of the research on compatibility and relationship success as a function of these traits has been done on long-term, married couples, but it is still relevant here, given the stresses and intensity of travel. The traits of agreeableness and emotional stability (the flip side of neuroticism) are highly related to relationship satisfaction.[3] These traits promote smooth interpersonal interactions and willingness to compromise and are related to fewer instances of heated conflict.[4]

Indeed, ability and willingness to communicate your needs in a calm and respectful way may well be the overarching trait underlying happy travel. Two people need not share the same interests, sense of adventure, or sleep-wake cycle in order to travel well together. But they *do* need to be able to convey their goals for the trip, voice their concerns, and compromise when planning. They need to be able to regulate their emotions when tensions inevitably run high. In short, agreeableness and emotional stability are of paramount importance.

Sizing Up Traits

It's probably a bit too heavy-handed to give a potential partner a battery of personality tests before you commit to traveling together. But maybe you can get a sense of their key traits more indirectly. They *do* have a way of playing out in everyday life. For example, in one intensive exploratory study, undergraduate participants agreed to have two days worth of their daily conversations recorded with an unobtrusive voice recorder.[5] A group of judges who didn't know the people they were rating were given the daunting task of listening to the entirety of these conversations, and then made their best guesses as to where the speakers would fall on each of the Big Five personality traits. Because the original set of participants had completed a validated measure of the Big Five before the recording phase had begun, the researchers could then see how well the judges' impressions aligned with reality.

They found that even though they were privy to only a thin slice of information about the participants, the judges were fairly accurate at guessing most of the traits.

So what are the clues? Some are very much what you might expect: extroverts talk more, and spend more time in the presence of others. Agreeableness was accurately assessed by language use, particularly the absence of curse words.[6] Because these two traits are very interpersonal in nature, they are fairly easy to assess in this kind of conversational data.

But there are a couple clues to the other, "quieter" traits as well: conscientiousness was related to time spent in class and on campus. (For nonstudents, assume you can generalize this to other socially prescribed responsible behaviors: time spent at work, running errands, exercising, etc.). There were surprisingly few reliable conversational clues to neuroticism, although time spent arguing was one of them. Openness was also tough for the judges to accurately detect. Time spent in public spaces like coffee shops and restaurants, rather than at home, did provide one indicator, but it was fairly weak. It's not that openness can't be detected in everyday life. It's more likely that given that it has a lot to do with a person's *inner* life (curiosity, intellect, wide-ranging interests), it might better reveal itself in nonconversational ways. For example, possessing a wide range of books, music, and art is a research-supported sign of openness.[7] So for this one, you might go beyond conversation and spend some time looking through the things that reflect a person's interests and inner life, like a bookshelf, magazine rack, or iTunes playlist.

Consider some other ways in which personality traits may reveal themselves in everyday situations:

Extroversion: This one's easy. How chatty is this person? Does she have a lot of friends and an active and varied social life? Does she seem to enjoy spending a lot of free time alone? At a social event, is she engaged in conversation or is she hanging back?

Agreeableness: If you're trying to decide on a restaurant or a movie, is the person willing to compromise? Is the person a good listener when you need advice or support? Does she express warmth and concern for a wide range of people?

Neuroticism: Does the person have frequent mood swings? Excessive anxiety? Stress over her decisions and their potential outcomes?

Conscientiousness: Is the person chronically late? Always financially strapped? Is her house or car constantly a mess?

Openness: Is the person willing to try ethnic restaurants and exotic foods? How about kayaking or caving? Accompany you to a modern art exhibit or experimental theatre performance? Is she open to political or religious perspectives that are not necessarily what she holds? Are new and exotic things of interest to her, or brushed off as "weird"?

Food, Wine, Views

Important and comprehensive as they are, the Big Five are very broad and general tendencies. According to personality psychologist Dan McAdams, when making sense of people, we often seek "a more detailed and nuanced description of a flesh-and-blood, in-the-world person, striving to do things over time, situated in place and role, expressing herself or himself in and through strategies, tactics, plans, and goals."[8]

Depending on the kind of trip you plan to take, you might want to get a little more specific, sleuthing out very precise and relevant things. Depending on what's most important to you, questions to work into conversation might include:

- Are you an early riser or a night owl?
- How physically active are you?

- What's your attitude toward spending money?
- Do you need to have some time to yourself most days?
- Do you travel light or pack everything but the kitchen sink?
- Do you plan to bring work along with you when you travel?
- Is it important to be able to connect to wifi and social media?

As was the case with directly sizing up another person's traits, these questions are undoubtedly blunt. Because an inquisition won't exactly endear a potential travel companion to you, the information needs to be gathered in a more subtle and socially appropriate way.

You can always make it about you. For example, I try (often in vain) to disconnect from social media when traveling, and it can be annoying when friends are constantly on their devices. To try and suss out whether a companion will be glued to her screen, I might say something like, "I am so burnt out on Facebook. I can't wait to unplug" and see what the person says. I might check out her social media profiles. Does she post constantly, or more selectively? To feel out how active she might be, I might enthusiastically share a cool-sounding hike with her to gauge her reaction. And for all of my frugality, I know the emotional value of a killer meal and am more than willing to splurge on a taxi to my hotel after a red-eye flight. Traveling with someone who is an extreme penny pincher would be a huge drag for me. To gauge this one, I might suggest we make a reservation at a hot new restaurant that's on the pricey side, and see what she says. Or, for something this important, I might just be direct. "After a long flight, I like to get a cab to the hotel. Is that okay?"

Finally, try a more general and yet potentially revealing question: "What was the best trip you ever took?" "What's your perfect travel day?" Or even, "What three words define your vision for this trip?"

When we planned our first vacation together, my friend Kate and I jokingly crafted what would become our travel mantra: "Food, wine, views." There's a lot of information in those three little words. It told me that spending a lot of money in restaurants was going to happen, but we cared less about staying in fancy hotels and buying souvenirs. We wouldn't be hitting a ton of museums or historical sites, and we'd probably prioritize pretty seaside or mountain villages over loud cities. Turns out, all of this came to pass, and without really trying, we'd communicated our goals in a lighthearted way with these three little words.

Another Piece of the Equation: You

Before your trip, you also have to be honest about your own foibles and idiosyncrasies. We all have them. While travel can be transformative and while you might feel compelled to push yourself out of your comfort zone, *you are still you*, even in a foreign country.

So if you know from past experience that staying in youth hostels or couchsurfing is just not your thing, you should tell your budget-minded friend this right away. If you can't possibly have a conversation before your first cup of coffee, let that be known too.

Perhaps most importantly, if you're an introvert and need your alone time, be clear about that up front. Especially for those of us who spend a lot of time by ourselves, suddenly being with someone 24/7 can be jarring, no matter how much we cherish that person. Indicate up front that your need to have some time alone doesn't signify any kind of a problem; it's just part of who you are. Similarly, be clear about your specific interests and goals for the trip. You may want to exercise in the mornings while your travel partner would rather sleep in, or you might love art museums while your partner doesn't. It's important that you both get to pursue your own interests, or resentment may slowly build. As the moments play out in real time, these things can easily become fodder for conflict. If made known ahead of time, they can be filed away as personal quirks that can be planned around.[9]

A Final Test

Before you take the plunge, here is a quick true-or-false test you and your potential travel partner can use to check in with yourselves:

1. We have successfully traveled together in the past.
2. We're on the same page with where we'd like to spend our money (restaurants, lodging, shopping, etc.).
3. We have similar attitudes about crowded places.
4. We have similar standards for comfort and security.
5. We are pretty similar in our need for adventure.
6. We've discussed how to break up our shared expenditures, like a hotel room, cab ride, or restaurant bill.
7. We share similar views on transportation (taxis versus public transit versus walking).
8. We both value good food and drink.
9. We are similar in our need for structure and planning.
10. We have similar energy and activity levels.
11. We are both able to laugh in the face of stress or setback.
12. We feel comfortable sharing our opinions with one another.
13. We are both willing to compromise.
14. We match on how much alone time versus time spent together we need.
15. We have successfully managed conflict in the past.

If you answered "true" to most or all of these questions, it sounds like you are well-prepared to travel together. If your reaction was largely one of uncertainty and head-scratching, sounds like you have some more research to do. And if most of your responses were "false!" well, it sounds like you have quite a lot of negotiating ahead of you.

Of course, not everything on this list will matter to everyone in the same way. What jumped out as a must-have? What seems less central?

Different attitudes toward spending money may jump out as a deal-breaker, while differing energy levels could be something you could work with. This process of prioritizing may help you decide what to focus on the most.

Want a more true-to-life test of travel compatibility? How about taking a brief getaway before plunging into something bigger? A car trip of a few hours before a cross-country road trip. A fairly close-by weekend away before two weeks in a foreign country. The more you can mimic what your vacation will be like, the better you'll be at determining how this person may be as a longer-term travel companion.

COPING WITH THE INEVITABLE

Even if you and your travel partners are exceeding agreeable, emotionally stable, and fundamentally compatible, tensions are likely to arise. Why? Because travel is stressful and intense. Things that might roll off your back while at home can become all-consuming when you're together constantly, on a trip that you've invested in heavily.

For one, the simple act of getting to your location is physically taxing and draining in ways that are hard to fully anticipate. Jet lag makes us moody and tired, yet all the advice tells us to ignore our exhaustion and push through so that we can get set on our new time zone. Nothing like utter exhaustion and disorientation to fan the flames of romance and connection! Even a road trip, which is far less jarring to our bodies, can make us grumpy and weary as the endless miles are accompanied by clashing music tastes, incompatible bathroom and hunger schedules, and a whiny chorus of "Are we there yet?"

And as you settle into your travels, problems may continue to pop up. The pressure to compromise on the day's activities and meals can be a source of tension. Constant togetherness in the confines of a small hotel room can wear you down even further. And heat, hunger, and fatigue can push you over the edge. In these tense moments, minor nuisances and grievances have the potential to erupt into serious conflict.

Damage Control

If (or, more likely, when) you find yourself in conflict while traveling, it is best to address it as soon as possible. First, identify the problem as you see it. Is your partner being too controlling? Chronically running late? Being a tightwad? Complaining excessively about the local culture? Only wanting to eat McDonalds and Starbucks?

After you've identified a specific problem, broach the subject with a calm, level-headed mindset, while in a calm and quiet location. Approaching him with an angry, accusing tone on a crowded subway car is less likely to be successful, so resist the urge. Clearly communicate the problem, and be specific, offering complaints ("I'm disappointed that we haven't tried any of the local foods") rather than general criticisms ("You are so unadventurous!").[10]

Ask questions to get to the root of the problem. Deep down, he might be anxious and uncomfortable in this new place and seeking out familiar things, like that Big Mac, might help ease his anxiety.[11] Once you know the problem, you will be better able to work through it successfully. For instance, maybe you can ease into the local food scene, going to one of those places that caters to tourists and has a menu in English. Once he warms to that, you can continue to baby-step your way toward the level of adventure you seek.

Alternatively, one or both of you may be misattributing the source of a bad mood. It's all too easy to get unknowingly tired, dehydrated, hungry, or overheated during a day of travel, and just as easy to take it out on whomever is in the line of fire. If you start to feel grumpy, check in with yourself. Could it be due to something inside of yourself, something physical? And if your partner is suddenly acting incredibly and strangely sullen, it may have nothing to do with you. He may just need a snack, some water, or a catnap.

Finally, let me stress that you might just need a break from one another, to diffuse tension, to pursue unique interests, or just to have some room to breathe. Canadian couple Dalene and Pete Heck learned this lesson when they decided to travel the world together and found their marriage being put to the test.

> When we first began our travels, we went from seeing each other only a few hours a day to being together 24/7. It was a major adjustment, and in our first few months in South America, we struggled . . . We bickered, we snapped, and we wondered if this was truly going to make us or break us. After a few months we learned a valuable lesson: Alone time is essential. When we want to take time for ourselves, we no longer worry that it's because of something the other said or did, but just that we need some space . . . Every week or so we go in our separate directions for a few hours. Pete grabs his camera and hits the streets; I usually find a quiet corner in which to write or read. And almost six years later, we're happier in our marriage than we ever thought possible.[12]

Even these experts, named *National Geographic's* Travelers of the Year in 2014, are vulnerable to the pressures of constant togetherness and really had to strategize on how to protect their relationship from the stresses of travel.

JOY DOUBLED

All of this talk of conflict and communication might call for a revision of Sartre. Hell isn't other people . . . hell is *traveling with* other people. Is it mere social convention and clever marketing that makes us believe that spending hours together in a confined space—be it car, plane, or hotel room—is the stuff of familial or romantic bliss? What does traveling with others really buy us?

Quite a lot, it appears. A Swedish proverb states that a joy shared is a joy doubled, and research confirms this idea. Positive experiences such as a sweeping mountain vista, a grand cathedral, a white sand beach, amazing food—so many of the things we seek out while traveling—are better shared.

In one study, undergraduates tasted chocolates alongside another student (who they didn't know).[13] When the other student tasted the chocolate at the exact same time, participants rated the chocolate as tastier than when the other student was present but not tasting the chocolate. This was true even though the students weren't communicating with one another.

However, not *all* experiences are better shared: having a negative experience together made it worse. A second study found that unpleasantly bitter chocolate was rated as even more unpleasant when another student ate it at the same time (as compared to when the other student was engaged in another task). Sharing an experience with someone else simply intensifies it, for better or for worse.

Why might this be? It seems to have something to do with the power of shared attention. Another line of research found that when looking at pleasant images and videos with a close other, participants attended more fully to what was before them, particularly when they thought the other person was also paying close attention.[14] They also reported feeling happier after. This was not the case when the close other experienced the same thing at a slightly different time. It was also not the case when sharing an experience with a stranger. An ordinary example is when you attend more fully to a TV program or a movie when watching it with a loved one, versus watching it alone or even when the two of you watch separately and then discuss it later. Not only will your enjoyment be ratcheted up, but so might your fear or sadness. There is something special about sharing reality with someone with whom we connect.[15]

Therefore, the joys of travel will be intensified when you share them with a close other, preferably someone who really gets you (on the flipside, the sorrows and anxieties—if they are felt together—may also be amplified). Do note that, in order to isolate and control key variables, these studies were conducted in the stark laboratory of a university rather than on a beach or a mountaintop. But given the comparative richness and intensity of the real world, you might reasonably argue that these effects could be even *stronger* outside of the lab. So stand on the mountaintop or beach alongside your friend. Take that first sip of wine at the same time as your partner. It might just make a positive experience even richer.

How Travel Makes the Heart Grow Fonder

Travel provides an escape from the daily grind and allows for relaxation, adventure, and personal growth, sure. But what can it do to fan the flames of romance?

Studies suggest that it can do quite a lot.

Perhaps by breaking out of their daily roles and routines, vacationing couples can see one another in a different and more romantic light; not as coparents or financial partners, but as footloose, fancy-free, sexy partners-in-adventure. Indeed, 90 percent of American couples embarking on a cruise reported that sex was the top activity on their itinerary. Perhaps not surprisingly then, 80 percent returned home feeling more connected to their partners, while 67 percent reported feeling more in love.[16] Another study revealed that couples reported being intimate more on a one-week vacation than they did during two months at home. That's essentially *eight times more often!*

Of course, one could argue that couples who opt to take a romantic vacation together are probably not the ones struggling with deep dissatisfaction. And while causal conclusions are hard to draw here (meaning, does a romantic vacation *cause* increased satisfaction, connection, and fireworks?), several studies provide strong suggestive evidence. Arthur Aron's experimental research on the inner workings of love, passion, and commitment has found that couples, even those married for a long time, show reignited excitement and satisfaction with their relationships when doing a novel activity with their partners.[17] What seems to happen is that as you engage in new and exciting activities with a partner, you can't help but extend and generalize the positive feelings associated with the activity to that person. This may be especially true for physiologically arousing kinds of activities: a roller coaster ride, a scary movie, or a vigorous hike. It happens without us knowing, yet the effects can enliven our relationships in powerful and surprising ways.[18] Because these studies were done under rigorous constraints in the laboratory, the novel activity was something akin to a three-legged race. But outside of the lab, what is more novel than the stuff of travel—exploring a foreign city, trying an exotic cuisine, or learning to scuba dive? It's yet another argument for adding some challenge and novelty into a vacation!

Want to supplement your vacation with even more relationship-enhancing techniques? Consider the work of psychologist Shelly Gable, who studies the phenomenon of *capitalization*. She's found that when one person in a couple shares something good that's happened to him, it provides the other with the opportunity to express understanding and share in his enthusiasm. Let's say you and your husband decide to spend a few hours apart during one day of your vacation. When you meet up for dinner and he tells you that he had a fantastic time at a contemporary art museum, how do you respond?

Gable has found that partners can respond in a number of ways, some of which are hazardous to the health of the relationship. You might actively squash his enthusiasm with something like, "Why would you want to be inside a stuffy museum on such a beautiful day?" or one-up him by telling him that your afternoon round of golf was far superior. A much better choice would be to capitalize on his enthusiasm and use this as an opportunity for relationship-building. Express your happiness that he had such a nice afternoon. Ask questions to draw him out and get specifics. What was it about this museum that so moved him? You might learn something new about your partner in this conversation, while also making him feel understood and validated. At least in the course of everyday life, couples who use capitalization-type responses in their daily interactions report higher levels of intimacy and satisfaction with their marriages. So in addition to working them into your travels, it wouldn't hurt to try these techniques at home, too.[19]

By extension, also notice what side of your partner (or friend, or family member) you're seeing highlighted in your travels. Maybe a latent talent for navigating new places or a knack for choosing the best hole-in-the-wall dinner spot? Clara Bensen told me,

> My partner Jeff and I have traveled to 16 countries together and one thing that strengthens our relationship is carving out roles that each of us "specialize" in. Jeff is incredible with directions and can strike up a friendship with a complete stranger in under a minute, even if there's no shared language. He covers navigation and gets us into bizarre situations I'd be too shy to initiate. I'm the researcher, which typically means I handle language, history, and the scouting of off-the-beaten path destinations. Although we have vastly different personalities, we truly respect each other's skills and take the time to tell each other so. Giving each other space to do what we do best has helped us build a strong partnership on the road (and back home).[20]

So don't just notice it. When it feels appropriate and authentic to do so, play it up! Tell him he does this well, and bonus: he or she may want to keep playing this role, just to receive such warm reinforcement. Thank him for doing it, too, for an extra dose of connection and good feelings.[21]

A Beachside Breather

Less exciting but just as important is the fact that travel may also diffuse or neutralize everyday conflict, allowing couples to come at their deeper issues from a calmer state. One survey of British married couples found that 67 percent reported not arguing at all while they traveled together, even though 54 percent of them reported arguing *every day* before they'd left.[22] A different survey of British adults found that most believed that a vacation provided an ideal opportunity to discuss major life decisions. And although these discussions take place far from home and could reasonably be more fantastical than practical ("This hot tub is so relaxing. We really ought to get one installed on our back deck!"), most of them actually inspired real change once the couple resumed ordinary life.[23]

Another study suggested that it's not only the already-happy couples who can benefit from traveling together. The Second Honeymoon Program, which began in 2010 and is funded by the Malaysian government, provides free vacations to Malaysian couples on the verge of divorce. These vacations, spent on a tropical island resort with access to counselors, appear to be highly effective, with all participants in the program reporting still being married. Improved communication between spouses is thought to be a key reason for the program's success. Again, causality is impossible to establish here, but it may just be that the escape from daily stressors allows the couples to reconnect while also identifying and working on their problems.[24]

In short, images of happy couples walking hand-in-hand on the beach and gazing into each other's eyes over cocktails are more than just clever marketing. Breaking away from everyday life, with all of its stresses and expectations, allowing time for connection, and sharing in novel, exciting experiences may be just the ticket to rejuvenating a romance.

Taking the Kids

The topic of traveling happily with kids is one that could fill a book of its own.[25] While traveling as a family can draw its members closer, some fundamental incompatibilities can pose a challenge. For one, parents often seek relaxation, while kids want activity.[26] And adults have to manage their expectations. A friend of mine, who recently traveled for several weeks around Europe with her husband and two children under the age of twelve, stressed the importance of not being too achievement-oriented when laying out the day's itinerary. Don't expect to tick off multiple attractions and activities per day. Have one or two goals: "Today, we'll go to the beach." A trip with the kids is going to be wholly different than a romantic weekend with your partner or a carefree girls' weekend, and acceptance of this fact is key to enjoyment.

What do parents get for their troubles? Greater feelings of connectedness to their families. Laughter. Playfulness. A wealth of warm memories.[27] The opportunity to see the world through the eyes of their children. While there is surprisingly little research on the benefits of travel for young children, many parents, as well as many children who grew up traveling, might agree with the journalist Hodding Carter, who noted that "two of the greatest gifts we can give our children are roots and wings."

THE ALLURE OF TRAVELING ALONE

Despite the benefits of traveling with loved ones, opting to see the world solo is becoming an increasingly popular choice. One 2015 survey of over 13,000 travelers from twenty-five different countries found that 24 percent traveled alone on their most recent leisure trip, the vast majority of these being women.[28] A surprising number are first-time travelers. Tour companies have been slowly awakening to this new market of travelers, creating tours just for singles, reducing or eliminating the dreaded single supplement, and creating cruise ship cabins just for solo travelers.[29]

Why the rise? There is a singular appeal of solo travel, one that goes beyond mere resignation at not having a partner. Solo travelers report having an easier time immersing themselves in a culture, seeing what they want to see without having to worry about compromise, and simply having no one to worry about or please beyond themselves. One survey of nearly a thousand British households found that travel had the longest lasting impact on the solo traveler, compared to those traveling with friends or family.[30]

As solo travel gains in popularity, maybe people are gradually realizing that traveling alone isn't as awkward or uncomfortable as they might have thought. One study found that fear of being seen alone in public doing something pleasurable but stereotypically social, such as eating in a restaurant, walking through an art gallery, or going to a movie, was off-putting enough to deter them from going.[31] It's not that they thought the meal, exhibit, or movie wouldn't be enjoyable; they mostly dreaded the potential humiliation of being seen enjoying it *alone*. Turns out, though, if they pushed through their fear and actually did it, they had a far better time than they expected. While the researchers didn't examine longer-term experiences like travel, the effect may hold for those as well, and could help explain the fact that 59 percent of women who take a trip on their own are eager to take another one soon.[32] It's far more fun than they may have expected.

I have felt the highs and lows of both solo and paired travel. When traveling with a group of over thirty peers in college, my favorite moments were ones of solitude: an early morning walk, sitting alone in a piazza with my journal, staring out the bus window while others slept. The freedom and anonymity were a joy. But on subsequent trips, I recall moments of boredom and loneliness after too many days spent on my own in a foreign country. Plus, with the right person, I cherish memories of laughter as we find ourselves in various absurd situations. I recall feeling exceedingly grateful to have someone to share a meal with or a view with, knowing that I would never be able to convey the experience second-hand.

In her essay "The Luxury of Solitude," Linda Holmes captures the trade-off between traveling solo and traveling with a companion:

> The experience of good company is in part the experience of matching your wishes to someone else's; that's part of what makes it great. You

build a common wish with another person: to go somewhere, to meet, to have sushi instead of steak. And those shared wishes are profound. But if you collaborate constantly, both professionally and personally, it's easy to forget what undiluted self-determination feels like, and there's something to be said for remembering.[33]

Interestingly, due to mismatched schedules or vastly different interests, committed partners are opting to take separate vacations with increasing frequency.[34] Is this you? Are you dying to embark on a solo trip but getting some pushback from your partner? Eager for some of the relaxation, feelings of authenticity, and close connections that can only be found in a girlfriends' getaway?[35] You might tell him or her that the time apart might actually make the two of you newly grateful for one another! According to researchers Katherine Jacobs Bao and Sonja Lyubomirsky, short periods of absence can make the heart grow fonder by making the relationship seem fresh again.[36] We adapt to the sameness of our romantic relationships just like we do to other things, and inserting a break can give you each the time and perspective to step back and appreciate one another anew.

HAPPY TRAVEL TIPS FOR RELATIONSHIP SATISFACTION AND ENHANCEMENT

It's easy to let yourself get swept away in the excitement of a potential vacation. But when it comes to choosing a companion, it pays to be picky. Before you commit to traveling with someone, don't forget to ask yourself some key questions.

- Do I have a good sense of this person's core personality traits? Is he or she agreeable and emotionally stable? Is at least one of us fairly conscientious?
- Do we match in important ways?

- Do we have similar goals for this trip?
- When conflict arises, do I know how I'm going to deal with it?
- Have I scouted out some new and exciting activities that I can do with my partner?
- Ultimately, will this person and I have a productive and enjoyable time together? And will we still like each other at the end of it?

EIGHT

ALL GOOD THINGS MUST END: HOW TO WIND DOWN FROM A TRIP WITHOUT DREADING THE RETURN TO DAILY LIFE

Why do you go away? So that you can come back. So that you can see the place you came from with new eyes and extra colors. And the people there see you differently, too. Coming back to where you started is not the same as never leaving.

—Terry Pratchett, *A Hat Full of Sky*

Red Delicious apples. Iceberg lettuce. Yellow mustard. Individually wrapped American cheese slices. I opened my parents' refrigerator and scoffed, silently judging their unsophisticated foods and, by extension, everything else about Reading, Pennsylvania. It all seemed so uninspired, so distasteful, and—I admit—so *below* me. You see, I was twenty-one and I had just spent the summer of my junior year of college studying Renaissance and Reformation art in Europe. This made me cultured in a way that—I believed—few others could understand.

In the days and weeks prior, I felt myself transform as I stood before the works of Botticelli, da Vinci, and Rembrandt, ate my weight in gelato, smoked my first cigarette, learned to love espresso, walked a hole into the sole of my Birkenstocks, and laughed with my new-found friends late into the night. I gazed with envy at effortlessly stylish Italian women, cruising along on candy-colored Vespas, wondering exactly how I could remake myself in their image. My identity was expanded from small-town college student to world traveler as I learned just how independent, open-minded, and adventurous I could be.

And each day was lived with a sense of urgency; time was a precious commodity not to be squandered. I woke at dawn to go for a solitary walk in each new city we visited. I never allowed myself to nap on the multi-hour bus rides though the Dolomites, Swiss Alps, or even on the German autobahn, lest I miss a once-in-a-lifetime view. Gradually, I became so sleep-deprived that I nodded off on brief subway rides and even on a bench in Amsterdam's Van Gogh museum, where I was promptly roused by an unhappy security guard. Because I was in Europe on a scholarship and couldn't imagine if or when I'd ever return, I savored to the point of exhaustion. This trip was an absolute whirlwind and I had loved every moment of it. *This* was what life should be, I decided.

Making it even sweeter was the fact that, after the three-week class officially ended, my new and amazingly fun friend Megan and I planned to take our program director up on his offer to change our flights in order to extend our stay in Europe. After much careful consideration, she and I agreed on a few days in London and a couple of weeks in Scotland. We had purchased British Rail passes and had made a list of youth hostels to stay in, two concepts that, to me, rang deeply of cool. We talked late into the night about what we might experience in places like Edinburgh, Glasgow, and the Isle of Skye. We would hike the Scottish Highlands, think profound thoughts as we gazed out of train windows, flirt with cute Scottish boys, and maybe even sample some haggis. We couldn't wait to start on the next part of our journey.

The day before the class ended and our big, bold adventure was to begin, our program director gathered us around our London hotel's lobby for some announcements. Amidst some information about the evening's group dinner, our final course grades, and the room checkout protocol, he nonchalantly mentioned that he wasn't able to change our plane tickets to allow us to extend our stay after all. Megan and I locked eyes. *What did he just say?* Some nonsense about the lettered code on our plane ticket making it unchangeable?

To this day I don't know exactly what happened, and in the pre-Internet era there wasn't a whole lot we could do to investigate. Instead, we became enraged at this buffoon who was about to spoil our Scotland adventure with utter impunity. We frantically called the airline from one of London's famous red telephone booths, the charm of this completely lost on us as we unsuccessfully begged the person on the other end to show us some mercy. Eventually, we had no choice but to call our parents and arrange to be picked up the next day (*the next day?!*) at Philadelphia International Airport. Then we cried and hugged and cried some more, promised we would go to Scotland together someday, and proceeded to gorge ourselves on fish and chips.

Stunned to be back home in Pennsylvania twenty-four hours later, I couldn't help but compare everything to the magnificent places I had just been, but also to the place I should have been but wasn't—Scotland. Instead of hikes and haggis, I was now picking up extra hours as a cashier at the grocery store and subjected to a curfew. (Did my parents care that I had just spent a month wandering foreign cities alone, you might ask? No, they did not.) I was grumpy as hell and I'm sure no one wanted me back in Europe as much as my family did. For me, in that moment, British novelist Fanny Burney said it best: "Travelling is the ruin of all happiness. There's no looking at a building here after seeing Italy."

This is the exact opposite of a happy homecoming. You might call it an extreme homecoming *fail.* Because my trip's ending was abrupt, frustrating, and uncontrollable, I returned home from Europe feeling sullen and antsy rather than happy and transformed. There wasn't a lot of opportunity for gratitude, reflection, or closure amidst all of that last-day chaos, and my sense of resentment stayed with me for longer than I care to admit. However, in the subsequent years, I have come to learn that the postvacation blahs are far from inevitable. In fact, while I'm always a little sad to come home, I've learned to see travel as a springboard for positive change and increased self-awareness. In this chapter, I will tell you how to ease back into regular life much more successfully than I did after that summer in Europe.

ATTEND TO THE END

"Begin with the end in mind," advised famed author Stephen Covey.[1] Sound advice indeed, but advice we travelers seldom heed. While we put so much time and energy into planning the perfect vacation, we spend far less time, or maybe no time at all, thinking about how best to wind it down. It's a bit of a downer, for one. Why dwell on the return to work stress and household drudgery when we could be visualizing another day at the beach or more time sipping cappuccinos in Italy? We also may simply fail to grasp its importance. Coming home is coming home. It's familiar and predictable. What's there to think about? And yet, we should always consider how we will wrap up our travels, especially if overall happiness and positive memories are important goals.

Let's say you've had the good fortune to experience your ideal beach vacation. You avoided major travel snafus. You spent your money wisely. You've gotten along beautifully with your companions and felt alternating moments of awe, absorption, relaxation, and joy. You crafted an epic final day, ending on a high note. You've followed all of the happy travel rules.

One downside lingers: because you had such an amazing time away, you dread coming home. Now, instead of lazy mornings, you'll once again be a slave to the 6 a.m. alarm and face the frenzied rush to get the kids out the door and yourself off to work. There will be emails to answer, bills to pay, and household chores to tackle. Concrete will replace white-sand beach and the sounds of traffic will take the place of the crashing waves. After spending time in a relative utopia, ordinary life can't help but seem depressingly . . . ordinary.

As a result, you choose not to rain on your own parade by thinking about your trip's end. This may save you some moments of sadness while traveling—denial exists for a good reason—but it could also detract from a happy homecoming. Instead, consider beginning with the end in mind and give the wind-down as much attention and planning as the trip itself.

Give Yourself a Treat

In chapter 4, we discussed the importance of anticipating your travels, when you spend time basking in all of the upcoming pleasures. You can apply this idea to your homecoming, too. What little treat might you be able to build into your arrival to help soften the blow? Maybe you could stop at your favorite ice cream place or restaurant on your way home from the airport. Maybe you could order a little goodie online to be waiting for you when you get home. Or, with some careful planning, you might relish coming home to a clean house, stocked refrigerator, and a bed with fresh, crisp sheets.

Maximize Your Buffer

When discussing trip-planning back in chapter 4, I also stressed the importance of leaving a buffer, a period of time in which you gradually ease back into your ordinary life. The tendency to maximize the amount of time you're away is well-intended, but you might discount the stress of having to dive immediately back into work and other routines.[2] You'll likely find that the rapid turn-around is a shock to the system that leaves you grumpy and discombobulated. Recall a central tenet of happy travel: *more time away is not always better.*

This can be tough advice to follow. Believe me, I constantly feel the pressure to stay away as long as possible, especially when the flight costs no extra. Really, if a flight from Washington, DC to Copenhagen costs $1,200 regardless of whether I stay two weeks or three, it's extremely easy to justify staying longer to get my money's worth.

However, there is a psychological cost to running your trip down to the wire, if not an obvious financial one. One survey examined German teachers before and after a two-week Easter vacation. They reported more energy and engagement with work following the vacation (regardless of whether they actually traveled anywhere), but it faded after about a month. Crucially, though, it faded out more slowly for those teachers who used postvacation evenings and weekends to relax.[3] Those who skipped this relaxing segue into reality did not feel reenergized for long once work resumed.

Okay, so back at home, imagine you've followed the advice and left yourself a buffer, a free day or two before resuming your responsibilities. Good job. What should you do with this time? Laundry? Binge-watch Netflix? Go through the stack of accumulated mail? Strategically nap until you're back in the proper time zone? Maybe. But also use this time to reflect on the many curiosities of being home.

THE OFF-KILTER FEELING
OF TRAVERTIGO

Let's be real. Coming home from a really great vacation doesn't always lend itself to favorable comparisons. We can find ourselves viewing our suburban neighborhood in sorry contrast to the vibrant city we just spend two weeks exploring. The local grocery store's mass-produced bread can't possibly compare to fresh Parisian baguettes. The air at home feels less crisp, the sky less blue, the greenery less lush. Absent daily housekeeping service, we can't help but notice the dust bunnies that have accumulated and grimace at the sink full of dirty dishes we left in our haste to make an early morning flight. It can all seem so uninspiring, so lackluster, particularly if we come home already feeling deflated.

Depending on how long we've been separated from ordinary life, this feeling can hit hard. Some have called it reverse culture shock. Others have coined cute terms like travertigo, discombobulocation, deja-new, or—for the pessimists among us—deja-ew. This disorientation is a hard thing to study, as it is far too complex an experience to capture in the traditional questionnaire method favored by researchers. Yet we travelers know it's real. The thing is, *we don't always know what to do with it.*

This is actually a unique and valuable time, not something to merely suffer through or shove out of awareness. While it can't compare with the Seven Wonders of the World, coming home can still be positive, if you cultivate the right mindset. Consider the following seven positive outcomes of homecoming.

THE SEVEN WONDERS
OF HOMECOMING

I. Altered Perceptions

Coming home often brings with it a unique and hard-to-describe feeling, a disorienting sense of novelty. The ordinary is, suddenly and strangely, somehow not quite ordinary. There's your house, your car, your stuff. You know it, but it looks and feels ever-so-slightly different. Because *you* are different. Your assumptions and perspective have been altered by your time away. One friend calls this traveler's haze and says, "When I have returned from trips outside of the US, I marvel at the size of everything—BIG—from coffee cups to cars, roads, buildings, people, you name it . . . everything is so BIG in the US. It usually lasts a few days. As I go about my day, I am dazed just looking at the enormity of *everything.*" Others have felt disoriented in their own homes, seeing their bookshelves, furniture arrangements, kitchen pantries, or closets not as they were, but in subtle contrast to the environment they'd been inhabiting. It might just feel *off.* Last year, after stepping out of Dulles International Airport after two months in Europe, I had to laugh at how very odd American license plates looked. They looked so big, the font so elongated and strange. A life-changing observation, it was not. But it was fascinating and jarring in its own very small way.

Emotion researchers might say that you've un-adapted to your regular life. Adaptation can work both ways, after all. We all know that traveling to a new place captures our attention and wows us like home simply cannot. Time and distance are powerful transformers, even of the most ordinary things. Yet we are surprised and sometimes at a loss for words when stepping back into our old world, taking it all in, and seeing it as a stranger might. These altered perceptions are not inherently good or bad, but they do provide a unique perspective. T. S. Eliot described this feeling well: "The end of all our exploring will be to arrive where we started and know the place for the first time."

There isn't much you can do to force this experience; it tends to happen naturally. The best way to facilitate it is by simply being open and receptive. Don't stare at your phone immediately upon emerging from the airport. Don't be so distracted by the business of coming home—hailing a cab, opening the mail, or unpacking—that you miss these small perceptual shifts.

2. Heightened Appreciation

Sometimes, travertigo is a mere curiosity, a quirky side effect of being separated from the norm. Things initially look and feel a little strange, but the feeling dissipates as real life resumes. Other times, though, we experience the best version of travertigo—one that comes with a sense of appreciation of the once-ordinary.

While coming home can be a sad reminder of the fact that crisp mountain air or a professionally maintained living space are not the stuff of daily life, it can also highlight things about daily life that we *can* appreciate, if we take advantage of the rare opportunity to see it through unadapted eyes. Last summer I returned from two months of summer travel and, after jump-starting my dead car battery, I was surprised to be appreciative of the simple act of driving. Driving! At best, this was something that I had previously taken for granted. At worst, it's something I avoid whenever possible. So it was shocking how, after a significant time away from it, that feeling of freedom, of being able to leave the city for the countryside without a hassle, to hug the curves of mountain roads, and to spontaneously stop for ice cream (don't judge), was newly prized. Even my first trip to my usual grocery store was a little thrilling as I suddenly had access to the foods I missed (even while I mourned the European delights I could no longer find). Later, I relished the fact that I could cook these things in my own kitchen, cramped and basic as it is. I loved being able to sleep in my own bed, see newly released movies, and do laundry in my own home. Yes, travel made me happy about *doing laundry*. Being away had un-adapted me from the very mundane activities that I take for granted.

Did this last forever? Is laundry still an occasion for joy? No, but it was a valuable part of the travel experience, however short-lived. And when daily life starts to lose its luster, I spark some appreciation for these subtle pleasantries by trying to see them as my traveling-self might.

3. Relishing Small Comforts and Routines

Because travel takes us far from the many comforts of home, I always marvel at the extremely common, cozy things I miss while away. My fuzzy bathrobe. A programmable coffee maker. My Ninja blender that quickly and quietly chops and mixes my morning smoothie. Vanilla candles. An entire closet full of clothes and shoes that don't need to be constantly packed and repacked. Reliable Internet. And, of course, the ability to do laundry. These are some of the easiest things to take for granted in daily life. They are ever-present and pleasant enough, but certainly not euphoria-inducing. And yet, when we enter a world that is devoid of these predictable comforts, we come to miss them.

Even the habits afforded by daily life—the schedules and routines that can make it all seem so dull and predictable—can be newly savored upon returning home. For all of the wonders of travel, being out of our comfort zones can require us to spend time and effort deliberating over pretty insignificant matters: Where to get the morning coffee. How to operate the shower. How to get to the museum, or the beach, or the restaurant we've scouted out for the day. Where to find a gas station, or a drug store, or the bus stop. Even how to communicate. While it's fun to be pushed out of our day-to-day routines and be forced to take nothing for granted, spending all of that mental energy on small tasks can also be a little exhausting.[4] Predictability does have its advantages, and coming home makes that apparent like little else can.

4. Gratitude

Let's face it: we travelers are a privileged lot. And as you're home and reflecting on your travels, you might spontaneously be made aware of this good fortune. You might also be struck by the fact that not everyone has such an opportunity to explore the world. You might feel this gratitude as you look back through photographs or a journal. Maybe it'll hit you as you relay some of your favorite moments from the trip. It may even be a byproduct of others' expressions of jealousy. Anything that reminds you of the great privileges of travel can be a source of gratitude.

You might also feel grateful for people who have made your travels more seamless: the neighbor who watered the plants, the friend who looked in on your cat, the sister who lent you her new suitcase, the coworker who picked up some of the slack in the office, the husband who picked you up from the airport.

The Japanese have a word I love—*amae*—which is difficult to translate into English but is best described as "indulgent dependence" or "feeling

loved because you are taken care of."[5] It is a key component of loving relationships in Japan but is far more elusive in Western nations, where autonomy
and self-reliance are so prized.[6] But because travel can leave us vulnerable—
away from our homes, cars, and offices—we may be required to call upon
others for all kinds of unusual assistance. This can feel awkward, especially
for those of us who pride ourselves on independence. However, we might
also get to witness a generosity that we seldom get to see. In fact, travel
may be one of the times when we get to feel the sweet dependence of *amae*.
Gratitude for being truly and deeply known, understood, and cared for is
often a surprising and underappreciated aspect of travel.

5. Reconnection

We can adapt to the people in our lives in the same way that we adapt to
our physical environments: we inadvertently get used to them and take
them for granted.[7] Often, it is when they are removed from our lives that
their importance is most deeply felt. That's why one of the great pleasures of coming home is the ability to reconnect with friends and family.

And the reconnection can suddenly feel so manageable. In ordinary
life, it's easy to buy into the "I'm too busy" myth. Most of us *are* busy,
and there's always tomorrow, or next week, or next month. However, this
type of all-too-common excuse reveals itself as being awfully flimsy after
we return home from a great distance. Carving out an hour or two for a
coffee date ten minutes from home seems much easier from this perspective. Upon returning home, having your loved ones nearby can suddenly
feel like a wonderful gift.

Happy Travel Tips for Capitalizing on Travertigo

Coming home unadapted—from people, from your everyday environment,
from small comforts and routines—is a rare and powerful mental and emotional experience. It is also one that we often fail to recognize and capitalize

on. But you can, in fact, actively take steps to make it happen. It can start before you even get back. As you're driving or flying home, perhaps feeling a little blue, turn your attention to what you've missed or are looking forward to about being back home. Surely, those things exist. They just need to be called to mind. You could write about them, not merely listing the things you appreciate but going into some detail. A simple prompt like, *"Think about your life at home, the people, places, and objects of your everyday life. What are you looking forward to, once you get home? Why? Go into detail about why they are so great."* As you reflect, big things might spring to mind: you miss your pets or your close friends. But small and seemingly trivial things may pop up as well, like my coffeepot, smoothie maker, and fuzzy robe.

This exercise can also spark discussion with your travel companions. You can have this conversation without sounding ungrateful for the trip you just took. You might even phrase it as, "I've been feeling a little sad that our trip is over. Why don't we talk about some of the things we miss at home?"

While you can encourage this process, sometimes it takes awhile for sources of appreciation and gratitude to reveal themselves, and it may happen without effort or forewarning. You may wake one morning and suddenly feel grateful to smell the coffee already brewing, thanks to your trusty old programmable Mr. Coffee. You may receive a text from a friend, asking if you can meet up for a spontaneous after-work cocktail, and feel grateful to have a social network so easily accessible. Revel in these moments. They are an important part of the extended travel experience.

You can, of course, take more active steps to engage with meaningful or pleasurable things when you get home, especially the things that make home unique and personal and yours. Relish an ordinary routine, such as popping into your favorite coffee shop. Make a date with a friend you miss to catch up over dinner, perhaps at a restaurant you also missed. Plan to go see the new movie you've been hearing about. Throw a dinner party with food made in your own kitchen. Take your car out on some country roads and savor the freedom of driving. Dance around the laundry room as you delight in having clean clothes. Sometimes, this newfound appreciation for the ordinary hits you unexpectedly as you reacquaint yourself with home, but you don't have to leave it completely up to chance.

6. Meeting a New You

As a social psychologist, I know just how much our environments impact our thoughts, feelings, and behaviors. While our personalities are fairly stable—say, an extrovert will be more likely to talk to strangers than an introvert—the situations we place ourselves in also exact tremendous pressure: an extrovert will be more likely to openly chat with an airplane seatmate than he would a TSA agent. It follows that dramatically altering the situations we're in, breaking away from the routines of daily life and putting ourselves in brand-new places, can encourage important realizations and foster new habits. This is, after all, one reason we travel.

To capitalize on this, use the return period as a time for serious reflection. What did you like about your life while you were away? Consider behaviors and activities that really called to you. You might realize that not having constant connectivity to email was incredibly freeing, and allowed you to think more creatively. It might hit you that you loved walking to your destination rather than mindlessly hopping in the car like you do at home. Maybe you came to love a new food, leisure activity, or cultural practice. Perhaps your curiosity has been piqued and you're eager to learn more about the people and places you visited. You think that these opportunities ended when your flight landed. Not so! You can recreate these elements of your trip in daily life.

Consider, too, what you saw in *yourself*, free from the people and places that constrain, define, and shape your identity. Is your travel-self different from how you think, feel, and behave in everyday life? How so, exactly?

Maybe you learned that you can be more brave, more outgoing, or more full-of-life than you realized. On the other hand, maybe you felt out-of-shape, excessively rigid, or unexpectedly anxious. The negatives are certainly less fun to explore, but hugely important and potentially valuable nonetheless.

F. Scott Fitzgerald mused, "It's a funny thing coming home. Nothing changes. Everything looks the same, feels the same, even smells the same. You realize what's changed is you." Ride the wave of this change. Don't wait. Upon arrival back home, take some time to think about the slightly different "you" that you encountered on the road. What did you like about him or her? What did you not like? Can this side of yourself be brought to life back home? How?

There is a small window of opportunity for change. Given the power of the situation, you're likely to fall back into the comfort of your mindless old habits: checking email constantly, eating dinner with the local news blaring in the background, driving everywhere, spending the weekends indoors. The days and weeks after travel are a potentially critical period for behavior change that you can capitalize on for personal betterment.

7. Lessons for Daily Life

This kind of deep reflection can and should also influence your future travels. From the trivial ("I should have packed more pants, fewer shorts") to the pretty major ("Guess I hate camping!"), when deciding where to go next, for how long, and with whom, past experiences are essential for learning who you are and what you need as a traveler. As much preliminary soul-searching and planning as you might do to pinpoint your specific travel personality, your needs, and your deal-breakers, there is always some element of trial and error. The more you travel, though, the more you will come to define the elements of your ideal trip. Note all of it and file it away.

Perhaps less obvious, but arguably even more important, is the fact that travel can teach you what can work better for you in *everyday life* as well as on the road. Maybe you woke each day of your trip feeling fully rested and energized, in a way you haven't in years. Perhaps you felt a reignited spark and deeper connection with your partner. Maybe your kids got along better than they had in ages. Ask yourself, what was responsible for that? Dissect it. You might think back on your vacation as a major life experiment. Away from all of your constraints and routines, what truly worked for you? What didn't? And—most importantly, what can you incorporate into your daily life?

Maybe as you reflect back on how beautifully your family got along, you realize that you were eating breakfast and dinner together everyday, a habit that has fallen to the wayside in your normal, busy lives. Further, the hotel's wifi was too spotty to allow for constant connectivity, and the television programs were in a foreign language. As a result, your family was forced to talk and listen to one another with dedicated focus.

You also note that you did many new and adventurous things together. More specifically, on that day you went white-water rafting, you recall banding together to keep the raft from tipping. You all cracked up when your guide slipped and fell out of the raft while demonstrating how to hold the paddle. You were a real team. You laughed together and shared your favorite memories from the day over dinner. And at the end of the day, you fell asleep, physically exhausted but also happy, and slept like a rock.

Can your family share meals with dedicated attention or white-water raft every day? Hardly. That's the stuff of vacations. But can you recreate some of the same thoughts and feelings of that time? That sounds more feasible. Family game nights. Challenging weekend hikes. Bike rides. Things that are more accessible in daily life, but might foster some of those same feelings of teamwork, challenge, bonding, shared laughter, and accomplishment. Can you prioritize technology-free family mealtime, if you've also identified this as a source of your travel happiness? Will there be some pushback? Probably. Old habits die hard. They're comfortable and so we cling to them, even when there may be something better for us out there.

Studies have found that postvacation bliss fades after about two to four weeks but perhaps we can make choices that slow it down.[8] By taking full advantage of the novelties of home and using the return to really hone in on all the pleasantries ordinary life affords, we can extend this blissful period. And the benefits go beyond good feelings. The return time can also be an important catalyst for personal development.

WHEN COMING HOME HURTS

For some travelers, returning home from an excellent travel experience can be more than just a little sad. For those who venture to exotic cultures for long periods of time, who experience a seismic shift in their worldview, or who feel their identities change as a result of being away, coming home can actually verge on the traumatic. Small Planet Studio, founded by Cate Brubaker, specializes in the very real experience of re-entry shock.[9] This can take several forms but is generally characterized by a feeling of no longer belonging in one's prior home, a continued sense of wanderlust, a critical assessment of things everyone else seems to take for granted, and a nagging sense that no one else really gets it. Brubaker notes that this is one of the unspoken challenges of travel, which seldom gets the attention and sympathy it deserves.

Looking back on my college Europe trip, I think that the transformative role it played in my life, plus the unexpectedly crummy way in which it ended, contributed to some re-entry shock. My family and friends back home, most of whom had never traveled, didn't know the right questions to ask, and I didn't know the right stories to tell to properly convey the impact my travels had on me. Sure, I could say the Roman Coliseum was really cool and that Italian gelato was creamy and delicious. But the deep feeling of freedom I felt when wandering the streets of Rome late at night? The sense of awe that came from looking at a building that dates back thousands of years? The connections I felt to my classmates after weeks of constant togetherness? I had no words for these feelings. This only contributed to my sense of alienation. On top of this was a feeling of guilt for not being constantly overjoyed and grateful. I had just returned from this amazing, rare gift of a summer, and I was acting like a brat.

If this sounds like you, it can actually be quite comforting simply to know that you are not alone. Many people struggle with the challenge of re-entry, making gratitude for home a real challenge. But there are ways to cope successfully with it. Brubaker has found that sharing your experiences with other travelers can cut back on a sense of alienation. She also suggests that travel be used as a means of self-exploration. What, exactly, about traveling was so captivating? What do you miss? Can any of that be found in daily life, even a modified or seemingly watered-down version of it?

The trick is to realize that there is much adventure and novelty to find sprinkled through everyday life: local Meetup groups that focus on practicing a foreign language or watching foreign films. Ethnic restaurants. Daytrips to small towns or natural areas you've never visited before. We often think that we must venture far from home to have our cultural curiosity and wanderlust satisfied, but as Marcel Proust argued, "The real voyage of discovery consists not in seeking new landscapes, but in having new eyes."

THE PARADOX OF ROSY RECALL

Let's say that you just got back from a week-long backpacking trip in Virginia's Blue Ridge Mountains. While you were initially flattered to receive the invitation from some athletic, adventurous friends, you quickly realized that you were ill-prepared to hike an average of twelve miles a day with a heavy backpack on your shoulders. To make matters worse, your new boots weren't properly broken in and you got some painful blisters. It rained buckets one day and much of your gear got soaked. The mosquitos made a meal of you, sleeping on the cold ground was awful, you constantly worried about encountering bears, and you got really sick of eating granola bars for both breakfast and lunch. You found asking yourself, "*How* many more days until this is over?" more than once.

But you have to admit that it wasn't *all* terrible. After a long, cold night, a steaming cup of coffee never tasted so good. The long daily slogs were punctuated by moments of sheer beauty, when the wooded trail would open up to a magnificent view of the valley below. These views were made even better by the fact that you had reached them on your own two feet. At the end of each day, you felt proud at the many miles you logged. You laughed and bonded with your hiking buddies over the campfire, and while dinners were far from gourmet, there was some gratification in knowing you prepared them yourself with such rudimentary tools. The trip ended on a bittersweet note. While the comforts of home have never been more seductive, you were also surprisingly sad to say goodbye to this singular experience.

You arrive home, take a long, hot, well-earned shower, scarf down a delicious home-cooked meal, and pack your camping gear away. The blisters and bites heal. Normal life resumes. Over dinner a month or so thereafter, a friend casually asks, "Hey, how was that backpacking trip you took recently?"

How do you answer what appears to be a very simple question? What information do you use to conclude that your trip was transcendent, miserable, or somewhere in between?

In order to give the most accurate possible answer, your best approach would be to mentally replay each moment of your trip, from mosquitos to mountain vistas, rate each of these moments on a scale from horrendous to joyful, average these moments together, and obtain your answer. But your dinner's getting cold, and your friend doesn't have that kind of time. What you do instead is do a quick replay of the week, extract a few key memories, and quickly make your judgment.[10] And which moments will your mind choose to extract? Probably the peaks and certainly the end.[11] Reaching a scenic overlook and looking out, awestruck, over the Shenandoah Valley and thinking, "I got myself here on my own two feet. I am a *badass*." Laughing with friends around the campfire at night. Feeling accomplished at the end of the trip as you realized you did something you didn't think possible. Stopping on your way home for a fast-food cheeseburger, declaring it the best thing you'd ever eaten. With these key moments in mind, you tell your friend that the trip was epic, amazing, and unforgettable.

But was it? Was it *really*? Epic moments aside, there was also a lot of misery, no? Remember the rain, the mosquitos, the painful blisters, the aching shoulders? How interesting that those were left out of the story. But it makes perfect sense when you think about the way our memories tend to operate.

First, recall the impossibility of conjuring up accurate memories of physical discomfort.[12] Yes, on a vague, conceptual level, you might remember times when you were cold, wet, and tired during the trip. You possess the knowledge that your feet hurt and that the mosquito bites itched. But, absent the actual physical feelings, it's easy and natural to shrug this off as unimportant. The broader sense of triumph and camaraderie you experienced is more easily accessible. So when you told your friend how amazing the backpacking trip was, you were probably giving priority to that sort of belief-based information while downplaying the physical discomfort you experienced.

And with the passage of even more time, the memory of your trip will come to increasingly resemble a highlight reel. Some of this happens unconsciously, as duration neglect kicks in and those peaks and ends come to dominate your memory of the experience. But it is also a motivated process, driven by the moments we elected to capture. You probably have numerous photos of mountains, scenic overlooks, wildflowers, and friends laughing around the campfire. You have far fewer of mosquito bites, blisters, and rainstorms. As a result of all of these fast, efficient, and largely unconscious processes, you weren't just grandstanding in that conversation with your friend. You truly came to believe that your trip was incredible.

These well-documented reconstructive memory processes will bias your recall of the trip. And usually, this is for the best. Travel is costly, and why not get the most bang for your buck by inadvertently constructing a highlight reel of all the best moments? You can keep this with you, play through the happy memories at will, and feel convinced that your trip was well worth the time, money, and effort you invested. Why not wear those rose-colored glasses with pride?

Take Two?

On the other hand, let's say that a year or two has passed and your hiking buddies invite you on another backpacking trip. Should you say yes? This brings up an interesting and important paradox. When calling to mind a past experience, it makes sense to highlight the positives. Why not? When faced with whether to put yourself in a similar experience in the future, the course is less clear. When it comes to decision-making, what would you rather be? Accurate or rosy?

Consider the following thought experiment. You can elect to have a week of reasonable misery, but it will be twisted and reshaped to provide you with the richest memories of your life. The arduous and impossible will morph into joy and triumph. Or you can choose a really fun, pleasurable week that will be remembered as mediocre. Which would you choose? There is no right or wrong answer to this question. The paradoxical disconnect between lived versus recalled experience is something that philosophers, behavioral economists, and psychologists have struggled with for decades. What may be surprising is the extent to which travel can be a real-life test of this thought experiment.

When reflecting back on the arduous backpacking trip, what we fail to realize is the amount of behind-the-scenes mental work that has taken place, acting quickly to neutralize intense emotions. Frigid cold, driving rain, and painfully sore feet become transformed into character-building experiences. We come to love the things we suffer for, and this is especially true when those things were freely chosen.[13]

An interesting sidenote: mild annoyances, like a cloudy day at the beach or slightly disappointing meals, often don't clear the threshold that is necessary for our internal rationalizer to kick in. As a result, these small irritations can linger while huge ones fade away or are transformed into something we can feel good about.[14] It's a curious side effect of how we cope with major disappointments. It turns out that you might feel all right concluding that a daytrip to the next town over was a disappointment. No big loss. But it really won't sit well to declare a tough week-long hiking trip or expensive vacation halfway around the world a huge bust. We would feel too foolish, too guilty. So we spin it: the more intensely upsetting an event, the more our defenses are triggered and the more we rationalize it. And given the fact that even the most awful of vacations is punctuated by some decent moments, this isn't too hard to do.

Assuming there's no pathological break with reality at play, there's nothing wrong with transforming the negative, creating and then reveling in positive memories. There's certainly something to be said for the value of a lifetime's worth of rich, positive memories that come at the expense of momentary pleasure. If you want these memories, you should say yes to the future backpacking trip. But if your primary goal is to avoid moments of crippling fatigue, uninspired food, and feeling cold and achy and stinky, perhaps you should think twice. Or consider the very reasonable middle ground. No one is saying the trip has to be exactly the same as the first. What did you love about it? Build in more of that. What did you hate? Minimize those things. Reflect on lessons learned: break in your boots before you leave, and don't forget the bug spray.

As you grapple with the decision, keep in mind that we are excellent rationalizers, skilled at protecting our precious self-esteem by putting a positive spin on our decisions. So you will, indeed, come to love what you've suffered for.

THE SOCIAL CAPITAL OF LOST LUGGAGE

Transforming our travel experiences into treasured memories is seldom a solitary process. It happens in a social context. As we share the stories of our past travel adventures, we naturally impose a narrative structure and shape them into something meaningful or hilarious.[15] The good, the bad, and the ugly all become material for unique social connection.[16]

When my friend Kate and I went to Italy a few years ago, her luggage got lost in the chaos of an extremely short layover. Upon landing in Milan and realizing the luggage wasn't there to meet us, we reported the loss to a very blasé agent and then hopped on the last train up to Lake Como. We had arranged to stay in an apartment in the gorgeous but remote and tiny lakeside town of Fiumelatte. Even for us, armed with maps and detailed directions, the place proved nearly impossible to find, tucked away in the hillside and accessible only via a series of small staircases blocked off by locked iron gates. Still, the airline had promised to deliver Kate's bag to us, at the needle-in-a-haystack apartment, "within a day or two."

For the next two days, she was housebound waiting for her bag, making fruitless attempts to contact the airline, and still wearing the same clothes she flew in. I ventured out a few times, but felt pretty guilty about leaving her behind. On the second day, we took turns sitting street-side, just in case the delivery person was unable to locate us on the hillside. Somewhere along the way, Kate thought it wise to learn the Italian phrase for "Do you have my luggage?"—"*Avete il mio bagaglio?"*—and would shout it indiscriminately and with increasing desperation anytime we heard footsteps approaching. It was getting grim. Finally, the luggage arrived, but by then, Kate had essentially lost two days of precious vacation time waiting around the apartment for it. The whole fiasco was maddening in the moment. However, we look back on it fondly. Those moments of misery became transformed, their upsides accentuated and the downsides suppressed, as if by magic. Indeed, to echo the renowned travel writer Paul Theroux, "Travel is glamorous only in retrospect."

How can this be? One reason was mentioned earlier: it would feel too crummy to regret the expensive, effortful trip to Lake Como, so we bright-sided it. But it's more than that. The lost luggage is part of a larger story: overcoming challenges. Bonding over shared difficulty. Keeping cool while waiting for a suitcase to arrive, drinking wine and browsing magazines. Wearing the same gross outfit for days on end and getting through it. We *want* these memories. We've earned them. They become part of us, part of our life stories. Both big and small, these trying events shape and enhance our identities, adding depth, complexity, and emotional richness. They don't just give us stories to tell. They help us craft our own story, a process of constant creation and revision that continues throughout life.[17]

The lost luggage also has social value for Kate and me as friends. It's a shared memory that is ours alone. Friends might ask "Why do you guys call luggage *bagaglio?"* and we'll crack up, recalling those couple of luggage-less days, drinking convenience-store chianti and shouting bad Italian to unsuspecting passersby. Traveling together provides so many of these priceless shared memories.[18] After the luggage debacle, Kate and I drank limoncello while gazing out at Lake Como. She started a late-night dance party in a town square in Florence. We took a winery tour through Chianti and learned to refer to swirling the wine around your glass as "shaking hands with the wine," a phrase we still use. We missed a train because I insisted on buying a soda from an uncooperative vending machine. I force-fed myself gelato three times in one day. And we became closer friends through these shared experiences, which ranged from the awe-inspiring to the despair-inducing to the straight-up ridiculous.

And beyond the two of us, these tales have their value. Research has found that one reason life experiences trump material purchases is because of the funny, meaningful, interesting stories they provide. People simply enjoy thinking back to a time when they spent money on a life experience, particularly when compared to money spent on a material possession. They also enjoy telling the tales of these life experiences much more than they enjoy talking about their material purchases. There are so many layers to a life experience, and so much to say. With a material possession, there's just not a lot. You need only to imagine a conversation about a new wristwatch versus a great meal, or a new car versus an epic trip, to feel the difference.

To examine the unique value of life experiences, researchers asked undergraduate participants to imagine either two vacation spots they'd really like to visit, or two material items they would really like to own.[19] There was always a clear favorite and a clear runner-up. Someone focusing on experiences might rate Australia as #1 and Ecuador as #2, while someone focusing on material possessions might rate a Rolex watch as #1 and a jet ski as #2. Then, to complicate matters, they asked them to further imagine that they could either have their first choice but would not be permitted to talk about it with others, or they could have their second choice and could talk about it all they wanted. In the case of material possessions, having the ability to talk about it didn't add much value. Therefore, people still preferred to have their original favorite. But in the case of vacations, people were more likely to opt for their second choice, provided they were allowed to talk about it. And their intuition was correct: life experiences are valuable in part because they give us something to talk about.

While we don't want our sharing to be seen as bragging—the normal rules of conversational give-and-take apply here—there is certainly social value in having rich and interesting stories. That person who's been scuba diving in Belize or who just got back from fly fishing in Montana? I want that person at my next dinner party. The guy who just bought a new Lexus? Not as much. In one study, participants were asked to chat with a stranger, either about a recent material purchase or about a recent life experience.[20] Afterward, those who discussed experiences reported enjoying their conversations more and liking their chat-partner more. One reason for this is that people who discuss their life experiences make a more positive impression than do people who discuss their possessions, coming off as adventurous and interesting rather than materialistic and braggy.

And when our life experiences overlap with another's, this fosters social connections like few other things can. Meeting someone new at a party and learning that she's been to Italy, too? Now you have fuel to spark a meaningful connection. And it turns out that even if that person had a much fancier trip than you did, say, staying at the Four Seasons while you bunked in a hostel, you still feel connected as adventurers who have experienced a place few others in your social circle have. Damaging social comparisons are far less likely to happen when thinking about and discussing your life experiences.[21]

On the other hand, meeting someone at a party and learning that he too was recently shopping for a new car? You might share a mutual eyeroll when commiserating on the misery of the process, but you're unlikely to feel deeply connected. Plus, if you learn that this guy just bought a sleek Mercedes while you had to settle for a sluggish Kia, you might actually feel more detached from him and dissatisfied with yourself. Doesn't sound like a very fun party to me.

THE ART OF POSITIVE MEMORY-MAKING

Positive memory-making happens naturally, often without awareness. However, you can consciously take the reins and encourage the process.

Go back through your photos from time to time. Tell the story of your travels. Reminisce with your travel companions and laugh at the fiascos you experienced—or maybe even caused.

Rather than posting your photos on social media while you travel, consider waiting until you get home, selecting your favorite moments, and posting your photos then. This way, you get to relive the experience and also see it through the eyes of others as the "likes" and comments come rolling in. It will prolong your enjoyment, and you also won't have devoted your precious travel time to this task.

Recall the idea of distributed anticipation from chapter 4, where you think about your trip, browse the Web, plan where you'll eat and what you'll do, strategically from time to time before you leave. This way, your excitement is maintained throughout what may be a long waiting period. Now that you're home, consider *distributed reminiscence*, where you revisit the memories of your trip from time to time. There are some obvious ways to do this: going through photos, re-reading your travel journal, and reliving it with travel companions spring immediately to mind.[22]

But there are less obvious tricks as well. You might leave a small memento in a pocket of your suitcase when you unpack: a brochure from a place you visited, a coin, a seashell, or a matchbook. You'll find it months later and the memories will rush back. You can try to recreate a favorite dish you ate on your trip, or watch a movie or TV show that was filmed there and be transported back. Yes, your nostalgia may come with a twinge of sadness as you look back on this precious time.[23] But the experience will be largely positive as old memories rush back. And, who knows, maybe this will light a fire under you as you realize that it's time to plan your next trip!

ONWARD!

Travel begets more travel. Once you start moving, seeing, and doing you want to move, see, and do all the time. Or, as Henry Miller said, "When you travel often, you will be addicted to it forever. Our destination is not the place, but [a] new way to see things."

We strive to make sound travel investments, but travel always contains an element of trial and error. Nothing teaches you what kind of traveler you are, and what works and does not work for you, quite like traveling itself. As you can't help but think ahead to the next trip, consider what you've learned on your recent one. What did you love, hate, or could do without? Because we know that memory has its limitations, you might look over your travel journal, if you kept one, as it will be free from reconstructive biases.

The way that we *remember* our travels carries special weight when debating whether to take a similar trip in the future. Researcher Derrick Wirtz and colleagues recruited a sample of college students who were taking a spring break vacation.[24] Two weeks before departing, they were asked to rate how much they expected to enjoy their trip, and to predict the intensity of their positive and negative feelings. They made similar predictions two-to-four days before their departure. They were each given a Palm Pilot (remember those?), and were told that they were going to be electronically paged, at random, numerous times per day during their vacation—it turned out to be seven times over a preselected thirteen-hour period: (9 a.m. to 10 p.m., or 11 a.m. to midnight). As soon as possible upon receiving the page, they were to report their current mood and level of enjoyment. Finally, after returning home, they were to return the Palm Pilot within two to four days and tell the researchers how much fun they remember having. In a follow-up five weeks later, they indicated how much they would like to take a similar trip again in the future. Interestingly, it was the *recalled* evaluation of the trip—their memories of how pleasant it was—that predicted whether they would want to do it again. Actual momentary experiences—how the spring breakers actually felt in the moments they were paged—were less important, despite the fact that they are arguably more objective and free from bias. The take-home here is that your memory of a trip matters, but your judgment might just be clouded.

Consult with your travel companions, especially if you're going to travel with them again, and determine the highs and lows of your past trip. Look over your photos and note which ones instill an immediate sense of longing in you. Are they cityscapes? Pictures of food? Of people? Of landscapes? Think back to the activities you most enjoyed. Were they cultural, like visiting museums? Were they adventurous, like hiking or zip-lining? Or were they relaxing, like swinging in a hammock with a book and a beer? Also note what didn't work for you. What was stressful or unpleasant? What splurges were worth the money, and what felt like a waste? And did you feel okay spending a lot of money on travel, or did you feel guilty and anxious?

No trip is perfect. There will always be disappointing hotel rooms and meals, arguments, grumpy children, and money poorly spent. All we can do is be aware of our missteps, file them away, and try to do better next time. Use the bad as lessons for the future, and take comfort in knowing that no matter what happens, the good will be what endures in your memory.

HAPPY TRAVEL TIPS
FOR COMING HOME

The task of wrapping up a trip is often tossed off as unimportant or ignored completely. But it's a vitally important part of the process. As your travels reach their inevitable end, ask yourself these key questions:

- *How will I wind down my trip?* Take advantage of the period of renewed appreciation and motivation that can happen when you return. Soon after you get home, reflect on what you liked about yourself, your family, and your routine on this trip. Plan how you can work some of this into daily life, then try it out.

- *What do I miss about my regular life?* Notice the people, places, and small pleasures that spring to mind. Plan to see these people, visit these places, and savor these pleasures soon after you get home.
- *How can I keep reliving this trip?* Tell the story of your travels. Enjoy the happy memories. Keep the memories alive by revisiting photos and mementos.
- *What have I learned about myself and my travel personality?* Use this information to help you plan your next trip!

Nine

The Art of the Staycation:
How to Live Every Day Like
a Happy Traveler

The sole cause of man's unhappiness is that he does not know how to stay quietly in his room.

—Blaise Pascal

The past December, my boyfriend and I decided to take a week-long Christmas trip to Costa Rica. We had done this the year before and loved it so much that after weighing other warm-weather, not-too-faraway options, we realized we wanted to see more of this country above all others.

We booked our flights, reserved hotel rooms, poked around TripAdvisor to read about restaurants and beaches, and looked over photos from the previous year with growing excitement. I got my suitcase out and started gleefully tossing in swimsuits, shorts, and sunscreen. I indulged in a pedicure and even scheduled a spray-tan. It had been a busy semester for me, and I was so looking forward to relaxing. In fact, when he asked me what my goals for the trip were, I thought for a minute and replied, "I just want to *be.*" He chuckled; that is *so* not me. But it was true. I wanted to be present-focused, aware and appreciative of my surroundings for a change. I didn't want to lose myself in web-browsing or social media, and I didn't want to think about work. I felt a deep need to reflect, to hit the pause button on my life for a few days. It seemed like a reasonable and worthy goal.

I never got to pursue it. About a week before the trip, life intervened and we had to cancel. We told ourselves all of the right things—Costa Rica will always be there, we'll save a bunch of money, et cetera—but the fact was, this was a big disappointment. I was so craving warm sunshine and cold beer, morning runs on the beach, and swinging idly in a hammock. But as I thought about it more, I recalled my goal, "I just want to *be*," and wondered why I assumed that this could only happen on a far-off beach. Because, as I've told you before, seldom am I really, truly relaxed on vacation. I'm a chronic planner who's always the first to ask what comes next. I'm wondering if I'm making the best use of my time. I'm taking myself out of lovely moments to photograph them to preserve for later. Given all of these questionable habits, I had to consider the very real possibility that my Costa Rica goal—to just *be*—was, ironically, more likely to be found at home than on the road.

Once my disappointment wore off—and it only took a couple of days—I decided to use our cancelled vacation as a little self-experiment. Maybe I could have my relaxation needs met perfectly well at home. With a degree of forethought that I seldom associate with leisure, I set out to craft an enjoyable vacation at home. I would definitely read a couple of novels. I'd watch the big hit of the winter, Netflix's *Making a Murderer*. I'd go to yoga classes at my gym, schedule lunch dates with friends, and try cooking some new dinner recipes. I'd take some of our Costa Rica money and make a reservation at a world-renowned restaurant an hour away so there would be something special to anticipate. I'd even post a vacation away message on my email.

How did I do? Well . . .

WHY SUCCESSFUL STAYCATIONS AREN'T SO EASY

Whether for financial reasons, a lack of planning, or an extra-busy schedule, many of us find ourselves spending our vacation days at home.

During the recent economic downturn, this became such a common trend that a new term was coined: *staycation*. A staycation is just what it sounds like: physically, you're at home, but mentally and emotionally, you've checked out. Sound easy?

Actually pulling off a successful staycation—that is, one that is relaxing and fulfilling and mimics a traditional vacation—might be more challenging than it initially seems. Being at home triggers numerous behaviors and thought patterns that aren't exactly conducive to rest and relaxation. These include, but are in no way limited to, waking up and immediately checking email, constantly tidying up the kids' toys, paying bills, or dealing with a dwindling refrigerator or growing laundry basket. It's all too easy to use your vacation time to clean out that closet, fix that broken shutter, or catch up on email, laundry, bills, appointments, grocery shopping, and life in general. On a traditional vacation, tidying up and cooking are someone else's responsibility. That's partly what you're paying for! At home, even if you'd sectioned off a day or week completely for yourself, it can be hard to abandon all of the things you normally do.

Another challenge lies in the fact that when we're at home for small bursts of leisure—a few hours here and there—we opt for passive, easy, relaxing things: TV, online shopping, or mindless web-surfing.[1] On a weekday evening or a stolen Saturday afternoon, these sorts of things can be fun and rejuvenating. But if we default to these passive routines while on a multiday staycation, we may have little more to show for ourselves than a sizable dent in the couch and a regrettable stack of boxes from Amazon.

And while it can be satisfying, is a clean closet really the goal of your vacation? Is watching all nine seasons of *How I Met Your Mother*? If you apply the same mindset you have for travel to the staycation, the answer is clear. A clean closet is not the goal. A close, personal connection with sitcom characters probably isn't, either. Not even close. Teaching yourself to think about home-time as akin to travel-time is a key part of the process, but also one of the biggest challenges.

And let's not forget about how even the most intense pleasures lose their emotional power and can fade into the background. As a result, even the exceptional or beautiful things that you see everyday can come to feel ordinary. Seeing them with a sense of wonder again requires focus and creativity. Here's what you can do to nudge yourself to see things anew, unrushed, and with a sense of appreciation.

Setting the Staycation Stage

If schedules, finances, or stamina dictate that this year's vacation days will be spent at home, it's important to set the stage for success, in the same way you might for a vacation far away. In fact, most tips from previous chapters apply, while some deserve special emphasis.

Importantly, *do some planning.* You probably wouldn't leave the details of "real" travel up to chance; you'd scope out some special things you might want to do. Do the same here. Any new restaurants you might want to try? Make a reservation. Novels you've been dying to read? Have them at the ready. A hiking trail or lake you want to visit? Know the details ahead of time. Make it easy to do these things so you don't find yourself accidentally losing a day to the couch and the television screen (unless, of course, that's what you truly want).

A concrete plan can be a surprisingly powerful motivator. Why? Consider something as simple as hiking. You love it, and every time you go to one of your local trails, you feel rejuvenated and committed to making it happen again. And yet it seldom does. When you get home at the end of the day, heading out again and exerting yourself just feels like too much work. Why? *Activation energy* may be to blame.

Psychologists use this phrase to refer to the amount of motivation needed to begin a task. The less activation energy required, the more likely we are to do something. Put bluntly: we are lazy. We opt for the easy thing, the thing requiring the least amount of activation energy. A lack of activation energy may explain why you don't hike as much as you'd like. It's just hard to get out the door and on the trail. Maybe you don't know exactly which trail you want to hike and become paralyzed with indecision. Maybe you don't know exactly how to get there or dread getting lost in the woods. Or you don't know where your hiking boots, first-aid kit, and daypack are, and the thought of digging through the garage to find them is just too exhausting to contemplate. As you consider each of these small but annoying steps in the process, at some point you just decide to stay home. Getting out there for that simple hike required too much activation energy.[2] It's far easier to reach for the remote or pick up a magazine. And, again, if that's what you really want to be doing, no shame. But if, at the end of the day, you felt regretful at how you spent your time, this might worth thinking about.

Fortunately, the fix is simple: *identify and eliminate these hurdles.* Know which hike you want to do and how to get there. Have your boots and other gear ready to go. Make it as easy as possible to enact the behavior you wish. So many of the most engaging experiences in life—those that promote flow, challenge, and growth—take some initiative to start up. And when that is the case, we might just default to the easy, passive, and generally inferior activity instead. So for a successful staycation that is full of novelty and excitement, make all the things you hope to do as easy to enact as possible.

Similarly, *do an honest assessment* of how you might be tempted to spend your time. Afraid you'll be constantly monitoring email? Put up an automatic away message. Worried that you'll spend most of your time doing household projects? Consider allotting just a few hours a day, and no more, to these tasks (after all, some of us can only really relax after we've accomplished something, and a staycation is unlikely to change that). Or do as much as you can before your break officially begins so you'll feel both accomplished and entitled to a rest. Or, hey, use some of the money you're saving and hire someone to do it for you! While you're at it, have your house professionally cleaned and arrange for meals to be delivered. Then it will *really* feel like a vacation.

Finally, *let yourself get excited!* The power of anticipation is not only reserved for expensive, far-flung adventures. Sure, on the surface, your time at home might not seem as exciting as, say, your brother's upcoming trip to Hawaii, but you have some decided advantages: no chance of delayed flights, lost luggage, or jet lag. Less stress. More money in the bank, or more to spend on special, nearby experiences. And managed expectations. You're far less likely to pressure yourself to have fun when you haven't invested gobs of time and money. If it rains one day, no big loss. If you want to spend half the day reading a novel in bed, no guilt or fear of missing out. A staycation can be an escape from the self-imposed pressures that can so often cast a shadow on our travels.

Maybe these are big "ifs," but *if* you can practice the art of savoring, *if* you can work in activities that are novel, engaging, and flow-promoting, and *if* you can meaningfully connect with your partner during a staycation, you might just be happier than your brother in Hawaii!

A LIFELONG STAYCATION

I've been talking about a staycation as something that is bracketed in time, with a clear beginning and end date. Two weeks. One week. One day! Whatever you choose to do with that time, the secret lies in applying the elements of happy travel—eager anticipation, active engagement, savoring, connection, making rich memories—to an experience that, on the surface, can appear quite mundane.

I'm going to push you even further, urging you to use what you've learned about travel to enhance your everyday life, not just during those few days you've deliberately earmarked for pleasure. There are two gigantic, internal pressures to consider: *adaptation* and *lack of motivation*. We need to see and savor the ordinary, despite life's many distractions and demands. And we need the stamina to do the new, challenging, and sometimes scary thing. This is by no means easy, but some reflection, planning, and perspective can help lay the groundwork for living like a traveler in our daily lives.

Never Be Bored

The security of home is wonderful in so many respects, ensuring comfort, safety, and predictability. But all of this can nudge us into complacency, posing a serious challenge to being a happy traveler at home. Home can be unchallenging. Uninspiring. Boring. And yet, as comedian Louis C. K. bluntly put it, "'I'm bored' is a useless thing to say. I mean, you live in a great, big, vast world that you've seen none percent of. Even the inside of your own mind is endless; it goes on forever, inwardly, do you understand? The fact that you're alive is amazing, so you don't get to say 'I'm bored.'"

Clara Bensen, author and frequent traveler, shared with me one of the most valuable lessons of travel that she and her partner Jeff have learned: "I'm a huge believer that the sense of openness and adventure that travel sparks is available to anyone, anywhere—not just when you've shelled out a bunch of money for a big overseas trip. It's a state of mind as much as anything. Jeff and I try to foster a sense of exploration where we live in Austin. Sometimes that's as simple as going for a walk in a neighborhood we're not familiar with. We have a train track that runs right past our apartment and one day, after months of wondering where it went, we decided to follow the tracks for an hour. We painted our nails with red nail polish we found along the track. We found bottles and hammers and odd-shaped pieces of metal. It felt like we'd gone some place completely different. Actively exploring together—wherever we happen to be—is a great way of continually introducing energy into our relationship. We're never bored."[3]

Indeed, seeing the nuances and layers of complexity in what can seem so mundane is the secret to maintaining wonder and appreciation for home. But how?

Learning to See

In *On Looking,* author Alexandra Horowitz argues that, due to a lack of dedicated attention and a set of rigid expectations, we so often fail to notice what is all around us:

> We all have the capacity to really see what is in front of us. On moving to a new home, one's first approach is wide eyed—with senses alert to the various ways that this new block differs from one's old home: the trees provide more shade, or the cars are more plentiful, or the sidewalks are cleaner, or the buildings are more deeply set back from the street. It is only after we have moved in, after we have walked the same street again and again, that we fall asleep to the block . . . The capacity to attend is ours; we just forget how to turn it on.[4]

Multiple times throughout this book, I've implicated hedonic adaptation—the tendency to grow accustomed to the constant pleasures around us—as a primary challenge to happy travel. It's the perfect villain. It's stealthy: slowly operating behind the scenes of our conscious awareness, diverting our attention from the background pleasantries around us. And yet for all of its subtlety, it's formidable. Without apology, it will diminish even the most potent of joys—new love, a sought-after promotion, or a dream home. Pushing back against this process requires vigilant use of an arsenal of tools, from gratitude journaling to actively savoring to injecting novelty into our relationships.

Throughout *On Looking,* Horowitz experiments with yet another approach to undoing adaptation to the most ordinary of things: her Manhattan neighborhood. Simply by walking the streets with different companions, she learns to see her immediate surroundings from a variety of viewpoints.

Through the wide eyes of her small child, who toddles along fascinated, she gained some appreciation for the pigeons, drainpipes, and construction vehicles that drew his gaze. From the learned perspective of a geologist, an expert on the millions of years of tectonic forces that formed the foundation of her neighborhood, she saw the world through the rich lens of geologic time. Through the keen eye of a field naturalist, she learned about the startlingly abundant insect life on her street. With a blind woman, she considered a new world of nonvisual sensory input: the surprisingly nuanced sounds of Manhattan traffic and the change in the breeze that signaled that she was passing by an alleyway or approaching an intersection; information that contributed to a wholly different sort of mental map. Even her dog, with his awareness of all the smells and sights at ground-level, taught her new lessons about the sensory information we naturally filter out of awareness and, by definition, out of the realm of appreciation.

For advice on learning to see the ordinary in a new way, Horowitz advises shaking things up by deviating from your typical path. Walk on a different side of the street. Take the scenic route. Even tilt your head to a different angle. And move slowly enough to really look. To this I would add, *get the backstory*. For five years, I've lived in a historic district in downtown Charlottesville. And for five years, I've existed in a state of vague aesthetic appreciation but historical ignorance. On a whim, I recently decided to take a one-hour walking tour of my neighborhood offered by the local historical society. It cost five dollars and started three blocks from my house. Of the five of us on the tour, four were tourists from out-of-state, and my presence seemed baffling to all. As she imparted her wisdom, our guide would often pause and look at me. "I'm sure you already know this," she would say. Nope! My shame was mitigated by the fact that I was pretty sure none of my local friends would have known it either.

So what did I learn? Here are just a few snippets: the downtown area that I currently inhabit once housed a hospital for Civil War soldiers. What is now a nondescript office building once was an opera house.

A gorgeous 1814 red brick mansion around the corner was originally the home of a prominent slave-owner and the founder of one of Virginia's first banks, while the library a few doors down was once the court house and then the post office. Even my own block was full of surprises. A hundred years ago, it featured a mansion that was demolished around 1920 and a six-story apartment building was put in that spot soon after.[5] In one short hour, my neighborhood went from a pleasant, tree-lined place with some pretty brick buildings to one rich in stories and history. I truly saw it differently.

Do we always *want* to see the world with such detail? Can every walk down the street be an occasion for lingering and careful analysis? Should it be? No. When reflecting back on her walks, Horowitz herself reports having moments of sensory overload. But by going deeper, seeing the ordinary from a new perspective can encourage attention and appreciation that might not happen otherwise.

The Power of a Microadventure

Another way to see home differently is to shake yourself out of your routine by trying out some new activities. Travel guide publisher Lonely Planet offers fun and concrete tips on finding new experiences in your hometown.[6] Some things to consider include following the suggestions of a local guidebook, taking a guided tour of a local attraction, letting your kids plan an entire day of activities, and getting up to watch the sunrise—easy, inexpensive things that we seldom do. Or join a free Meetup group. Even my small town of Charlottesville boasts hundreds of options: wine groups, book groups, hiking groups, language groups, and many more. These carry multiple benefits: connecting you with new and possibly like-minded people, promoting active engagement in an activity, and even showing you a whole new side of your hometown.

Similarly, author and adventurer Alastair Humphries sings the praises of the "microadventure," which is something that is close to home, simple, cheap, and brief. Suggestions are practically limitless but include camping in nearby woods, swimming in a lake under the stars, or cooking dinner over a campfire. While his recommendations are geared toward the outdoors as an escape from urban life, his argument is more general: adventures lie around every corner, if we have our eyes open to them. And we don't need to wait for vacation time or even the weekend to have them. They can be worked in around work, family, and other obligations.[7] But remember activation energy: we often need some oomph to get these things started.

Here's an example of a microadventure. Last summer, on some random Wednesday night, I caught wind of a 5K trail race. The starting line was in a park that was a ten-minute drive from my house. I had nothing to do that night. I needed some exercise. In other words, I had no excuses.

Two minutes after the starting gun fired and the race began, I was shocked to find myself completely disoriented. Where *was* I? I couldn't be too far from anything familiar. As the crow flies, I was extremely close to a shopping mall and a slew of new subdivisions. And yet I had no sense of place. Despite their embarrassingly close proximity to my home, I had never been on these trails before. I shrugged off my confusion and settled in with a pack of runners. Then, a mile or so into the race, the skies quickly clouded over. Like they so often do in the humid Virginia summers, a flash thunderstorm rolled in. Suddenly, I was drenched and running with new urgency through the woods. The trail quickly became a mud bath, and a few slips and falls made me into a muddy mess as well. Panic and prissiness gave way to resignation and then, ultimately, laughter. I met eyes with strangers and we shared looks of sympathy and camaraderie as we urged each other forward. I crossed the finish line sweaty, muddy, and disgusting but with this sense of pride and badassery that I had thought unattainable in the confines of home. Now, while I wouldn't advise going for a run in the woods in a thunderstorm, that evening was the ultimate microadventure: close to home but out of my comfort zone. Fun, challenging, perspective-shifting, and most definitely memorable.

Thirty Days and Counting

Want to seize the everyday but lacking the motivation to do so? Here's a thought experiment for you. Imagine that you suddenly had to move far from your current hometown in a month. What would rise to the top of your must-do list? Certain restaurants, coffee shops, parks, museums, natural areas, and tourist attractions might naturally spring to mind, and if you can really cultivate the mindset that time is running out, you might just be motivated to make the extra effort to seek these things out. Use the power of scarcity as a motivator. Dubious? Consider some of my own recent research which shows that even *imagined* scarcity can be a powerful tool.

In one study, we instructed a group of freshmen and sophomores to imagine moving away from their college town in thirty days, to see if this would motivate them to make the most of their time.[8] We asked them to think about the sorts of things they would want to do if they really did have only thirty days left—who would they spend this time with? What would they do? They checked in with us weekly, reporting on their actions and feelings. In one of these check-ins, one student reported, "During this week I enjoyed the beautiful campus I live on by doing many different things. I walked around campus to classes instead of taking the bus. I sat on the Quad and enjoyed the scenery. I also visited Skyline Drive off-campus with my boyfriend to stargaze. We went to dinner off-campus in downtown Harrisonburg. I went shopping and spent time with my roommate watching movies and eating Taco Bell . . . focusing on others gives me a sense of purpose . . . I did well on my health exam after studying very hard which was a great accomplishment. I was productive but didn't spend too much time doing work without spending time with friends."

Compared to a neutral control group who simply kept track of their daily activities, those living the month like it was their last showed a significant increase in happiness. Interestingly, this effect was driven by fulfillment of the core psychological needs—autonomy, competence, and interpersonal relatedness—that are related to well-being.[9] Perhaps these students felt like more active agents in their daily decision-making as time's scarcity helped to clarify their priorities. The student I mentioned previously saw that studying was important, but her relationships didn't need to be sacrificed—or simply would not be!— in order to do well. Students were choosing activities they felt skilled at and were also allowing themselves to socialize with meaningful others. These are all the kinds of things we do when time is *actually* scarce, but this study suggests that just *imagining* time running out—essentially, living each day as if it were your last—may bring a similar benefit.[10]

But I Can Always Go Next Year!

In fact, one of the challenges to making the most of every day—like a traveler might—is the persistent belief in time's abundance. Because of this, we lack the motivation to capitalize on the wonders that surround us. I experienced this first-hand when I was living in southern California for a couple of years. I was pretty certain that, barring a lasting romantic relationship and long-term employment, my time there had a clear expiration date. So I essentially lived like a traveler, taking weekend drives up the Pacific Coast Highway to Big Sur and south into Mexico. I drove two hours to Santa Barbara for the sole purpose of finding a taco stand that was generously praised by Julia Child. I took that aforementioned trip to Vegas. I ate my way through the Los Angeles Zagat guide, walked on as many beaches as possible, and made a point of going to as many national parks as I could. The ticking clock gave me the stamina to see and do so much more than I would have otherwise.

One Friday, I was wrapping up some work and gearing up to spend a weekend in Yosemite National Park. I'd never been there before and still had to research exactly where I'd go and what I'd do there. Luckily, or so I thought, a colleague of mine, born and bred in California, walked into the mailroom just as I was finishing up some copying. "Hey, I'm going up to Yosemite this weekend! Any suggestions on favorite hikes or restaurants?" I asked. He looked at me blankly. "I've never been there," he said. I was shocked. "But you've lived here your entire life!" He thought for a moment and then mumbled, "I guess I figure I can always go next year."

Bingo. For all of its majesty, Yosemite was five-plus hours away. Not exactly convenient. And it isn't going anywhere. Like with so many things, we simply tell ourselves we'll do it later.

Procrastination doesn't only apply to term papers and income taxes. One study found that we tend to put off even those experiences that promise to be pleasant, if doing them takes some initiative or activation energy. Residents of several big cities, such as Chicago and London, were simply asked to note which of their city's major landmarks and tourist attractions they had visited.[11] Then, a sample of tourists briefly visiting the same cities were polled. It was revealed that the tourists were more likely to have visited the major attractions than were the residents! Presumably, those who perceived having all the time in the world to go to Westminster Abbey or Buckingham Palace figured they could always just do it later. Delving further, the researchers found that it wasn't that the residents were less interested in seeing major attractions than were the tourists (a reasonable assumption, since they were two fundamentally different sets of people). Residents reported having visited the notable attractions when traveling to *other* cities. Just not while in their own.

This effect seems to be driven by the perceived abundance of time. Having a lot of time removes pressure, so we tell ourselves—like my California colleague—that we can always do it later. The end result? We may do it never. The researchers concluded with, "We find that the average two-week visitor has seen significantly more than the average resident who has lived in a city for up to a year."[12]

A Tour Guide at Home

Interestingly, although not surprisingly, sixty percent of the residents' landmark visits happened while they were hosting out-of-town guests. Part of that is surely driven by urgency. As a London resident, you might have a lifetime in which to tour Westminster Abbey, but your visiting cousin has only one week. So you go.

But there's probably more at play here than merely a hastened timeline. As you walk around the city with your cousin, shepherding her to the key attractions and landmarks, the landscape before you may become subtly transformed. One morning, on your way to your neighborhood subway station, you pass a colorfully painted house, a lively café, and a carefully tended flower garden. Having lived in the neighborhood for years, none of it registers with you. You've adapted. And so you walk to the subway station in your typical fashion: quickly, purposefully, with your head down and your attention turned to the business of the day. But your cousin lags behind, forcing you to slow down. She might ask you to tell her about the quirky, colorful house, making you consider it with a more analytical eye. She might want to pop in the café or stop and photograph the flower garden. Her sense of wonder as she does all of this is palpable and contagious.[13] As you look at it all from her fresh perspective, you can't help but feel it too. You're newly aware of and grateful for what had become so very ordinary. For a burst of motivation and a renewed appreciation for the everyday, then, letting yourself see it through the eyes of a newcomer is a great strategy.

I recently started investigating whether this idea of "playing tour guide" can be an effective tool for savoring experiences. To do so, I randomly assigned a sample of sophomores and juniors at James Madison University to write a hypothetical letter to either an incoming freshman, one who is seeing the campus through new eyes, or to a peer who has been at JMU about as long as they have been.[14] Specifically, they were told, "In this study, you are going to be writing a letter to an incoming freshman. You can begin with 'Dear new student' and—beyond that—we are going to allow you to choose what you write about. Take your time with this and show them your excitement, as well as specific things you love about college. Before you start writing, take a moment and imagine what it might feel like to be entering this specific university as a new freshman—basically, someone with much less knowledge and experience of what it is like here."

Those in the peer-condition were given similar instructions but were asked to write to someone who has been at the university about the same amount of time as they have, presumably without the starry-eyed perspective of a brand-new freshman. Those in a third condition, which served as a control, wrote about what they do on a typical weekday, which is a standard neutral writing prompt. After twelve minutes of writing, I found that those writing to a new freshman showed enhanced appreciation for college life compared to those in the other two conditions.

These are preliminary results and I don't want to overstate them, but they do seem to be consistent with people's actual experiences. Consider one of my former research assistants, who served as a campus tour guide while at JMU, showing incoming freshmen and their families around campus. She reflects, "On days when I don't give tours, I can walk around campus all day without really taking in my surroundings or the unique features of my school. However, on tour days, I get to re-experience my school through the eyes of an incoming freshman. I notice the small things I fell in love with on *my* first tour at JMU and in my first few months as a new student here. I honestly feel that I have had a better undergraduate experience and greater appreciation for my university as a result of this position."

Another real-life example comes from Leo Bormans, a Dutch writer and speaker who created the concept of "hapspots."[15] A hapspot is just what is sounds like: the place in your hometown that makes you the happiest, for whatever reason. The concept has been implemented in several ways. In a few European cities, hapspot markers have been put in various locations for visitors to find. Other times, volunteers have been enlisted to stand at their particular hapspot, giving visitors a briefing on the location and why it is so special and meaningful. These projects have been centered mostly in France, Belgium, and the Netherlands, but the idea can be implemented anywhere. Just imagining standing in a few of my favorite places in Charlottesville—the coffee shop where I met my boyfriend, a winery that has one of most gorgeous views around, or where I crossed the finish line of a grueling ten-mile race—and telling people the story of why I love these specific spots fills me with renewed appreciation. In her quest to fall in love with her new town of Blacksburg, Virginia, Melody Warnick discusses some key determinants of "place attachment"—feeling an emotional connection to your home. She suggests you ask yourself, "What about this place would I want to show off to visitors?" as a way of zeroing in your home's special features and biggest selling points.[16]

And of course, the advice here goes both ways. When you're visiting out-of-town friends or family, share your enthusiasm for what they may consider ordinary. You might resist in an attempt to look cool or sophisticated, but your perspective may end up being a far greater hostess gift than any bottle of wine or flower bouquet could ever be.

LESSONS FROM A PERFECT DAY

And, finally, a question: if you were asked to describe and live your perfect day, one that is possible for you to experience right now, what would it look like? How would you spend your time? With whom would you spend it?

This is one of the initial assignments in my undergraduate positive psychology course. First, students have to sit down and really ask themselves, "What would be the 'perfect day' for me, right now?" (I realize that "perfect" is an impossible standard. This fact just gives us more to talk about.) They describe in detail what this day would look like to them. Then, they go out and attempt to live this day.

When we discuss it later, common themes emerge. Time spent with friends tops many of their lists, and catching up on sleep is also way up there. Food always has a privileged spot, too. Not particularly fancy or expensive food, but some favorite meal or snack that's thoughtfully chosen and savored. I'm always surprised at how often "a long, hot shower" is mentioned. An episode of a favorite TV show with roommates before bed is common. If schedules and finances allow, there's sometimes a special outing in the mix: a winery, a hike, or even a trip to Target. Schoolwork is notably absent.

When students are attempting to enact their perfect days, many of them are working under conditions that are less than ideal: a big exam, an unexpected rainstorm, or a long shift at a part-time job. Or they've inadvertently chosen a day when their close friends are all too busy to spend time with them. Many express regret at not being able to see their long-distance partners, close family members, or even their pets. To me, this is when it gets interesting. Can they manage to carve out moments of pleasure, engagement, and meaning even when their circumstances are anything but perfect? Many find that, yes, with the right mindset, they can. But they also learn that too much pressure, the quest for absolute perfection, can be totally counterproductive and can rob them of enjoyment.[17]

Later, when we debrief as a class, another big discussion point is how elements of their perfect days can be incorporated into their daily lives. Because, really, much of what they chose to do wasn't terribly extraordinary. This is great news, actually. It suggests that peak moments can be found in the dining hall and on the local nature trail just as easily as at a Michelin-starred restaurant or at the Louvre.

It's the *intention* with which students lived out their moments that was so key. It's a *mindset*. The activity takes them off of auto-pilot for the day, reminding them that so much of what they seem to most value—ordinary foods, their friends and roommates, a good night's sleep, a hot shower— are ever-present. The difference, most often, lies within their own hearts and minds. For this assignment, they are simply taking the time and making the effort to live with thoughtful intention, seeing the ordinary as an opportunity for a wealth of good feelings.

But layered on top of all of this and further complicating matters is the persistent belief that they are all so darn *busy*.[18] Surely, you can relate. One reaction that I've always remembered was from an especially bright, motivated senior who was in the middle of applying to medical school while also finishing up her last semester of intense coursework. A highlight of her perfect day was simply spending ten minutes standing on the balcony of her apartment, watching the sunset. Even in the frenzied stress-fest that her life had recently become, she felt relaxed and grateful in that moment. When I asked her if that's something she could see herself doing more regularly, she paused and quietly remarked, "Well, maybe. But I'm just so busy." She couldn't fathom taking ten minutes to relax and appreciate, even though it cost nothing and seemed to bring her such happiness.

This is one of the primary challenges of happy traveling through life: noticing and taking ownership of these moments, not while on vacation, but in the day-to-day, when we *are* busy. It's about giving ourselves permission to carve out moments of wonder, connection, joy, peace, and gratitude, even when life is far from perfect and distractions, to-do lists, and demands take hold.

Think back to *your* perfect day. Not one spent on a far-off beach or in a foreign city, but one that you could reasonably live out *today*. If you haven't yet done so, map it out, from beginning to end. You can try to live it, sure. Or you can just step back and look at what you've written. What things on that list are possible for you to incorporate into your real, imperfect life right now? If you're not doing them, why not? Too busy? Too stressed? Could you be feeling like my former student, too overburdened to even take ten minutes out of the day to watch a sunset? Your challenge is to suppress that belief and try it out. Not just on vacation, but every single day.

Anticipation, awe, savoring, flow, deep connection, and treasured memories are not only the stuff of vacations. They are the ingredients of a well-lived life. While this book has been a series of empirically supported lessons in enhancing travel, it's also a collection of advice on daily living. All of the strategies discussed here can be applied to our daily lives. Maybe the stakes are lower. Maybe it's less intense, less urgent. And therein lies the challenge.

HAPPY TRAVEL TIPS FOR EVERY DAY

Trying to revive your enthusiasm for home? Try asking yourself the following:

- *What would I miss most if I had to move far away from my current town in a month or so? What things would I regret not having done?* This is important information! Seek out those places, people, and experiences.
- *If people were to visit me from out of town, what would I be most excited to show them?* Play tour guide. Even if you're not up for houseguests, craft a day or even an afternoon of your favorite things, and introduce them to someone else. It might even be a fun way to spend the day with your partner, friends, or children.
- *Do I know the backstory of my city? Or even my immediate neighborhood?* Peel back some of the unexplored layers of a place. Take a tour of a local attraction, or read up on local history.

- *How can I inject more novelty and adventure into my everyday life?* Adventures and excitement don't need to be reserved for vacation or even for the weekend! Walk into that new ethnic restaurant or funky new boutique. Smile at a stranger. Join a Meetup group. Learn something new. Pitch a tent. Drive down a new road. Live an experientially rich life!

The Twelve Rules for Happy Travel

1. More time away is not always better. Quality over quantity.
2. Location matters less than your attitude in that location.
3. Let the anticipation build. Planning and researching are part of the fun.
4. When planning a trip, map out how a typical day might look, from beginning to end.
5. You always pack yourself—your personality, anxieties, and habits—with you on your trip.
6. Anticipate the fact that no matter how beautiful or exciting the location, you will get used to it after a couple of days. Plan to vary your experiences.
7. Go deeper: get the backstory on the people you meet and places you visit.
8. Use technology selectively and with intention.
9. Traveling with others is intense, in the best and worst ways. Consider travel compatibility before booking.
10. End on a high note. Craft a special last day or evening.
11. Coming home can be shaped into a good thing. Relish coming home and see it as an opportunity for gratitude and positive change.
12. With attention and motivation, you can be a happy traveler even at home.

ACKNOWLEDGMENTS

———

To my dedicated and creative agent, Maria Ribas of Stonesong—a huge thank you for taking a chance on me and patiently and expertly teaching me so much about this new world of nonacademic writing. Abby Gross, my editor at Oxford, you have my undying gratitude for your faith in this project, your craftsmanship, and your good humor while guiding me through my first book. The entire team at OUP has been a dream to work with: thank you.

One upside of somehow being into midcareer is that I have the perspective to say that when it comes to teachers and mentors, I hit the jackpot. Back in Schuylkill Valley High School's AP art history course, my caring and passionate teacher Evelyn Braun was planning a summer trip to Europe for her students and covertly called my mother at work to strongly suggest that I go along. Mrs. Braun, along with my selfless parents, set this whole thing into motion. Know that I am forever grateful. At Millersville University, Professors Al Forsyth, Susan Luek, and John Osborne gave me a much-needed dose of confidence while my undergraduate mentor, Tae Woo, constantly opened her door to me, took me under her wing, and—with her singular wisdom and hilarity—taught me more than she could ever know about academic life and how psychology is alive and well in the real world. Tim Wilson at the University of Virginia expertly taught me the art and science of conducting experimental research and perfectly modeled how to write elegantly for both academic and nonacademic audiences. And now, at James Madison University, my colleagues and friends in the Department of Psychology have been tremendously supportive of me and of this project. I have been extremely fortunate to have spent my career in the presence of such gifted, inspiring, dedicated mentors and colleagues.

To the JMU research team who helped along the way: Demitra Bivens, Rachel Jones, Anna Lacy, Alexis Morse, Maria Camila Restrepo Chavez, Erik Simmons, and Alyssa Welch—thank you for being with me from square one. To my study abroad students, you have unknowingly taught me so many lessons in how to be a happy traveler. I love seeing the world through your grateful, fun-loving, wide-open eyes. And a very special thanks to Briana Craig, Kayla Filipour, Megan Mischinski, and Allison Piotrowski for carefully weeding through my rough drafts. Your thoughtful and tactful corrections and suggestions made the final product far better than it ever would have been otherwise, and I am forever grateful for your hard work and discerning eyes.

To the colleagues and friends who helped me craft my very early, very rough ideas into a proposal and, ultimately, a final product—Sara Algoe, Robert Biswas-Diener, Dana Dunn, Liz Dunn, Kristin Layous, Alan Levinovitz, Gabi Logan, Sonja Lyubomirsky, and Shige Oishi—I so appreciate you generously sharing your expertise and knowledge of the book-writing process.

In Charlottesville and beyond, I've been fortunate to have a family of friends and supporters who've kept me going through this process with any or all of the following: red wine, Lifetime movies, long lunches, Saturday morning runs, free lodging, encouraging words, tough love, and wonderful anecdotes about happy and not-so-happy travel: Christina Ball, Jean Flores, Steve Grace, Jim Harder, Holly Hom, Michelle Majorin, Jan Parker, Doug Schneider, Tracie Skipper, Dan Stern, Miller Murray Susen, Becky Tassone, Lynn Thorne, Suzanna Turanyi, Edward Warwick White, and Gary Warwick White. For so many reasons, I appreciate you tremendously. And to Mark Lorenzoni and the Charlottesville running community: I thank you for keeping me from becoming an utter couch potato during this process.

Writing about the hazards of traveling with others has made me relish my own travel companions all the more. Jessica Irons, Kate Lambert, and Hung Cam Thai, the memories I have of our adventures and mishaps could fill a thousand pages, and they've shaped what I know happy travel to be. From lazy days in beachside hammocks to frenzied sprints to make a flight, from wine and lobster to convenience-store Combos, and from gilded opera houses to smoky karaoke bars, you make it all unbelievably fun.

To my biggest cheerleaders: my mom, Mary Kurtz, my brother, Ryan Kurtz, and my nana, Marion Kurtz. Your faith in me keeps me going. To my aunt, Jane Schmeider, you opened up my world on all of those childhood car trips and I am finally taking the opportunity to thank you. And to my dad, Butch Kurtz, I continuously feel your pride from the great deer camp in the sky. This one's for you.

Finally, a special thanks to Joe Harder, with his knack for creative acronyms and his eagle eye for typos and grammatical impropriety. (Note: he did not read this section, so you can blame him for any errors.) He was with me every step of the way, from encouraging me to pursue my kernel of a notion of an idea for a psychologically based travel guidebook to line-editing each and every chapter. He's been the most agreeable travel partner imaginable, navigating six countries with me and smiling through my stubborn jet lag, height-induced panic attacks, inability to drive a stick shift, and poor choices in footwear. He indulges my constant insistence that, "Yes, of course I know the way!" and never says "I told you so" when I'm proven wrong. The reason there are few personal accounts in my traveling-with-your-partner-is-hard chapter is largely because of him. I simply have nothing to gripe about, and—truth be told—I don't want to make you all jealous.

And that brings me to my final happy travel tip. The next time you have to endure an early morning cross-country flight, I strongly suggest you devote some of that time to thinking about all of the generous, inspiring people who have nurtured and supported *you* over the years. As I sit here in 23B—a *middle seat*—with the person in front of me fully reclined and my seat mate monopolizing the armrest, somewhere above Kansas, I am amazed to be feeling nothing but gratitude.

NOTES

―――

PROLOGUE

1. In one of the first books on modern positive psychology, Marty Seligman describes "the good life" as one that is pleasurable, engaging, and meaningful. These terms nicely describe what I mean by "happy travel" as well. See Martin E. P. Seligman, *Authentic Happiness: Using the New Positive Psychology to Realize Your Potential for Lasting Fulfillment* (New York: Free Press, 2002).

2. Barry Schwartz, *The Paradox of Choice: Why More Is Less* (New York: Ecco, 2004). Iris B. Mauss, Maya Tamir, Craig L. Anderson, and N. S. Savino, "Can Seeking Happiness Make People Unhappy? Paradoxical Effects of Valuing Happiness," *Emotion* 11 (2011): 807–815.

3. Charlie Lankston, "The Wild Effect: Hundreds of Women Follow in Cheryl Strayed's Footsteps and Take on 2,600-Mile Pacific Crest Trail Made Famous in Her Best-Selling Novel," *The Daily Mail Online*, December 16, 2014, www.dailymail.co.uk/femail/article-2876281/The-Wild-Effect-Hundreds-women-follow-Cheryl-Strayed-s-footsteps-2-600-mile-Pacific-Crest-Trail-famous-best-selling-novel.html#ixzz4EpYkIywZ.

4. Jason Wilson, "Under the Crushing Weight of the Tuscan Sun," *The New Yorker*, March 11, 2016, www.newyorker.com/books/page-turner/under-the-crushing-weight-of-the-tuscan-sun?mbid=social_facebook.

5. Amit Kumar, Matthew A. Killingsworth, and Thomas Gilovich,"Waiting for Merlot: Anticipatory Consumption of Experiential and Material Purchases," *Psychological Science* 25 (2014): 1924–1931; Jeroen Nawijn, Miquelle A. G. Marchand, Ruut Veenhoven, and Ad J. Vingerhoets, "Vacationers Happier, but Most Not Happier After a Holiday," *Applied Research in Quality of Life* 5 (2010): 35–47.

6. Dalia Etzion, "Annual Vacation: Duration of Relief from Job Stressors and Burnout," *Stress and Health* 16 (2003): 213–226; Jessica de Bloom, Sabine A. E. Geurts, and Michiel A. J. Kompier, "Effects of Short Vacations, Vacation Activities and Experiences on Employee Health and Well-Being," *Stress Health* 28 (2012): 305–318; Ondrej Mitas, Careen Yarnal, Reginald Adams, and Nilam Ram, "Taking a 'Peak' at Leisure Travelers' Positive Emotions," *Leisure Sciences* 34 (2012): 115–135.

7. William W. Maddux and Adam D. Galinsky, "Cultural Borders and Mental Barriers: The Relationship Between Living Abroad and Creativity," *Journal of Personality and Social Psychology* 96 (2009): 1047–1061; Julia Zimmermann and Franz J. Neyer, "Do We Become a Different Person When Hitting the Road? Personality Development of Sojourners," *Journal of Personality and Social Psychology* 105 (2013): 515–530; Angela M. Durko and James F. Petrick, "Family and Relationship Benefits of Travel Experience: A Literature Review," *Journal of Travel Research* 52 (2013): 720–730; Niels van de Ven, Leon van Rijswijk, and Michael M Roy, "The Return Trip Effect: Why the Return Trip Often Seems to Take Less Time," *Psychonomic Bulletin and Review* 18 (2011): 827–832; Leaf Van Boven and Thomas Gilovich, "To Do or to Have? That is the Question," *Journal of Personality and Social Psychology* 85 (2003): 1193–1202; Karl Pillemer, *30 Lessons for Living: Tried and True Advice from the Wisest Americans.* (New York: Hudson Street Press, 2011); Bronnie Ware, *The Top Five Regrets of the Dying: A Life Transformed by the Dearly Departing* (Carlsbad, CA: Hay House, 2012).

8. For a discussion of the lack of dialogue between psychologists and tourism researchers, see Svein Larsen, "Aspects of a Psychology of the Tourist Experience," *Scandinavian Journal of Hospitality and Tourism* 7 (2007): 7–18.

CHAPTER 1

1. Daniel Gilbert, *Stumbling on Happiness* (New York: Vintage, 2006); Adam Waytz, Hal E. Hershfield and Diana I. Tamir, "Mental Simulation and Meaning in Life," *Journal of Personality and Social Psychology* 108 (2015): 336–355.

2. James G. March, "Bounded Rationality, Ambiguity, and the Engineering of Choice," *Bell Journal of Economics* 9 (1978): 597–608.

3. Timothy D. Wilson and Daniel T. Gilbert, "Affective Forecasting: Knowing What to Want," *Current Directions in Psychological Science* 14 (2005): 131–134.

4. Daniel T. Gilbert, Elizabeth C. Pinel, Timothy D. Wilson, Stephen J. Blumberg, and Thalia P. Wheatley, "Immune Neglect: A Source of Durability Bias in Affective Forecasting," *Journal of Personality and Social Psychology* 75 (1998): 617–638; George F. Loewenstein, Ted O'Donoghue, and Matthew J. Rabin, "Projection Bias in Predicting Future Utility," *Quarterly Journal of Economics* 118 (2003): 1209–1248; Barbara A. Mellers and A. Peter McGraw, "Anticipated Emotions as Guides to Choice," *Current Directions in Psychological Science* 10 (2001): 210–214; Timothy D. Wilson, Thalia P. Wheatley, Jonathan M. Meyers, Daniel T. Gilbert, and Danny Axsom, "Focalism: A Source of Durability Bias in Affective Forecasting," *Journal of Personality and Social Psychology* 78 (2000): 821–836.

5. Dale W. Griffin, David Dunning, and Lee Ross, "The Role of Construal Processes in Overconfident Predictions About the Self and Others," *Journal of Personality and Social Psychology* 59 (1990): 1128–1139.

6. Philip Brickman, Dan R. Coates, and Ronnie Janoff-Bulman, "Lottery Winners and Accident Victims: Is Happiness Relative?" *Journal of Personality and Social Psychology* 36 (1978): 917–927.

7. Harry Helson, "Current Trends and Issues in Adaptation-Level Theory," *American Psychologist* 19 (1964): 26–38; Allen Parducci, *Happiness, Pleasure, and Judgment: The Contextual Theory and Its Applications* (Hillsdale, NJ: Lawrence Erlbaum, 1995); Ed Diener, Richard E. Lucas, and Christie Napa Scollon, "Beyond the Hedonic Treadmill: Revising the Adaptation Theory of Well-Being," *American Psychologist* 61 (2006): 305–314.

8. Kennon M. Sheldon and Sonja Lyubomirsky, "The Challenge of Staying Happier: Testing the Happiness Adaptation Prevention Model," *Personality and Social Psychology Bulletin* 38 (2012): 670–680.

9. Bill Bryson, introduction to *The Best American Travel Writing* (Boston: Houghton Mifflin, 2000).

10. Alexandra Horowitz, *On Looking: A Walker's Guide to the Art of Observation.* (New York: Simon & Schuster, 2014), 30.

11. Jessica De Bloom, Sabine A. E. Geurts, and Michiel A. J. Kompier, "Vacation (After-) Effects on Employee's Health and Well-Being, and the Role of Vacation Activities, Experiences and Sleep," *Journal of Happiness Studies* 14 (2013): 613–633.

12. Timothy D. Wilson and Daniel T. Gilbert, "Explaining Away: A Model of Affective Adaptation," *Perspectives on Psychological Science* 3 (2008): 370–386.

13. For some amazing examples of the disconnect between the real and the ideal, see Matt Hershberger, "Hilarious Photos Show the Difference Between Travel Expectations and Travel Reality," February 19, 2016, http://matadornetwork. com/life/hilarious-photos-show-difference-travel-expectations-travel-reality/.

14. David A. Schkade and Daniel Kahneman, "Does Living in California Make People Happy? A Focusing Illusion in Judgments of Life Satisfaction," *Psychological Science* 9 (1998): 340–346; Timothy D. Wilson, Thalia P. Wheatley, Jonathan M. Meyers, Daniel T. Gilbert, and Danny Axsom, "Focalism: A Source of Durability Bias in Affective Forecasting," *Journal of Personality and Social Psychology* 78 (2000): 821–836.

15. Derrick Wirtz, Justin Kruger, Christie N. Scollon, and Ed Diener, "What to Do on Spring Break? The Role of Predicted, On-line, and Remembered Experience in Future Choice," *Psychological Science* 14 (2003): 520–524.

16. Yaavoc Trope and Nira Liberman, "Construal Level Theory," *Psychological Review* 110 (2003): 403– 421.

17. Katherine L. Milkman, Todd Rogers, and Max H. Bazerman, "I'll Have the Ice Cream Soon and the Vegetables Later: A Study of Online Grocery Store Purchases and Lead Time," *Marketing Letters* 21 (2010): 17–35; Katherine L. Milkman, Todd Rogers, and Max H. Bazerman, "Highbrow Films Gather Dust: Time-Inconsistent Preferences and Online DVD Rentals," *Management Science* 55 (2010): 1047–1059.

18. Thomas Gilovich, Margaret Kerr, and Victoria H. Medvec, "Effect of Temporal Perspective on Subjective Confidence," *Journal of Personality and Social Psychology* 64 (1993): 552–560.

19. Timothy D. Wilson, Thalia P. Wheatley, Jonathan M. Meyers, Daniel T. Gilbert, and Danny Axsom, "Focalism: A Source of Durability Bias in Affective Forecasting," *Journal of Personality and Social Psychology* 78 (2000): 821–836.

20. Daniel L. Schacter, "Memory," in *Foundations of Cognitive Science*, ed. Michael I. Posner (Cambridge, MA: MIT Press, 1989), 683–725.

21. Terence R. Mitchell, Leigh Thompson, Erika Peterson, and Randy Cronk, "Temporal Adjustment of the Evaluation of Events: The 'Rosy View,'" *Journal of Experimental Social Psychology* 33 (1997): 421–448.

22. Robert I. Sutton, "Feelings about a Disneyland Visit: Photographs and Reconstruction of Bygone Emotions," *Journal of Management Inquiry* 1 (1992): 278–287.

23. George Loewenstein, "Out of Control: Visceral Influences on Behavior," *Organizational Behavior and Human Decision Processes* 65 (1996): 272–292.

24. Kristi Lemm and Derrick Wirtz, "Exploring 'Rosy' Bias and Goal Achievement in Marathon Runners," *Journal of Sport Behavior* 36 (2013): 66–81; Eran Chajut, Avner Caspi, Rony Chen, Moshe Hod, and Dan Ariely, "In Pain Thou Shalt Bring Forth Children: The Peak-and-End Rule in Recall of Labor Pain," *Psychological Science* 25 (2014): 2266–2271.

25. Leon Festinger, *A Theory of Cognitive Dissonance* (Redwood City, CA: Stanford University Press, 1957).

26. W. Richard Walker, John J. Skowronski, and C. P. Thompson, "Life is Pleasant—and Memory Helps to Keep It That Way!," *Review of General Psychology* 7 (2013): 203–210.

27. Olga Khazan, "Why Mistakes Are Often Repeated," *The Atlantic*, February 25, 2016, www.theatlantic.com/science/archive/2016/02/why-mistakes-are-often-repeated/470778/?utm_source=SFFB.

28. Derrick Wirtz, Justin Kruger, Christie N. Scollon, and Ed Diener, "What to Do on Spring Break? The Role of Predicted, On-line, and Remembered Experience in Future Choice," *Psychological Science* 14 (2003): 520–524.

29. Alain De Botton, *The Art of Travel* (New York: Pantheon, 2002), 19.

30. Kennon M. Sheldon and Sonja Lyubomirsky, "Achieving Sustainable Gains in Happiness: Change Your Actions, Not Your Circumstances," *Journal of Happiness Studies* 7 (2006): 55–86.

31. Daniel T. Gilbert, Matthew A. Killingsworth, Rebecca N. Eyre, and Timothy D. Wilson, "The Surprising Power of Neighborly Advice," *Science* 323 (2009): 1617–1619.

32. Dale W. Griffin, David Dunning, and Lee Ross, "The Role of Construal Processes in Overconfident Predictions About the Self and Others," *Journal of Personality and Social Psychology* 59 (1990): 1128–1139.

33. Sheena S. Iyengar and Mark R. Lepper, "When Choice is Demotivating: Can One Desire Too Much of a Good Thing?," *Journal of Personality and Social Psychology* 79 (2000): 995–1006.

34. Timothy D. Wilson and Jonathan S. Schooler, "Thinking Too Much Can Reduce the Quality of Preferences and Decisions," *Journal of Personality and Social Psychology* 60 (1991): 181–192.

35. Neal Roese, "Counterfactual Thinking," *Psychological Bulletin* 121 (1997): 133–148.

36. Sheena S. Iyengar, Rachael E. Wells, and Barry Schwartz, "Doing Better but Feeling Worse: Looking for the 'Best' Job Undermines Satisfaction," *Psychological Science* 17 (2006): 143–150.

37. Barry Schwartz, Andrew Ward, John Monterosso, Sonja Lyubomirsky, Katherine White, and Darrin R. Lehman, "Maximizing Versus Satisficing: Happiness is a Matter of Choice," *Journal of Personality and Social Psychology* 83 (2002): 1178–1197. Copyright © 2002 American Psychological Association. Reproduced with permission. No further reproduction or distribution is permitted without written permission from the American Psychological Association.

38. Barry Schwartz, *The Paradox of Choice: Why More Is Less* (New York: Ecco, 2004).

39. Just trying to select examples of the too-many-choices problem presents a choice overload. Amazon.com offers over 200,000 wristwatch options, over 50,000 suitcases, and over 5,000 toilet bowl brushes. Your local supermarket may well offer over 200 types of breakfast cereal. The 2013 car issue of Consumer Reports examined 281 different models. A few examples in the context of travel: New York City currently has over 16,000 rentals available on Airbnb, and over 51,000 restaurants reviewed on Yelp. Even my own small city of Charlottesville, Virginia boasts 240 rental options and 507 restaurants.

40. Jeong-Yeol Park and Soo Cheong Jang, "Confused by Too Many Choices? Choice Overload in Tourism," *Tourism Management* 35 (2013): 1–23.

41. But note the large gap between the ten-option and twenty-option condition. The sweet spot may actually lie somewhere in this range. Another study, which had participants taste and rate different types of strawberry jam or chocolates, found that trying six options led to a satisfying choice, while twenty-four or thirty overwhelmed; see Iyengar and Lepper, "When Choice is Demotivating." Twenty vacation options still seems like an awful lot in real life.

42. Herbert A. Simon, "Rational Choice and the Structure of the Environment," *Psychological Review* 63 (1956): 129–138.

43. Schwartz, Ward, Monterosso, Lyubomirsky, White, and Lehman, "Maximizing Versus Satisficing: Happiness is a Matter of Choice."

44. Your score can range from 13 to 91. The average score here is about a 50. While there is no precise cutoff point, if your total score is above a 65, you're clearly in the maximizing camp. Below 40, you tend toward satisficing.

45. Thomas D. Gilovich and Victoria H. Medvec, "The Experience of Regret: What, When, and Why," *Psychological Review* 102 (1995): 379–395.

46. Jane Beattie, Jonathan Baron, John C. Hershey, and Mark D. Spranca, "Psychological Determinants of Decision Attitude," *Journal of Behavioral Decision Making* 7 (1994): 129–144.

47. Gilbert, Killingsworth, Eyre, and Wilson, "The Surprising Power of Neighborly Advice."

48. Barry Schwartz, "Self-Determination: The Tyranny of Freedom," *American Psychologist* 55 (2000): 79–88.

49. Max H. Bazerman, Don Moore, Ann E. Tenbrunsel, and Kimberly A. Wade-Benzoni, "Explaining How Preferences Change across Joint Versus Separate Evaluations," *Journal of Economic Behavior and Organization* 39 (1999): 41–58; Christopher K. Hsee and Jiao Zhang, "Distinction Bias: Misprediction and Mischoice Due to Joint Evaluation," *Journal of Personality and Social Psychology* 86 (2004): 680–695.

50. Daniel Kahneman, Jack L. Knetsch, and Richard H. Thaler, "Experimental Tests of the Endowment Effect and the Coase Theorem," *Journal of Political Economy* 98 (1990): 1325–1348.

51. Daniel T. Gilbert and Jane E. Ebert, "Decisions and Revisions: The Affective Forecasting of Changeable Outcomes," *Journal of Personality and Social Psychology* 82 (2002): 503–514.

CHAPTER 2

1. Ed Diener, Randy J. Larsen, and Robert A. Emmons, "Person-Situation Interactions: Choice of Situations and Congruence Response Models," *Journal of Personality and Social Psychology* 47 (1984): 580–592.

2. Ashley Fulmer, Michele Gelfand, Arie Kruglanski, Chu Kim-Prieto, Ed Diener, Antonio Pierro, and E. Tory Higgins, "On 'Feeling Right' in Cultural Contexts: How Person-Culture Match Affects Self-Esteem and Subjective Well-Being," *Psychological Science* 21 (2010): 1563–1569; Richard Florida, *Who's Your City?* (New York: Basic Books, 2008); Markus Jokela, Wiebke Bleidorn, Michael E. Lamb, Samuel D. Gosling, and Peter J. Rentfrow, "Geographically Varying Associations Between Personality and Life Satisfaction in the

London Metropolitan Area," *Proceedings of the National Academy of Science* 112 (2015): 725–730; Shigehiro Oishi, "Goals as Cornerstones of Subjective Well-Being: Linking Individuals and Cultures," in *Cross-Cultural Psychology of Subjective Well-Being*, eds. Ed Diener and Eunkook M. Suh (Cambridge, MA: MIT Press, 2000), 87–112.

3. Brent W. Roberts and Richard W. Robins, "A Longitudinal Study of Person-Environment Fit and Personality Development," *Journal of Personality* 72 (2004): 89–110.

4. Robert D. Bretz and Timothy A. Judge, "Person-Organization Fit and the Theory of Work Adjustment: Implications for Satisfaction, Tenure, and Career Success," *Journal of Vocational Behavior* 44 (1994): 32–54.

5. Kennon M. Sheldon and Andrew J. Elliot, "Goal Striving, Need-Satisfaction, and Longitudinal Well-Being: The Self-Concordance Model," *Journal of Personality and Social Psychology* 76 (1999): 482–497; Kennon M. Sheldon and Tim Kasser, "Coherence and Congruence: Two Aspects of Personality Integration," *Journal of Personality and Social Psychology* 68 (1995): 531–543.

6. Sandra Basala and David Klenosky, "Travel Style Preferences for Visiting a Novel Destination: A Conjoint Investigation across the Novelty-Familiarity Continuum," *Journal of Travel Research* 40 (2001): 172–183.

7. Alan E. Kazdin, *Encyclopedia of Psychology* (Washington, DC: American Psychological Association, 2000).

8. Paul T. Costa and Robert R. McCrae, "Set Like Plaster? Evidence for the Stability of Adult Personality," in *Can Personality Change?*, eds. T. F. Heatherton and J. L. Weinberger (Washington DC: American Psychological Association, 1994), 21–40.

9. Robert Biswas-Diener, P. Alex Lindley, Helen Dovey, John Maltby, Robert Hurling, Joy Wilkinson, and Nadezhda Lyubchik, "Pleasure: An Initial Exploration," *Journal of Happiness Studies* 16 (2015): 313–332. For another brief measure of the Big Five, see Samuel D. Gosling, Peter J. Rentfrow, and William B. Swann, "A Very Brief Measure of the Big-Five Personality Domains," *Journal of Research in Personality* 37 (2003): 504–528.

10. Paul T. Costa and Robert R. McCrae, "Four Ways Five Factors Are Basic," *Personality and Individual Differences* 13 (1992): 653–665; Paul T. Costa and Robert R. McCrae, "A Five Factor Theory of Personality," in *Handbook of Personality Theory and Research*, eds. L. Pervin and O. John (New York: Guilford Press, 1999), 139–153.

11. The other Big Five traits have implications for happy travel as well, although there is less research on the topic. Agreeableness and neuroticism certainly relate to traveling well with others, which is the topic of chapter 7. Conscientiousness, with its focus on organization and responsibility, certainly relates to successful planning. You haven't read the last of the Big Five!

12. Note that items 4, 5, 6, and 7 are reverse-scored. After reverse-scoring, higher numbers indicate a tendency toward allocentrism.

13. Because the full measure was a bit too long for this brief demonstration, I shortened it by removing seven slightly redundant items. I conducted a pilot test of 171 people and found that this measure maintained some key psychometric properties. Internal consistency, the average correlation of each item with each other item, dropped from $\alpha = .79$ to .65, which is partly a mathematical artifact (having fewer items lowers this number). Both the full measure and condensed measure provided here moderately and significantly correlate with a measure of openness to experience. For the full measure, see Jeff Jiang, Mark E. Havitz, and Robert M. O'Brien, "Validating the International Tourist Role Scale," *Annals of Tourism Research* 27 (2000): 964–981.

14. Andrew Yiannakis and Heather Gibson, "Roles Tourists Play," *Annals of Tourism Research* 19 (1992): 287–303; Erik Cohen, "Towards a Sociology of International Tourism," *Social Research* 39 (1972): 164–182; Stanley C. Plog, "Why Destination Areas Rise and Fall in Popularity," *Cornell Hotel and Restaurant Quarterly* 14 (1972): 55–58.

15. Thomas Bieger and Christian Laesser, "Market Segmentation by Motivation: The Case of Switzerland," *Journal of Travel Research* 41 (2002): 68–76; Bae-Haeng Cho, "Segmenting the Younger Korean Tourist Market: The Attractiveness of Australia as a Holiday Destination," *Journal of Travel and Tourism Marketing* 7 (1998): 1–19; Laurie E. Loker and Richard R. Perdue, "A Benefit-Based Segmentation of a Nonresident Summer Travel Market," *Journal of Travel Research* 30 (1992): 30–35; Thomas E. Muller, "Using Personal Values to Define Segments in an International Tourism Market," *International Marketing Review* 8 (1991): 57–70.

16. Stanley C. Plog, "Understanding Psychographics in Tourism Research," in *Travel, Tourism and Hospitality Research*, eds. R. Ritchie and C. Goeldner (New York: Wiley, 1987).

17. Pierre Filiatrault and J. R. Brent Richie, "The Impact of Situational Factors on the Evaluation of Hospitality Services," *Journal of Travel Research* 26 (1988): 29–37.

18. Mervyn S. Jackson and Gerald N. White, "Personality Type and Predicting Tourist Behaviour," in *Tourism and Hospitality on the Edge*. eds. C. Pforr and J. Carlsen, Proceedings of the 2002 CAUTHE Conference, Part 30. Norma P. Nickerson and Gary D. Ellis, "Traveler Types and Activation Theory: A Comparison of Two Models," *Journal of Travel Research* 30 (1991): 26–31.

19. Seppo E. Iso-Ahola, "Towards a Social Psychological Theory of Tourism Motivation: A Rejoinder," *Annals of Tourism Research* 9 (1982): 256–262.

20. Shigehiro Oishi, Minha Lee, and Thomas Talhelm, "Personality and Geography: Introverts Prefer Mountains," *Journal of Research in Personality* 50 (2015): 55–68.

21. As the kids say, you only live once.

22. Robert M. Yerkes and John D. Dodson, "The Relation of Strength of Stimulus to Rapidity of Habit-Formation," *Journal of Comparative Neurology and Psychology* 18 (1908): 459–482.

23. Daniel Pink, *Drive: The Surprising Truth About What Motivates Us* (New York: Riverhead, 2011).

24. Morgan R. Frank, Lewis Mitchell, Peter S. Dodds, and Christopher M. Danforth, "Happiness and the Patterns of Life: A Study of Geolocated Tweets," *Scientific Reports* 3 (2013): 1–23.

25. Philip L. Pearce and Uk-Il Lee, "Developing the Travel Career Approach to Tourist Motivation," *Journal of Travel Research* 43 (2005): 226–237. Philip L. Pearce, *Tourist Behaviour: Themes and Conceptual Schemes* (Clevedon, UK: Channel View Publications, 2005).

26. Julia Zimmermann and Franz J. Neyer, "Do We Become a Different Person When Hitting the Road? Personality Development of Sojourners," *Journal of Personality and Social Psychology* 105 (2013): 515–530.

27. Lynn Minnaert, "Social Tourism Participation: The Role of Tourism Inexperience and Uncertainty," *Tourism Management* 40 (2014): 282–289.

28. Ibid., 248.

29. Vanessa A. Quintal, Julie A. Lee, and Geoffrey N. Soutar, "Risk, Uncertainty and the Theory of Planned Behaviour: A Tourism Example," *Tourism Management* 31 (2010): 797–805.

30. Joyce Ehrlinger, Ainsley L. Mitchum, and Carol S. Dweck, "Understanding Overconfidence: Theories of Intelligence, Preferential Attention, and Distorted Self-Assessment," *Journal of Experimental Social Psychology* 63 (2016): 94–100.

31. John L. Crompton, "Motivations for Pleasure Vacations," *Annals of Tourism Research* VI, no. 4 (1979): 408–424.

32. To quantify these qualitative accounts, they are then coded for content, a factor analysis is often conducted, and common themes tend to emerge in people's responses; Sebastian Filep and Luke Greenacre, "Evaluating and Extending the Travel Career Patterns Model," *Tourism* 55 (2007): 23–37.

33. Anna Lacy, Rebecca McCallister, Allison Piotrowski, and Jaime L. Kurtz, "Why Do We Travel? Extraversion and Openness Relate to Specific Travel Motives," poster presented at the annual meeting of the Virginia Psychological Association, Virginia Beach, VA, April, 2015.

CHAPTER 3

1. Richard Easterlin, "Does Economic Growth Improve the Human Lot? Some Empirical Evidence," in *Nations and Households in Economic Growth: Essays in Honor of Moses Abramovitz*, eds. Paul A. David and Melvin W. Reder (New York: Academic Press, 1974).

2. Elizabeth W. Dunn, Daniel T. Gilbert, and Timothy D. Wilson, "If Money Doesn't Make You Happy, Then You Probably Aren't Spending It Right," *Journal of Consumer Psychology* 21 (2011): 115–125.

3. Timothy D. Wilson, Jay Meyers, and Daniel T. Gilbert, "Lessons from the Past: Do People Learn from Experience That Emotional Reactions Are Short Lived?" *Personality and Social Psychology Bulletin* 27 (2001): 1648–1661.

4. Leaf Van Boven and Thomas Gilovich, "To Do or to Have: That Is the Question," *Journal of Personality and Social Psychology* 85 (2003): 1193–1202.

5. This is reminiscent of the decision-making challenges mentioned in chapter 1, but now applied specifically to spending money.

6. Elizabeth Becker, *Overbooked: The Exploding Business of Travel and Tourism* (New York: Simon & Schuster, 2013).

7. According to guidebook author Rick Steves, this is a huge red flag if you're seeking an authentic and reasonably priced dining experience.

8. Elizabeth Dunn and Michael Norton, *Happy Money: The Science of Smarter Spending* (New York: Simon & Schuster, 2013).

9. John L. Lastovicka, Lance A. Bettencourt, Renée Hughner-Shaw, and Ronald J. Kuntze, "Lifestyle of the Tight and Frugal: Theory and Measurement," *Journal of Consumer Research* 26 (1999): 85–98.

10. Matt Kepnes, *How to Travel the World on $50 a Day: Travel Cheaper, Longer, Smarter* (New York: Tarcher Perigee, 2015); Lonely Planet, *Lonely Planet's Southeast Asia on a Shoestring* (Melbourne: Lonely Planet, 2013); Robert Wells. *How to Live in a Car, Van or RV—And Get Out of Debt, Travel and Find True Freedom* (Scotts Valley, CA: CreateSpace, 2014).

11. Using the Dollar Times Inflation Calculator, five dollars in 1957 had the same buying power as $42.85 does in 2016. It's still not a lot.

12. When 5:00 came and the host finally got to us, he told us we could be seated around 10 p.m. We found another restaurant.

13. Yaacov Trope and Nira Liberman, "Construal Level Theory," *Psychological Review* 110 (2003): 403–421.

14. Ashley V. Whilans, Aaron C. Weidman, and Elizabeth W. Dunn, "Valuing Time Over Money Is Associated with Greater Happiness," *Social Psychological and Personality Science* 7 (2016): 213–222.

15. Timothy D. Wilson and Daniel T. Gilbert, "Explaining Away: A Model of Affective Adaptation," *Perspectives on Psychological Science* 3 (2008): 370-386.

16. Jordi Quoidbach and Elizabeth W. Dunn, "Give It Up: A Strategy for Combatting Hedonic Adaptation," *Social Psychological and Personality Science* 4 (2013): 563-568.

17. Michael Pollan, *Food Rules: An Eater's Manual* (New York: Penguin, 2009).

18. Robert Cialdini, *Influence: Science and Practice* (Boston: Pearson Education, 2009).

19. Of course, always know the rules of taking things like this from a location, especially a delicate or endangered habitat. I checked with the rangers on our way out.

20. Mihaly Csikszentmihalyi and Eugene Rochberg-Halton, *The Meaning of Things: Domestic Symbols and The Self* (New York: Cambridge University Press, 1981).

21. Amos Tversky and Daniel Kahneman, "Advances in Prospect Theory: Cumulative Representation of Uncertainty," *Journal of Risk and Uncertainty* 5 (1992): 297–323; Nicholas Epley and Thomas Gilovich,

"Putting Adjustment Back in the Anchoring and Adjustment Heuristic: Differential Processing of Self-Generated and Experimenter-Provided Anchors," *Psychological Science* 12 (2001): 391–396.

22. Kathleen D. Vohs, Nicole L. Mead, and Miranda R. Goode, "The Psychological Consequences of Money," *Science* 314 (2006): 1154-1156.

23. Jordi Quoidbach, Elizabeth W. Dunn, K.V. Petrides, and Moira Mikolajczak, "Money Giveth, Money Taketh Away: The Dual Effect of Money on Happiness," *Psychological Science* 21 (2010): 759-763.

24. But read the fine print, as "all-inclusive" is a loose term. Airfare, excursions, spa services, gratuities, and other add-ons can cost extra. Look for the dreaded asterisk that points you to these extra costs.

25. Barbara L. Fredrickson and Daniel Kahneman, "Duration Neglect in Retrospective Evaluations of Affective Episodes," *Journal of Personality and Social Psychology* 65 (1993): 45–55.

26. Donald A. Redelmeier, Joel Katz, and Daniel Kahneman, "Memories of Colonoscopy: A Randomized Trial," *Pain* 104 (2003): 187–194.

27. Daniel Kahneman, Barbara L. Fredrickson, Charles A. Schreiber, and Donald A. Redelmeier, "When More Pain Is Preferred to Less: Adding a Better End," *Psychological Science* 4 (1993): 401–405.

28. Amy M. Do, Alexander V. Rupert, and George Wolford, "Evaluations of Positive Experiences: The Peak-End Rule," *Psychonomic Bulletin and Review* 15 (2008): 96-98.

29. Dan Ariely and Ziv Carmon, "The Sum Reflects Only Some of its Parts: A Critical Overview of Research about Summary Assessment of Experiences," in *Time & Decision: Economic & Psychological Perspectives on Inter-temporal Choice*, eds. George Loewenstein, Daniel Read, and Roy Baumeister (New York: Russell Sage Press, 2003): 323–350.

30. Simon Kemp, Christopher D. B. Burt, and Laura Furneaux, "A Test of the Peak-End Rule with Extended Autobiographical Events," *Memory & Cognition* 36 (2008): 132–138.

31. Researchers stated that all participants were maxed-out on happiness ratings at their reported peak, and that a more nuanced or fine-grained measure could have better detected differences.

32. Jeroen Nawijn, Miquelle Marchand, Ruut Veenhoven, and Ad J. Vingerhoets, "Vacationers Happier, But Most Not Happier After a Holiday," *Applied Research in Quality of Life* 5 (2010): 35-47.

33. Tversky and Kahneman, "Advances in Prospect Theory"; Epley and Gilovich, "Putting Adjustment Back in the Anchoring and Adjustment Heuristic."

CHAPTER 4

1. Becky Krystal, "A Mystery Tour with a Surprise Ending," *Washington Post*, February 27, 2014, www.washingtonpost.com/lifestyle/travel/a-mystery-vacation-with-a-surprise-ending/2014/02/27/8f3f5bde-847e-11e3-bbe5-6a2a3141e3a9_story.html.

2. Daniel T. Gilbert, Matthew A. Killingsworth, Rebecca N. Eyre, and Timothy D. Wilson, "The Surprising Power of Neighborly Advice," *Science* 323 (2009): 1617–1619.

3. Timothy D. Wilson, David B. Centerbar, Deborah A. Kermer, and Daniel T. Gilbert, "The Pleasures of Uncertainty: Prolonging Positive Moods in Ways People Do Not Anticipate," *Journal of Personality and Social Psychology* 88 (2005): 5–21.

4. But also see Jaime L. Kurtz, Timothy D. Wilson, and Daniel T. Gilbert, "Quantity Versus Uncertainty: When Winning One Prize is Better Than Winning Two," *Journal of Experimental Social Psychology* 43 (2007): 979–985; Erin R. Whitchurch, Timothy D. Wilson, and Daniel T. Gilbert, "He Loves Me, He Loves Me Not: The Effects of Uncertainty on Romantic Attraction," *Psychological Science* 22 (2011): 172–175.

5. Christopher K. Hsee and Bowen Ruan, "The Pandora Effect: The Power and Peril of Curiosity," *Psychological Science* 27 (2016): 659–666.

6. Jeroen Nawijn, Miquelle A. G. Marchand, Ruut Veenhoven, and Ad J. Vingerhoets, "Vacationers Happier, but Most Not Happier After a Holiday," *Applied Research in Quality of Life* 5 (2010): 35–47.

7. Jordi Quoidbach, Alex M. Wood, and Michel Hansenne, "Back to the Future: The Effect of Daily Practice of Mental Time Travel into the Future on Happiness and Anxiety," *Journal of Positive Psychology* 4 (2009): 349–355.

8. Amit Kumar, Matthew A. Killingsworth, and Thomas D. Gilovich, "Waiting for Merlot: Anticipatory Consumption of Experiential and Material Purchases," *Psychological Science* 25 (2014): 1924–1931.

9. George Loewenstein, "Anticipation and the Value of Delayed Consumption," *Economic Journal* 97 (1987): 666–684.

10. Kumar, Killingsworth, and Gilovich, "Waiting for Merlot."

11. Ibid.

12. Leaf Van Boven and Laurence Ashworth, "Looking Forward, Looking Back: Anticipation is More Evocative Than Retrospection," *Journal of Experimental Psychology: General* 136 (2007): 289–300.

13. These included Thanksgiving holidays, menstruation, and listening to the piercing sound of a dial-up modem.

14. Eugene M. Caruso, Leaf Van Boven, Mark Chin, and Andrew Ward, "The Temporal Doppler Effect: When the Future Feels Closer Than the Past," *Psychological Science* 24 (2013): 530–536.

15. Eugene M. Caruso, Daniel T. Gilbert, and Timothy D. Wilson, "A Wrinkle in Time: Asymmetric Valuation of Past and Future Events," *Psychological Science* 19 (2008): 796–801; Julia A. Weiler, Boris Suchan, and Irene Daum, "When the Future Becomes the Past: Differences in Brain Activation Patterns for Episodic Memory and Episodic Future Thinking," *Behavioural Brain Research* 212 (2010): 196–203.

16. In light of this, travel professionals would do well to market a trip as one that lies ahead ("Imagine yourself, six months from now, relaxing on this beach") rather than as one that happened in the past ("Think back on the vacation you took six months ago, when you were relaxing on the beach"). This subtle difference can have a real impact on people's excitement and perhaps even on their desire to take a trip.

17. Steven M. Nowlis, Naomi Mandel, and Deborah B. McCabe, "The Effect of a Delay Between Choice and Consumption on Consumption Enjoyment," *Journal of Consumer Research* 31 (2004): 502–510.

18. Elizabeth Dunn and Michael Norton, *Happy Money: The Science of Smarter Spending* (New York: Simon & Schuster, 2013).

19. Leif D. Nelson and Tom Meyvis, "Interrupted Consumption: Disrupting Adaptation to Hedonic Experiences," *Journal of Marketing Research* 45 (2008): 654–664.

20. Metin Kozak and Mike Rimmington, "Tourist Satisfaction with Mallorca, Spain, as an Off-Season Holiday Destination," *Journal of Travel Research* 38 (2000): 260–269.

21. Timothy D. Wilson, Thalia P. Wheatley, Jonathan M. Meyers, Daniel T. Gilbert, and Danny Axsom, "Focalism: A Source of Durability Bias in Affective Forecasting," *Journal of Personality and Social Psychology* 78 (2000): 821–836.

22. Neil D. Weinstein, "Unrealistic Optimism About Future Life Events," *Journal of Personality and Social Psychology* 39 (1980): 806–820.

23. See the website Flights from Hell (www.flightsfromhell.com)

24. Julie K. Norem, *The Positive Power of Negative Thinking* (New York: Basic Books, 2001).

25. Shawn Achor. "When a Vacation Reduces Stress—And When It Doesn't," *Harvard Business Review*, February 14, 2014, https://hbr.org/2014/02/when-a-vacation-reduces-stress-and-when-it-doesnt/.

26. Caterina Gawrilow, Katrin Morgenroth, Regina Schultz, Gabriele Oettingen, and Peter M. Gollwitzer, "Mental Contrasting with Implementation Intentions Enhances Self-Regulation of Goal Pursuit in Schoolchildren at Risk for ADHD," *Motivation and Emotion* 37 (2013): 134–145; Sylvaine Houssais, Gabriele Oettingen, and Doris Mayer, "Using Mental Contrasting with Implementation Intentions to Self-Regulate Insecurity-Based Behaviors in Relationships," *Motivation and Emotion* 37 (2013): 224–233; Gertraud Stadler, Gabriele Oettingen, and Peter M. Gollwitzer, "Physical Activity in Women: Effects of a Self-Regulation Intervention," *American Journal of Preventive Medicine* 36 (2009): 29–34; Gertraud Stadler, Gabriele Oettingen, and Peter M. Gollwitzer, "Intervention Effects of Information and Self-Regulation on Eating Fruits and Vegetables Over Two Years," *Health Psychology* 29 (2010): 274–283.

27. See the WOOP My Life website at www.woopmylife.org.

28. Susan Folkman, "Personal Control and Stress and Coping Processes: A Theoretical Analysis," *Journal of Personality and Social Psychology* 46 (1984): 839–852; Robert Sapolsky, *Why Zebras Don't Get Ulcers* (New York: St. Martin's Griffin, 1994).

29. Shawn Achor, "When a Vacation Reduces Stress—And When It Doesn't."

30. Gerhard Strauss-Blasche, Franziska Muhry, Michael Lehofer, Maximillian Moser, and Wolgang Marktl, "Time Course of Well-Being After a Three-Week

Resort-Based Respite from Occupational and Domestic Demands: Carry-Over, Contrast and Situation Effects," *Journal of Leisure Research* 36 (2004): 293–309.

31. Suzanne Greist-Bousquet and Noah Schiffman, "The Effect of Task Interruption and Closure on Perceived Duration," *Bulletin of the Psychonomic Society* 30 (1992): 9–11.

CHAPTER 5

1. Leigh Ann Henion, *Phenomenal: A Hesitant Adventurer's Search for Wonder in the Natural World* (New York: Penguin, 2015), 52.

2. "New Writer, Same Goal: Exploring the World on a Budget," *New York Times*, February 10, 2016, www.nytimes.com/2016/02/14/travel/budget-travel-tips.html.

3. This may actually be another fun way to build your anticipation!

4. See the Experiment in International Living's website at www.experiment.org/.

5. See the US Travel Association's website at www.ustravel.org/.

6. Keiko Otake and Kenji Kato, "Subjective Happiness and Emotional Responsiveness to Food Stimuli," *Journal of Happiness Studies* (2016) 1–18.

7. Belle Cushing, "Anthony Bourdain Thinks You're Crazy for Eating Airplane Food," *Bon Appetit*, May 9, 2016, www.bonappetit.com/people/celebrities/article/anthony-bourdain-parts-unknown.

8. Kurt Lewin, *A Dynamic Theory of Personality* (New York: McGraw-Hill, 1935.)

9. Roy F. Baumeister and Mark R. Leary, "The Need to Belong: Desire for Interpersonal Attachments as a Fundamental Human Motivation," *Psychological Bulletin* 117 (1995): 497–529.

10. Nicholas Epley and Juliana Schroeder, "Mistakenly Seeking Solitude," *Journal of Experimental Psychology: General* 143 (2014): 1980–1999.

11. In the extroverted condition, participants were instructed to act "bold, talkative, energetic, active, assertive, and adventurous" or, in the introverted condition, to act "reserved, quiet, lethargic, passive, compliant, and unadventurous"; William Fleeson, Adriane B. Malanos, and Noelle M. Achille, "An Intraindividual Process Approach to the Relationship Between Extraversion and Positive Affect: Is Acting Extraverted as 'Good' as Being Extraverted?" *Journal of Personality and Social Psychology* 83 (2002): 1409–1422; John M. Zelenski, Deanna C. Whelan, Logan J. Nealis, Christina M. Besner, Maya S. Santoro,

and Jessica E. Wynn. "Personality and Affective Forecasting: Trait Introverts Underpredict the Hedonic Benefits of Acting Extraverted," *Journal of Personality and Social Psychology* 104 (2013): 1092–1108.

12. Gillian M. Sandstrom and Elizabeth W. Dunn, "Social Interactions and Well-Being: The Surprising Power of Weak Ties," *Personality and Social Psychology Bulletin* 40 (2014): 910–922.

13. Elizabeth W. Dunn, Jeremy C. Biesanz, Lauren J. Human, and Stephanie Finn, "Misunderstanding the Affective Consequences of Everyday Social Interactions: The Hidden Benefits of Putting One's Best Face Forward," *Journal of Personality and Social Psychology* 92 (2007): 990–1005.

14. I think his name was Eric. Thank you, Eric.

15. Robyn K. Mallett, Timothy D. Wilson, and Daniel T. Gilbert, "Expect the Unexpected: Failure to Anticipate Similarities When Predicting the Quality of an Intergroup Interaction," *Journal of Personality and Social Psychology* 94 (2008): 265–277.

16. Thomas F. Pettigrew and Linda R. Tropp, "A Meta-Analytic Test of Intergroup Conflict Theory," *Journal of Personality and Social Psychology* 90 (2006): 751–783.

17. Kostadin Kushlev, Jason Proulx, and Elizabeth W. Dunn, "Just Google It: Relying on Smartphones for Information Compromises Trust and Social Connectedness," presentation, Happiness and Well-Being Preconference of the Annual Convention at the Society for Personality and Social Psychology, Long Beach, California, 2015.

18. The brain region was the right posterior hippocampus. Eleanor A. Maguire, Katherine Woollett, and Hugo J. Spiers, "London Taxi Drivers and Bus Drivers: A Structural MRI and Neuropsychological Analysis," *Hippocampus* 16 (2006): 1091–1101.

19. Julia Frankenstein, "Is GPS All in Our Heads?" *New York Times*, February 2, 2012, www.nytimes.com/2012/02/05/opinion/sunday/is-gps-all-in-our-head.html.

20. Stephanie Rosenbloom, "Reclaiming the Age-Old Art of Getting Lost," *New York Times*, April 16, 2015, www.nytimes.com/2015/04/19/travel/19EssayLostEurope.html.

21. Elizabeth K. Nisbet and John M. Zelenski, "Underestimating Nearby Nature: Affective Forecasting Errors Obscure the Happy Path to Sustainability," *Psychological Science* 22 (2011): 1101–1106.

22. The study was done in Canada, where sometimes tunnels are built so that people can stay inside as much as possible during the harsh winters. Research was, however, conducted in nice weather.

23. Gregory N. Bratman, Gretchen C. Daily, Benjamin J. Levy, and James J. Gross, "The Benefits of Nature Experience: Improved Affect and Cognition," *Landscape and Urban Planning* 138 (2015): 41–50.

24. Richard M. Ryan, Netta Weinstein, Jessey Bernstein, Kirk W. Brown, Louis Mastella, and Marylene Gagne, "Vitalizing Effects of Being Outdoors and in Nature," *Journal of Environmental Psychology* 30 (2010): 159–168.

25. Ruth Ann Atchley, David L. Strayer, and Paul Atchley, "Creativity in the Wild: Improving Creative Reasoning through Immersion in Natural Settings," *PLoS One* 7 (2012): e51474.

26. Peter James, Jaime E. Hart, Rachel F. Banay, and Francine Laden, "Exposure to Greenness and Mortality in a Nationwide Prospective Cohort Study of Women," *Environmental Health Perspectives* 124 (2016): 1344–1352.

27. Dacher Keltner and Jonathan Haidt, "Approaching Awe, A Moral, Spiritual, and Aesthetic Emotion," *Cognition and Emotion* 17 (2003): 297–314; Abraham H. Maslow, *Religions, Values, and Peak Experiences* (Columbus: Ohio State University Press, 1964.)

28. Michelle N. Shiota, Dacher Keltner, and Amanda Mossman, "The Nature of Awe: Elicitors, Appraisals, and Effects on Self-Concept," *Cognition and Emotion* 21 (2007): 944–963.

29. Paul K. Piff, Pia Dietze, Matthew Feinberg, Daniel M. Stancato, and Dacher Keltner, "Awe, the Small Self, and Prosocial Behavior," *Journal of Personality and Social Psychology* 108 (2015): 883– 899; Jia Wei Zhang, Paul K. Piff, Ravi Iyer, Spassena Koleva, and Dacher Keltner, "An Occasion for Unselfing: Beautiful Nature Leads to Prosociality," *Journal of Environmental Psychology* 37 (2014): 61–72.

30. Melanie Rudd, Kathleen D. Vohs, and Jennifer Aaker, "Awe Expands People's Perception of Time, Alters Decision Making, and Enhances Well-Being," *Psychological Science* 23 (2012): 1130–1136.

31. Given this, you may be curious how researchers study it in the decidedly nonawesome environment of a research lab. Some approaches involve asking people to think about a time when they recently felt awe or to watch a film clip that was shown

to elicit feelings of awe in the past (see Zhang et al., "An Occasion for Unselfing"). Want to see one? Try this: http://ggia.berkeley.edu/practice/awe_video.

32. Henion, *Phenomenal*, 16.

33. Giovanni B. Moneta, "On the Measurement and Conceptualization of Flow." *Advances in Flow Research*, ed. Stefan Engeser (New York: Springer Science, 2012), 23–50. With permission of Springer.

34. Mihaly Csikszentmihalyi, *Flow: The Psychology of Optimal Experience* (New York: Harper Collins, 1990).

35. Susan A. Jackson, "Athletes in Flow: A Qualitative Investigation of Flow States in Elite Figure Skaters," *Journal of Applied Sport Psychology* 4 (1992): 161–180; Sarah Sinnamon, Aidan Moran, and Michael O'Connell, "Flow Among Musicians: Measuring Peak Experiences of Student Performers," *Journal of Research in Music Education* 60 (2012): 6–25.

36. Jackson, "Athletes in Flow"; Sinnamon, Moran, and O'Connell, "Flow Among Musicians."

37. Kristin Diehl, Gal Zauberman, and Alixandra Barasch, "How Taking Photos Increases Enjoyment of Experiences," *Journal of Personality of Social Psychology* 111 (2016), 119–140.

38. I later was vindicated when I learned that this was a notoriously bad place to learn to surf.

39. Aaron M. Sackett, Tom Meyvis, Leif D. Nelson, Benjamin A. Converse, and Anna Sackett, "You're Having Fun When Time Flies: The Hedonic Consequences of Subjective Time Progression," *Psychological Science* 21 (2010): 111–117.

40. Mihaly Csikszentmihalyi, *Finding Flow: The Psychology of Engagement with Everyday Life* (New York: Basic Books, 1997), 65.

41. Thomas Mussweiler, "Comparison Processes in Social Judgment: Mechanisms and Consequences," *Psychological Review* 110 (2003): 472–489.

42. Rebecca K. Ratner, Barbara E. Kahn, and Daniel Kahneman, "Choosing Less-Preferred Experiences for the Sake of Variety," *Journal of Consumer Research* 26 (1999): 1–15; Leif D. Nelson and Tom Meyvis. "Interrupted Consumption: Adaptation and the Disruption of Hedonic Experience" *Journal of Marketing Research* 45 (2008): 654–664.

43. Christopher K. Hsee, Adelle X. Yang, and Liangyang Wang, "Idleness Aversion and the Need for Justifiable Busyness," *Psychological Science* 21 (2010): 926–930.

44. Timothy D. Wilson, David A. Reinhard, Erin C. Westgate, Daniel T. Gilbert, Nicole Ellerbeck, Cheryl Hahn, Casey L. Brown, and Adi Shaked, "Just Think: The Challenges of the Disengaged Mind," *Science* 345 (2014): 75–77.

45. Jonathan Schooler, Dan Ariely, and George Loewenstein, "The Pursuit and Assessment of Happiness Can Be Self-Defeating," in *Psychology and Economics, Volume 1*, eds. I. Brocas and J. Carrillo (Oxford: Oxford University Press, 2003), 41–70.

46. Iris B. Mauss, Maya Tamir, Craig L. Anderson, and N. S. Savino, "Can Seeking Happiness Make People Unhappy? Paradoxical Effects of Valuing Happiness," *Emotion* 11 (2011): 807–815. Copyright © 2011 American Psychological Association. Reproduced with permission. No further reproduction or distribution is permitted without written permission from the American Psychological Association.

47. Jeroen Nawijn, "Positive Psychology in Tourism: A Critique," *Annals of Tourism Research* 56 (2016): 128–163.

CHAPTER 6

1. Simone Fullagar, Kevin Markwell, and Erica Wilson, eds., *Slow Tourism: Experiences and Mobilities. Vol. 54* (Bristol, UK: Channel View Publications, 2012.)

2. Carl Honore, *In Praise of Slowness* (New York: HarperCollins, 2009.)

3. Kirk W. Brown and Richard M. Ryan, "The Benefits of Being Present: Mindfulness and Its Role in Psychological Well-Being," *Journal of Personality and Social Psychology* 84 (2003): 822–848.

4. I use "savoring" and "appreciating" somewhat interchangeably. Other synonyms include relishing, basking, luxuriating, and marveling.

5. Fred B. Bryant and Joseph Veroff, *Savoring: A New Model of Positive Experience* (Mahwah, NJ: Erlbaum, 2007).

6. Savoring our food is challenging for many of us. You can practice the art of slow and mindful eating with the structured "raisin activity" described at the Greater Good in Action website at http://ggia.berkeley.edu/practice/raisin_meditation. The basic idea of eating mindfully has been related not only to

enjoyment of food but also to maintaining a healthy body weight. See Brian Wansink, *Mindless Eating: Why We Eat More than We Think* (New York: Bantam, 2006) and Thich Nhat Hanh and Lilian Cheung, *Savor: Mindful Eating, Mindful Life* (New York: HarperOne, 2011).

7. For a comprehensive review of how savoring regulates and generates positive feelings, see Jordi Quoidbach, Moira Mikolajczak, and James J. Gross, "Positive Interventions, An Emotion Regulation Perspective," *Psychological Bulletin* 141 (2015): 655–693.

8. Bryant and Veroff, *Savoring*,

9. Delphine Nelis, Jordi Quoidbach, Michel Hansenne, and Moïra Mikolajczak, "Measuring Individual Differences in Emotion Regulation: The Emotion Regulation Profile-Revised (ERP-R)," *Psychologica Belgica* 51 (2001): 49–91.

10. Bryant and Veroff, *Savoring*,

11. Roy F. Baumeister, Ellen Bratslavsky, Catrin Finkenauer, and Kathleen D. Vohs, "Bad Is Stronger than Good," *Review of General Psychology* 5 (2001): 323–337.

12. These items are excerpted from the 60-item Ways of Savoring Checklist in Bryant and Veroff, *Savoring* 246.

13. This is adapted from the research on cultivating gratitude, which is a close cousin of savoring. For a foundational study on gratitude, see Robert A. Emmons and Michael E. McCullough, "Counting Blessings Versus Burdens: Experimental Studies of Gratitude and Subjective Well-Being in Daily Life," *Journal of Personality and Social Psychology* 84 (2003): 377–389. For practical advice on gratitude journaling, see Robert A. Emmons, *Gratitude Works! A 21-Day Program for Creating Emotional Prosperity* (New York: Jossey-Bass, 2013).

14. Sylvia Plath, *The Unabridged Journals of Sylvia Plath*. ed. Karen V. Kukil. (New York: Anchor, 2000), 178–179.

15. Barbara L. Fredrickson and Laura L. Carstensen, "Choosing Social Partners: How Old Age and Anticipated Endings Make People More Selective," *Psychology and Aging* 5 (1990): 335–347; Ed O'Brien and Phoebe Ellsworth, "Saving the Last for Best: A Positivity Bias for End Experiences," *Psychological Science* 23 (2012): 163–165.

16. Harvey Lemelin, Jackie Dawson, Emma J. Stewart, Pat Maher and Michael Lueck, "Last-Chance Tourism: The Boom, Doom, and Gloom of Visiting Vanishing Destinations," *Current Issues in Tourism* 13 (2010): 477–493.

17. Allen Salkin, "Tourism of Doom on the Rise," *New York Times*, December 16, 2007, www.nytimes.com/2007/12/16/world/americas/16iht-tourism.1. 8762449.html?pagewanted=all&_r=1&.

18. Jaime L. Kurtz, "Looking to the Future to Appreciate the Present: The Benefits of Perceived Temporal Scarcity," *Psychological Science* 19 (2008): 1238–1241.

19. Hal Ersner-Hershfield, Joseph A. Mikels, Sarah J. Sullivan, and Laura L. Carstensen, "Poignancy: Mixed Emotional Experience in the Face of Meaningful Endings," *Journal of Personality and Social Psychology* 94 (2008): 158–167.

20. This was in contrast to a group who was asked to think about all the reasons why they still had a fair amount of time left in college, and a control group who focused on something neutral and unrelated to graduation.

21. Laura L. Carstensen, Derek M. Isaacowitz, and Susan T. Charles, "Taking Time Seriously: A Theory of Socioemotional Selectivity," *American Psychologist* 54 (1999): 165–181.

22. There are many of these apps to choose from. I use Dreamdays, but there's also Countdown!, Event Countdown Free, and many others. In addition to reminding you to make the most of your travel moments, these can also help build anticipation in advance of your trip, giving you an easy way to countdown the days until you head out.

23. Jeff Galak, Joseph Redden, Yang Yang, and Ellie Kyung, "How Perceptions of Temporal Distance Influence Satiation," *Journal of Experimental Social Psychology* 52 (2014): 118–123.

24. Elliott Kruse, Joseph Chancellor, Peter M. Ruberton, and Sonja Lyubomirsky, "An Upward Spiral Between Gratitude and Humility," *Social Psychological and Personality Science* 5 (2014): 805–814.

25. Fred B. Bryant, "Savoring Beliefs Inventory (SBI): A Scale for Measuring Beliefs about Savouring," *Journal of Mental Health* 12 (2003): 175–196; Jordi Quoidbach, Elizabeth V. Berry, Michel Hansenne, and Moira Mikolajczak, "Positive Emotion Regulation and Well-Being: Comparing the Impact of Eight Savoring and Dampening Strategies," *Personality and Individual Differences* 49 (2010): 368–373.

26. Linda A. Henkel, "Point and Shoot Memories: The Influence of Taking Photos on Memory for a Museum Tour," *Psychological Science* 25 (2014): 396–402.

27. Kristin Diehl, Gal Zauberman, and Alixandra Barasch, "How Taking Photos Increases Enjoyment of Experiences," *Journal of Personality of Social Psychology* 111 (2016), 119–140.

28. Jaime L. Kurtz, "Seeing through New Eyes: An Experimental Investigation of the Benefits of Photography," *Journal of Basic and Applied Sciences* 11 (2015): 354–358.

29. Diehl, Zauberman, and Barasch, "How Taking Photos Increases Enjoyment of Experiences," 119–140.

30. Alain de Botton, *The Art of Travel* (New York, Vintage, 2008).

31. Myunghwa H. Kang and Michael A. Schuett. "Determinants of Sharing Travel Experiences in Social Media," *Journal of Travel & Tourism Marketing* 30 (2013): 93–107.

32. Hui-Tzu Grace Chou and Nicholas Edge, "'They Are Happier and Having Better Lives than I Am': The Impact of Using Facebook on Perceptions of Others' Lives," *Cyberpsychology, Behavior, and Social Networking* 15 (2012): 117–121.

33. Sonja Lyubomirsky and Lee Ross, "Hedonic Consequences of Social Comparison: A Contrast of Happy and Unhappy People," *Journal of Personality and Social Psychology* 73 (1997): 1141–1157; Jinhyung Kim, Emily K. Hong, Incheol Choi, and Joshua A. Hicks, "Companion Versus Comparison: Examining Seeking Social Companionship or Social Comparison as Characteristics That Differentiate Happy and Unhappy People," *Personality and Social Psychology Bulletin* 42 (2016): 311–322.

34. Patricia R. Hetz, Christi L. Dawson, and Theresa A. Cullen, "Social Media Use and the Fear of Missing Out (FoMO) While Studying Abroad," *Journal of Research on Technology in Education* 47 (2015): 259–272.

35. Gus Cooney, Daniel T. Gilbert, and Timothy D. Wilson, "The Unforeseen Costs of Extraordinary Experience," *Psychological Science* 25 (2014): 2259–2265.

36. Irene Scopelliti, George Loewenstein, and Joachim Vosgerau, "You Call It 'Self-Exuberance'; I Call It 'Bragging': Miscalibrated Predictions of Emotional Responses to Self-Promotion," *Psychological Science* 26 (2015): 903–914.

37. Doreen Carvajal, "In Tourist Destinations, a Picture of Excess," *New York Times.* July 11, 2015, www.nytimes.com/2015/07/12/world/europe/selfie-vacation-damage-majorca-paris-ibiza-rome.html.

38. Robert Huesca, "How Facebook Can Ruin Study Abroad," *Chronicle of Higher Education*, January 14, 2013, http://chronicle.com/article/How-Facebook-Can-Ruin-Study/136633/.

39. Dan Wang, Sangwon Park, and Daniel R. Fesenmaier, "The Role of Smartphones in Mediating the Touristic Experience," *Journal of Travel Research* 51 (2012): 371–387.

40. These restrictions don't come cheap, however. Author Pico Iyer notes, "I noticed that those who part with $2,285 a night to stay in a cliff-top room at the Post Ranch Inn in Big Sur pay partly for the privilege of *not* having a TV in their rooms; the future of travel, I'm reliably told, lies in 'black-hole resorts,' which charge high prices precisely because you can't get online in their rooms." Pico Iyer, "The Joy of Quiet," *New York Times*, December 29, 2001, www.nytimes.com/2012/01/01/opinion/sunday/the-joy-of-quiet.html?pagewanted=all.

41. Kostadin Kushlev and Elizabeth W. Dunn, "Checking Email Less Frequently Reduces Stress," *Computers in Human Behavior* 43 (2015): 220–228.

42. Josh Constine, "Instagram Hits 300 Million Monthly Users To Surpass Twitter, Keeps It Real With Verified Badges," *Tech Crunch*, December 10, 2014, http://techcrunch.com/2014/12/10/not-a-fad/

43. Sruthi Vijayan, "The 3 Ways Social Media Could Be Ruining Your Travel Experience," *Wanderful*, www.travelgogirl.com/blog/2015/02/11/three-reasons-social-media-ruining-travel-experience/.

44. Kennon M. Sheldon and Sonja Lyubomirsky, "How to Increase and Sustain Positive Emotion: The Effects of Expressing Gratitude and Visualizing Best Possible Selves," *Journal of Positive Psychology* 1 (2006): 73–82.

CHAPTER 7

1. Clara Bensen, *No Baggage: A Minimalist Tale of Love and Wandering* (Philadelphia: Running Press, 2016).

2. Robert Biswas-Diener, P. Alex Lindley, Helen Dovey, John Maltby, Robert Hurling, Joy Wilkinson, and Nadezhda Lyubchik, "Pleasure: An Initial Exploration," *Journal of Happiness Studies* 16 (2015): 313–332.

3. Michael D. Botwin, David M. Buss, and Todd K. Shackelford, "Personality and Mate Preferences: Five Factors in Mate Selection and Marital Satisfaction," *Journal of Personality* 65 (1997): 107–136; J. M. Malouff, E. B. Thorsteinsson,

N. S. Schutte, N. Bhullar, and S. E. Rooke, "The Five Factor Model of Personality and Relationship Satisfaction of Intimate Partners: A Meta-Analysis," *Journal of Research in Personality* 44 (2010): 124–127.

4. J. E. Bono, T. L. Boles, T. A. Judge, and K. J. Lauver, "The Role of Personality in Task and Relationship Conflict," *Journal of Personality* 70 (2002): 311–344; L. A. Jensen Campbell and W. G. Graziano, "Agreeableness as a Moderator of Interpersonal Conflict," *Journal of Personality* 69 (2001): 323–362.

5. Matthias R. Mehl, Samuel D. Gosling, and James Pennebaker, "Personality in Its Natural Habitat: Manifestations and Implicit Folk Theories of Personality in Daily Life," *Journal of Personality and Social Psychology* 90 (2006): 862–877.

6. This paper also points to some interesting sex differences. For women but not for men, participating in group conversations was related to extroversion. Arguing was a sign of disagreeableness for women only.

7. Samuel D. Gosling, Sei Jin Ko, Thomas Mannarelli, and Margaret E. Morris, "A Room with a Cue: Personality Judgments Based on Offices and Bedrooms," *Journal of Personality and Social Psychology* 82 (2002): 379–398.

8. Dan McAdams, "What Do We Know When We Know a Person?" *Journal of Personality* 63 (1995): 365–396.

9. Bente Heimtun and Fiona Jordan, "'Wish YOU Weren't Here!': Interpersonal Conflicts and the Touristic Experiences of Norwegian and British Women Travelling with Friends," *Tourist Studies* 11 (2011): 271–290.

10. John Gottman and Nan Silver, *The Seven Principles for Making Marriage Work* (New York: Three Rivers Press, 2002).

11. People who have moved a lot in their lives seem to take comfort in the familiarity of chain stores and restaurants. It may well hold for travelers, as well. See Shigehiro Oishi, Felicity F. Miao, Minkyung Koo, Jason Kisling, and Kate A. Ratliff, "Residential Mobility Breeds Familiarity-Seeking," *Journal of Personality and Social Psychology* 102 (2012): 149–162.

12. April Kilcrease, "Don't Get Hangry and 10 Other Tips on How to Travel as a Couple," *ZOZI*, February 13, 2015, www.zozi.com/journal/travel/traveling-together?&ed=2015-02-14&p=11&et=editorial_icons&c=FEB14_Vday_Journal&a=city-events&el=bulk&utm_source=EmailDirect.com&utm_medium=Email&utm_campaign=FEB14_Vday_Journal.

13. Erica J. Boothby, Margaret S. Clark, and John A. Bargh, "Shared Experiences Are Amplified," *Psychological Science* 25 (2014): 2209–2216.

14. Garriy Shteynberg, J B. Hirsh, E. P. Apfelbaum, Jeffery T. Larsen, Adam D. Galinsky, and Neal J. Roese, "Feeling More Together: Group Attention Intensifies Emotion," *Emotion* 14 (2014): 1102–1114.

15. A friend once said that you never realize how many curse words are in a movie until you watch it with your grandma.

16. Do note that this survey was commissioned by Royal Caribbean International Cruise Lines. L. Sierra, "Survey Says a Cruise Vacation Heats Up Romance for Couples," *PR Web*, February 10, 2012, www.prweb.com/releases/Royal_Caribbean/Romance_Survey/prweb9187956.htm.

17. Arthur Aron, Christina C. Norman, Elaine N. Aron, Colin McKenna, and Richard Heyman, "Couples Shared Participation in Novel and Arousing Activities and Experienced Relationship Quality," *Journal of Personality and Social Psychology* 78 (2000): 273–283.

18. Donald G. Dutton and Arthur Aron, "Some Evidence for Heightened Sexual Attraction under Conditions of High Anxiety," *Journal of Personality and Social Psychology* 30 (1974): 510–517; Katherine Jacobs Bao and Sonja Lyubomirsky, "Making It Last: Combating Hedonic Adaptation in Romantic Relationships," *Journal of Positive Psychology* 8 (2013): 196–206.

19. Although it's important to note that these relationships are correlational, not causal. See Shelly L. Gable, Harry T. Reis, Emily A. Impett, and Evan R. Asher, "What Do You Do When Things Go Right? The Intrapersonal and Interpersonal Benefits of Sharing Positive Events," *Journal of Personality and Social Psychology* 87 (2004): 228–245.

20. Clara Bensen in discussion with the author, May 2016.

21. Sara B. Algoe, Shelly L. Gable, and Natalya Maisel, "It's the Little Things: Everyday Gratitude as a Booster Shot for Romantic Relationships," *Personal Relationships* 17 (2010): 217–233.

22. C. Brown, "Majority of Couples Get Intimate More During One Week Holiday Than Two Months at Home," *Travel Daily News International*, November 19, 2010.

23. Angela M. Durko and James F. Petrick, "Family and Relationship Benefits of Travel Experience: A Literature Review," *Journal of Travel Research* 52 (2013): 720–730.

24. G. Chen, "Malaysia Moves to Bolster Marriage," *Khabar Southeast Asia*, August 30, 2012, http://khabarsoutheastasia. com/en_GB/articles/apwi/articles/features/2012/08/30/feature- 03

25. And many exist! Most popular guidebooks contain a section focusing on kid-friend activities. Fodors has an entire line of books focusing on things to do with kids in various parts of the world. For a general guide, see Lonely Planet's guide *Travel with Children* (Melbourne: Lonely Planet, 2011).

26. Malene Gram, "Family Holidays, a Qualitative Analysis of Family Holiday Experiences," *Scandinavian Journal of Hospitality and Tourism* 5 (2005): 2–22.

27. Durko and Petrick, "Family and Relationship Benefits of Travel Experience."

28. Visa Global Travel Intentions Study, 2015, www.visamiddleeast.com/ae/en-ae/aboutvisa/research/travelintentions.shtml.

29. Stephanie Rosenbloom, "Travel Industry Responds to Rise in Solo Sojourners," *New York Times*, May 15, 2015, www.nytimes.com/2015/05/17/travel/travel-industry-responds-to-rise-in-solo-sojourners.html?_r=0.

30. Zoe Alexander, Ali Bakir, and Eugenia Wickens, "An Investigation into the Impact of Vacation Travel on the Tourist," *International Journal of Tourism Research* 12 (2010) 574–590.

31. Rebecca K. Ratner and Rebecca W. Hamilton, "Inhibited from Bowling Alone," *Journal of Consumer Research* 42 (2015): 266–283.

32. "I Want to Be Alone! 72 Percent of American Women Will Vacation Solo This Year," Yahoo Travel, www.yahoo.com/style/the-rise-of-the-solo-lady-traveler-by-the-numbers-85084024117.html.

33. Linda Holmes, "The Luxury of Solitude," *NPR*, November 3, 2014, http://www.npr.org/sections/monkeysee/2014/11/03/361124560/the-luxury-of-solitude.

34. Rosenbloom, "Travel Industry Responds to Rise in Solo Sojourners."

35. Liza Berdychevsky, Heather J. Gibson, and Heather L. Bell, "Girlfriend Getaways and Women's Well-Being," *Journal of Leisure Research* 45 (2013): 602–623.

36. Jacobs Bao and Lyubomirsky, "Making It Last."

CHAPTER 8

1. Stephen R. Covey, *The 7 Habits of Highly Effective People* (New York: Simon & Schuster, 1989).

2. Jessica De Bloom, Sabine A.E. Geurts, and Michiel A. J. Kompier, "Vacation (After-) Effects on Employee Health and Well-Being, and the Role of Vacation Activities, Experiences and Sleep," *Journal of Happiness Studies* 17 (2012): 613–633.

3. Jana Kuhnel and Sabine Sonnentag, "How Long Do You Benefit from Vacation? A Closer Look at the Fade-Out of Vacation Effects," *Journal of Organizational Behavior* 32 (2011): 125–143.

4. Mark Muraven and Roy F. Baumeister, "Self-Regulation and Depletion of Limited Resources: Does Self-Control Resemble a Muscle?" *Psychological Bulletin* 126 (2000): 247–259.

5. Takeo Doi, *The Anatomy of Dependence: The Key Analysis of Japanese Behavior*, English trans. John Bester, 2nd ed. (Tokyo: Kodansha International, 1981).

6. Harry C. Triandis, "Individualism-Collectivism and Personality," *Journal of Personality* 69 (2001): 907–924.

7. Katherine Jacobs Bao and Sonja Lyubomirsky, "Making It Last: Combating Hedonic Adaptation in Romantic Relationships," *Journal of Positive Psychology* 8 (2013): 196–206.

8. De Bloom, Geurts, and Kompier, "Vacation (After-) Effects on Employee and Well-Being."

9. See the Small Planet Studio website at www.smallplanetstudio.com.

10. Norbert Schwarz and Fritz Strack, "Reports of Subjective Well-Being: Judgment Processes and Their Methodological Implications," in *Well-Being: The Foundations of Hedonic Psychology*, eds. Ed Diener, D. Kahneman, and N. Schwarz (New York: Russell Sage Foundation, 1999), 61–84.

11. Barbara L. Fredrickson and Daniel Kahneman, "Duration Neglect in Retrospective Evaluations of Affective Episodes," *Journal of Personality and Social Psychology* 65 (1993): 45–55.

12. George Loewenstein, "Out of Control: Visceral Influences on Behavior," *Organizational Behavior and Human Decision Processes* 65 (1996): 272–292.

13. Elliot Aronson and Judson Mills, "The Effect of Severity of Initiation on Liking for a Group," *Journal of Abnormal and Social Psychology* 59 (1959): 177–181.

14. Daniel T. Gilbert, Matthew D. Lieberman, Carey K. Morewedge, and Timothy D. Wilson, "The Peculiar Longevity of Things Not So Bad," *Psychological Science* 15 (2004): 14–19.

15. Dan P. McAdams, *The Redemptive Self: Stories Americans Live By* (New York: Oxford University Press, 2006); James W. Pennebaker, *Opening Up: The Healing Power of Confiding in Others* (New York: Morrow, 1990).

16. James S. Coleman, "Social Capital in the Creation of Human Capital," *American Journal of Sociology* 94 (1988): S95-S120.

17. Dan P. McAdams, "The Psychological Self as Actor, Agent, and Author," *Perspectives on Psychological Science* 8 (2013): 272–295.

18. Tim Wildschut, Constantine Sedikides, Clay Routledge, Jamie Arndt, and Filippo Cordaro, "Nostalgia as a Repository of Social Connectedness: The Role of Attachment-Related Avoidance," *Journal of Personality and Social Psychology* 98 (2010): 573–586.

19. Amit Kumar and Thomas Gilovich, "Some 'Thing' to Talk About? Differential Story Utility from Experiential and Material Purchases," *Personality and Social Psychology Bulletin* 41 (2015): 1320–1331.

20. Leaf Van Boven, Margaret C. Campbell, and Thomas Gilovich, "Stigmatizing Materialism: On Stereotypes and Impressions of Materialistic and Experiential Pursuits," *Personality and Social Psychology Bulletin* 36 (2010): 551–563.

21. Travis J. Carter and Thomas Gilovich, "The Relative Relativity of Material and Experiential Purchases," *Journal of Personality and Social Psychology* 98 (2010): 146–159.

22. Alice Good, Arunasalam Sambhantham, and Vahid Panjganj, "Looking Back at Facebook Content and the Positive Impact Upon Welbeing: Exploring Reminiscing as a Tool for Self Soothing," Proceedings of the 5th International Conference on Online Communities and Social Computing, Las Vegas, NV, 278–286, 2013; Ting Zhang, Tami Kim, Alison Wood Brooks, Francesca Gino, and Michael I. Norton, "A 'Present' for the Future: The Unexpected Value of Rediscovery," *Psychological Science* 25 (2014): 1851–1860.

23. Constantine Sedikides, Tim Wildschut, Jamie Arndt and Clay Routledge, "Nostalgia: Past, Present, and Future," *Current Directions in Psychological Science* 17 (2008): 304–307.

24. Derrick Wirtz, Justin Kruger, Christie N. Scollon, and Ed Diener, "What to Do on Spring Break? The Role of Predicted, On-Line, and Remembered Experience in Future Choice," *Psychological Science* 14 (2003): 520–524.

CHAPTER 9

1. Mihaly Csikszentmihalyi, *Finding Flow: The Psychology of Engagement with Everyday Life* (New York: Basic Books, 1997).

2. Shawn Achor, *The Happiness Advantage: The Seven Principles of Positive Psychology That Fuel Success and Performance at Work* (New York: Crown Business, 2010).

3. Clara Bensen in discussion with the author, May 2016.

4. Ibid

5. I took notes as quickly as I could, but please forgive very minor historical inaccuracies. The point is, I learned a lot about where I live!

6. Etain O'Carroll, "How to Be a Traveller Close to Home," *Lonely Planet*, January 9, 2015, www.lonelyplanet.com/off-the-beaten-track/best- of-off-the-beaten-track/content/travel-tips-and-articles/how-to-be-a-traveller-close-to-home.

7. Alastair Humphreys, *Microadventures: Local Discoveries for Great Escapes* (London: William Collins, 2014).

8. Kristin A. Layous, Jaime L. Kurtz, Joseph Chancellor, and Sonja Lyubomirsky, (in press). "Reframing the Ordinary: Imagining Time as Scarce Increases Well-Being." *Journal of Positive Psychology*.

9. Richard M. Ryan and Edward L. Deci, "Self-Determination Theory and the Facilitation of Intrinsic Motivation, Social Development, and Well-Being," *American Psychologist* 55 (2000): 68–78.

10. Laura L. Carstensen, Derek M. Isaacowitz, and Susan T. Charles, "Taking Time Seriously: A Theory of Socioemotional Selectivity," *American Psychologist* 54 (1999): 165–181; Jaime L. Kurtz, "Looking to the Future to Appreciate the Present: The Benefits of Perceived Temporal Scarcity," *Psychological Science* 19 (2008): 1238–1241.

11. For Chicago residents these included the Field Museum, the Art Institute, Lincoln Park Zoo, and the Sears (Willis) Tower. For Londoners, they included Madame Tussaud's Wax Museum, Big Ben, Kensington Palace, and the Tower Bridge. See Suzanne B. Shu and Ayelet Gneezy, "Procrastination of Enjoyable Experiences," *Journal of Marketing Research* 47 (2010): 933–944.

12. Ibid., 936.

13. Elaine Hatfield, John T. Cacioppo, R. L. Rapson, "Emotional Contagion," *Current Directions in Psychological Science* 2 (1993): 96–99; James H. Fowler and Nicholas A. Christakis. "Dynamic Spread of Happiness in a Large Social Network: Longitudinal Analysis over 20 Years in the Framingham Heart Study," *British Medical Journal* 337 (2008): 1–9.

14. The logic in using sophomores and juniors as participants is that they have adapted to being at college more so than the brand-new, starry-eyed freshmen, and they also aren't in the now-or-never mindset of seniors.

15. See the Hapspots website at www.hapspots.org/en/.

16. Melody Warnick, *This Is Where You Belong: The Art and Science of Loving the Place You Live* (New York: Viking, 2016).

17. This is in keeping with recent work on how the pressure to be happy can make you unhappy, as I mentioned at the end of chapter 5. This is one reason why I like to call this the "perfect day" activity. It highlights how this unnatural pressure and excessive monitoring of our affective states can be a stumbling block to lasting happiness. See Iris B. Mauss, Maya Tamir, Craig L. Anderson, and N. S. Savino, "Can Seeking Happiness Make People Unhappy? Paradoxical Effects of Valuing Happiness," *Emotion* 11 (2011): 807–815.

18. Brigid Schulte, *Overwhelmed: Work, Love, and Play When No One Has the Time* (New York: Harper, 2014).

INDEX